AF808035

Natural Law and the Constitution

The law of All Laws

Natural Law

and the Constitution

The Law of All Laws

Joan Neumann

Cover Illustration

Marion J Chard

Proud Daughter Publishing Alger, MI

Copyright © 2022 by Joan Neumann

All rights reserved. No part of this publication may be reproduced, distributed, or transmitted in any form or by any means, without prior written permission.

Proud Daughter Publishing
1460 Joy Street
Alger, Michigan 48610
www.prouddaughterllc.com

Socrates, Jesus and Freedom - 1st edition
Written by Joan Arnsteen
Socratesplace.com

Cover and book design @ Marion J Chard

ISBN - 978-0-578-61116-7
Library of Congress PCN - 2022907663

Dedication/Acknowledgment

This book Natural Law and the Constitution: The Law of All Laws is dedicated to my husband James T. Neumann, whose love and wisdom has brought me to the stage in my life where I was able to complete this project. "Do not be anxious about anything, but in everything, by prayer and petition, with thanksgiving, present your requests to God. And the peace of God, which transcends all understanding, will guard your hearts and your minds in Christ Jesus." (Philippians 4: 6-7 NIV).

I'd like to extend my thanks and appreciation to my editor/publisher, Marion J Chard, for her creative efforts, and dedication to this project. And to my husband for his steadfast belief in the creation of this book, and his patience with my absences as I "visited" our "Founding Fathers".

Table of Contents

Chapter 1

Natural Law and the Constitution of the United States

Lord, we pray, open our hearts to your Word and Your Name, and impress onto our souls the Natural Law so that we may bear witness to Your love and be fruitful for Your Glory.

"The tongue of the righteous is choice silver." (Proverbs 10:20)

Like the ancient apple tree whose roots are planted firmly and deeply in the earth, with its scarred and rough bark that has weathered many seasons of sun and storm; her fruit is the sweeter through time: God has planted us also in the fertile soil of natural law, so that we may grow stronger through our earthly trials and tribulations, and that our faith and love toward Christ may bear delicious fruit for the first offering to our King.

As I write this book, *Natural Law and The Constitution: The Law of All Laws*, our Nation has been under a Corona virus lock-down. As well as the lock-down and worry over the virus, our cities have been besieged by angry protesters who claim that the United States is not a virtuous nation, but a Nation founded by "systematic racism", inequality, white supremacy, cruelty, and exploitation. The protesters initially began with an outrage over the death of George Floyd after Minneapolis Police Officer, Derek Chauvin, put his knee into George Floyd's neck for almost eight minutes. Three other police officers were involved: J. Alexander Kueng, Thomas Lane, and Tou Thao, and all four now ex-police officers have been charged over the death of George Floyd. What began as protests over the death of George Floyd soon escalated into mob violence. Since the death of George Floyd, hooded and masked agitators in large cities have pulled down and defaced statutes commemorating historical figures, have destroyed and defaced federal property, have destroyed businesses and neighborhoods, have looted and rioted, have murdered, have beaten innocent bystanders, have called for an end to the rule of law and the abolishment of the police force, and have illegally established a "Capitol Hill Organized Protest" and encamped on six blocks in Seattle, Washington, where progressive leaders have used appeasement to try to disband the protesters. Angry mobs have burned major cities, looted businesses, threatened and injured (as well as killed) police officers, innocent bystanders, and innocent children. The deliberate destruction of American cities and property with the forced and deliberate "cancellation" of American culture, history, philosophy, religion, the rule of law, and our United States Constitution is instigated by progressive and Marxist anarchists who want to overthrow our free-market capitalism, our constitutional republic and rule of law, and replace it with a static and intolerant government of coercion run by powerful and elitist bureaucrats.

Our recent presidential election of 2020 has left seventy-four million American citizens disenfranchised, disheartened, and dispirited over the allegations of election fraud — seating a president who is surrounded with a cloud of accusations over his selling of the vice-presidential office for access and power to the enemy. It is not the aim of this book to name names (or provide the well-documented proof of this treason — a determined researcher can do this for him or herself. See, for example, the current publication by investigative journalist Peter Schweizer, *Red-Handed: How American Elites Get Rich Helping China Win*.) of all the leaders behind this fraud, deliberate destruction of The United States of America, and the disintegration movement used by wealthy backers to destroy the United States for personal financial gain, other authors have recently done an excellent job of this; for example, Mark R. Levin's *American Marxism*[1], but my goal is to point directly to natural law to remind the reader of the critical importance of getting back in touch with God's natural law to save ourselves and the American Republic that is so dear to us.

Joseph Biden's Inaugural Address on January 20th, 2021, called for unity and he promised his commitment to "truth before God, to defend the Constitution, defend democracy, and to defend America." This Inaugural Address was contradicted a few short hours later when he signed seventeen controversial Executive Orders that further divided the Nation by eliminating jobs when he cancelled the Keystone Pipeline while at the same time moving America away from energy independence, the oil will now have to be transported by rail, or will go to China, disbanding Trump's "The 1776 Commission" that prompted patriotic education to counter the false historical narrative of the 1619 Project that promotes a false ideology that American history was based on slavery, and that proclaims that Americans are not exceptional, construction at the Border Wall was stopped (Americans overwhelmingly support the Border Wall), rejoining the World Health Organization which Americans know helped China to cover up their role in the spread of the Corona virus, reversal of the travel ban on nations that support terrorist groups, and rejoined the Paris Climate Agreement. Biden's suspension of Trump's Executive Order for Bulk Power Systems will allow foreign adversaries to exploit any vulnerabilities in the Nation's bulk-power systems, which could lead to catastrophic effects for Americans. The Biden administration has generated a border crisis by not securing our southern border, along with an opioid crisis, a human smuggling crisis, a humanitarian, and a health crisis. The President has violated his oath to The Constitution of the United States in failing to secure our border, as well as ignoring the vast legislative body of laws that secure our borders and the legal parameters for entering the United States and gives non-citizens a legal path to citizenship. The majority of American citizens do not support the radical leftist ideology of the Democratic Party. There is such wide-spread knowledge of facts about the former vice-presidents' collusion, and corruption with foreign nationals that United States House Representative from Georgia, Marjorie Taylor Greene, has introduced Articles of Impeachment (House Resolution

57) against President Joseph Biden on January 21, 2021, for his corrupt actions and abuse of power by enabling bribery and other high crimes and misdemeanors. On March 5, 2021, the Articles of Impeachment against President Biden was referred to the Subcommittee on the Constitution, Civil Rights, and Civil Liberties. The House of Representatives has taken no action on the Articles of Impeachment since it was referred to the Subcommittee. Contrast these actions with the quick and aggressive attack by the Democrats against President Donald J. Trump when, on January 13, 2021, the Democratic leaders in the House filled Articles of Impeachment (their second unsuccessful attempt to impeach the popular president!) against President Trump even though there was no proven cause, and it is unconstitutional to impeach a president who is no longer in Office.

Contrary to the false claims of the radical left that the United States is a nation of racists and is not a good nation, the historical truth is that the United States of America has represented and delivered more individual liberties, Bill of Rights' freedoms, more opportunities, a higher standard of living, and happiness for its citizens than any other nation. The United States of America has also led the world in humanitarian aid for other nations, is a world leader in negotiating peace through diplomacy and strength, and American citizens can be said to be the most giving of both their time and money to assist others. Contrary to the liberal narrative of Americans being "systematically racist," Americans can be said to be the most loving and virtuous of human beings.

The ancient classical idea of "virtue" in the eighteenth-century America became a virtue of politeness, sociability, and civility. Today, as in the past, The Office of the President of the United States of America represents the highest integrity and virtue of a man or woman for leadership and wisdom. Although this book, *Natural Law and the Constitution: The Law of All Laws*, is not a book about the American political system, the current political problems must be briefly mentioned because of the current crises situations addressing our Nation: will we remain a free Nation or not, and who is responsible for the undoing of our Nation? God teaches us to obey His natural law, and part of that obedience to God and natural law is to be a responsible citizen. For answers to our questions, we examine President Biden's Executive Orders made within hours of his inauguration and clearly see that his policies do not benefit American citizens nor our Nation, and will violate our freedoms, our Bill of Rights' liberties, the integrity, viability, and independence of our natural resources, our economy, jobs, business opportunities, our children's education, our health needs, including an inconsistent response and forced mandatory vaccination for the pandemic, our ability to earn a living, our quality of life, our Sovereignty as a Nation and as citizens, and our safety and our security. Those of us who believe in God, believe in God's overall governance of our Nation and the world, believe in the maturity and activity of a God-given soul, and believe in natural law; we pray for our Nation, for our families, for the safety of all our citizens, and for our elected leaders. We American citizens and worshippers of the Lord pray that God will intervene so that any impostors who have entered the Peoples' house wearing the mantle of fraud will not be allowed to stay and do further damage to our Republic. "Blessed is the nation whose God is the Lord, the people he chose for his inheritance." (Psalm 33:12). Keep my hands in prayer, O Lord, for the healing of our Nation. Dark forces are attempting to tear our Republic apart. There is no more important time than now to turn our faces to heaven, and our hearts to the Lord, and swear our allegiance to the United States Constitution.

The United States history is driven by many forces: fidelity and obedience to the United States Constitution and laws, belief in natural law, morality, religion, individual freedom, family, love for our children, friendships, culture, tradition, history, leadership, philosophy, politics, patriotism, business, jobs, creative ideas, innovations and inventions, technology, education, free-market economics, natural resources, respect and love for nature, access to food, water, land, and property ownership. All these forces influence the nature of our historical society; however, there is no force that is more universal, basic, and true than natural law, and a commitment to a worship, and belief in God. The United States is a natural rights Nation, and these natural rights have an origin in natural law. Our founding documents — the *Declaration of Independence*, the Constitution, and the Bill of Rights — are natural law documents based upon natural law. Our individual moral patterns are the patterns of natural law. Our knowledge of natural rights are the dominant concepts that will confirm for us the existence of natural law. Natural law expresses God's eternal truth and is a creative force of nature. Natural law gives moral guidance to the individual. The energy of natural law strengthens civil society, and our society was thriving (before the Corona virus lock-down) with a successful free-market economy. American capitalism is a moral system because it generates a greater amount of good for the greatest number of people. Our constitutional culture of rights is maintained through the individual morality of a free people, the belief in natural law, and the freedom to worship God. The American Founder's ideas were based upon a belief in natural law, natural rights and the laws of nature, and these concepts are all born within the truths of natural law[2]. The founder's belief in the universal truth of natural law is the same truth that we seek today; that is, it is the truth of natural law that guides all our human actions, including our worship of God, our interactions with one another, love, our moral reasoning, our political thinking about our freedom-loving Nation, and the complex world that we inhabit. The individual opportunities and material goods that are available to us by our Nation are personally fulfilling; however, there is something more that is necessary for us to satisfy our deep spiritual growth. We yearn for a nearness to the spiritual nature of God — of the permanence of something that is universal, life-giving, and sustaining, true, good, and spiritual. The self-evident principle that holds everything together for our successful American society is also the universal principle that was the foundation of the United States of America, and that principle is natural law.

The doctrine of natural law has a rich tradition in the history of Western religion and philosophy. Natural law custom has a foundation in natural-law ethics that can be traced back to the ancient philosophers Socrates, Plato, and Aristotle, and the philosophic school known as the Stoics. Ancient Rome's codification of the laws was an influence on the American Founders[3]. English common law and Whiggish thought also had an influence on the Founders of our Republic. Natural law has a foundation in Christian religion, most markedly in the teachings of the Bible, and Christian theologians. We begin the search for natural law with a study of the ancient Greek philosophers Socrates, Plato, and Aristotle. We will continue the study of natural law with an examination of the 13th century Catholic philosopher and theologian St. Thomas Aquinas with a reading of the natural law passages from his book, *Summa Theologica*[4]. An examination of St. Thomas will help us in our understanding of God's governance of us, our American Republic, and the spiritual importance of natural law.

We inhabit natural law; natural law lives within us. We give thanks to the omniscience and omnipotent power of God Who bestowed upon us the gift of natural law. We can define natural law as a body of unchanging moral principles that can be regarded as the foundation for all our human conduct. These ethical moral principles are part of our nature and can be accessed and understood universally through reason. Natural law teaches us that we live in a purposeful world, and we can access this purpose through reason. Christians believe that God has instilled natural law within our hearts, and God has given us a rational nature whereby we can discern the principles of natural law. These ethical percepts guide our behavior and the life of our communities. Our goal on earth is human happiness and flourishing as moral creatures, and natural law guides us in the knowledge of what is a morally right or a morally wrong action. Our spiritual goal is eternal life in heaven. As God's creatures, we desire to prosper and bear sweet and delicious fruit that is pleasing to His glory. Natural law is the essential part of our nature and constitutes our essential being as a human. We are not isolated individuals, but are part of a family, a community, a State, and a Nation; therefore, we participate in activities that are compatible with our natural law. These intrinsic natural law norms guide us in our daily activities. Our purposeful action that is based upon natural law is a learned activity gained through our knowledge of what God desires of us, our obedience to divine percepts, God's rule of law, our wisdom, rational inquiry, attentiveness to the Divine Word, and revelation.

Is natural law an expression of divine order? The early Americans shared a vision of the nation, and a belief in a transcendent God that bound them as a people who believed in the principle of natural law. The American Republic was built on the foundation of a morality whose basic principle was natural law that was known by the individual's reasoning power. The Holy Bible and John Locke taught colonial Americans that natural law can be discerned through reason. Virtue, justice, liberty, goodness, and human happiness stem from the universal principle of natural law. Natural law is the essential part of our nature and constitutes our essential being as a human. Intrinsic and innate natural law norms, — for example, that we should not murder — guide us in our daily activities.

Our religious beliefs and belief in natural law are powerful forces and energy that will shape the world of our experience, who we are, and what actions we take as a moral person; as well as influencing our personal beliefs, our love for our family and family members will be strengthened and blessed. This love guided by natural law will extend to the respect and love that we have toward our neighbors and fellow human beings. God commands us to love one another. God's Word is a glorious word of love. Today, when we watch our fellow human beings riot, loot, destroy property, set fires, harass police officers and citizens who have a public service role, (even senators, representatives, governors, and mayors), injure others, and even murder our citizens, especially innocent young children, we pray to our Almighty God to protect our Nation. God's natural law teaches us not to hate, to never take a life, and to use our God-given reason to discuss, debate, converse, reasonably argue for our point of view and find solutions to any problems. The hatred that is being demonstrated against our Nation, our Constitution, our president, our police officers, our history, and our culture is being spread by those who hold an extreme leftist agenda — an ideology that is pushing for the downfall of our great Nation to amass power, riches, and control for themselves.

Natural law exerts a positive influence on our political beliefs in order that we may demonstrate how we will live within the political community that we have worked to create — the type of political community reflects the type of community that we desire for our family, for ourselves, and for others. Natural law beliefs entail a respect for human life so that our political choices will be those that select individual leaders who also believe in the sanctity of life. As citizens of a republican Nation, we have freedom to choose our political leaders, where we live, our lifestyle, where we work, who we marry, who we socialize with, what we eat, and our beliefs. Socrates taught us that choice is an activity of the soul. Therefore, when we act to protect our republican Nation, we are also acting to protect the activity of the soul. Our desire is to maintain our freedoms. The leaders behind the hate-filled activities of the rioters want to take away our freedoms so that complete power — cash, natural resources, and wealth — will pass into their hands. The Framers used the scientific concept of "interest" to describe the difficult notion of the soul. Instead of looking into our souls, the Framers wrote that we consult our "self-interest."[5] In *The Federalist No. 10.*, Madison writes with a realistic view of human nature. Madison addresses the factious spirit that had damaged the public administration. By faction, he means a number of citizens who are united by a common passion or interest that is not in the common interest of the majority of the community. To solve a faction, Madison writes that you either remove its cause or control it effects. Madison writes, "Men of factious tempers, of local prejudices, or of similar sinister designs, may, by intrigue, by corruption, or by other means, first obtain the suffrages, and then betray the interests of the people."[6] To remove the causes of faction would be harmful to our liberty, because there will always be factions; however, it is reasonable to control the effects of factions by the extension of the sphere of the Republic. When you take in a variety of interests you make it less probable that "a majority of the whole will have a common motive to invade the rights of other citizens; or if such a common motive exists, it will be more difficult for all who feel it to discover their own strength and to act in unison with each other."[7] Madison assumes that politicians will pursue individual self-interest, and that the structure of the republican government will set boundaries to check this behavior.[8] Madison was not entirely pessimistic about human nature, he did believe that we sometimes act for the broader public good, and a prime example of this action is the behavior of the delegates who attended the Constitutional Convention. Madison concludes *The Federalist No. 10,* with an Aristotelian means between two extremes, "The federal Constitution forms a happy combination in this respect; the great and aggregate interests being referred to the national, the local and particular to the State legislatures."[9] Madison's essays in *The Federalist* helped the Americans to understand the novel Constitution, and how the variety of interests of the citizens, and the size of the United States would guarantee stability and justice under the United States Constitution.

Do not confuse natural law with the laws of nature; natural law is a deep spiritual truth that governs our lives on an individual and moral foundation. The laws of nature govern everything in the universe, and all our physical activities. The universe and planetary rotations, the four forces of physics, i.e., gravity, electromagnetism, and the weak and strong nuclear forces,[10] physical objects, chemical compositions, animal instincts, amongst other things, are all covered under the laws of nature. The laws of nature presuppose that there are universal laws of nature that govern our universe, the planets and specifically (from our perspective), our earth. The laws of nature are subsumed under God's natural law which provide a moral guide for our human behavior. We obey the natural laws that are superior or "higher" than the laws of nature. The laws of nature are always in harmony with natural law. We obey the natural laws that are superior or "higher" than the positive laws (constructed by human beings) of the federal and state government. The laws that are enacted by the federal government, the states, and the communities where we live are the extrinsic norms of natural law, and are human made laws (positive laws) that should always be in harmony with natural law. Natural law (God-given law) can be distinguished from statutory law because statutory law is human made law; however, statutory law is always in harmony with natural law. Natural law is also distinct from the scientific "laws of nature" that express material phenomena because these laws govern our material world; natural law governs our spiritual world. However, the laws of nature are always in harmony with God's natural law.[11]

In this book *Natural Law and the Constitution: The Law of All Laws*, we will refresh our historical knowledge of the colonial era with a study of the philosophical ideas that helped to shape our government under the guidance of natural law and within the natural rights theory. I write about many of these thinkers within this book but mention just a few in this introduction: Hugo Grotius (1583-1645), Thomas Hobbes (1588-1679), John Locke (1632-1704), and Charles-Louis de Secondat, Baron de la Brede et de Montesquieu (1689-1755). James Madison, of course, was influenced by Montesquieu's political philosophy within *The Spirit of the Law* (1748) where the government's separation of powers into judicial, legislative, and executive powers will maximize individual liberty. As we are reminded by historian Paul A. Rahe, the goal of colonial Americans was individual liberty.[12] The authority of John Locke's moral and political philosophy, and the Lockean influence on the *Declaration of Independence*, and the Constitution of 1787 is without dispute.[13] During his lifetime, Locke was considered an authority on constitutional law, and an expert on English constitutionalism.[14] Locke's idea of natural law is within the tradition of classical natural law as represented earlier by St. Thomas; however, Lock's philosophy of natural law is different from the other thinkers on natural law. We will examine these seminal differences. Colonial Americans believed in natural law, and equality, and their theory of natural rights was entailed by the Lockean contract theory and consent of the governed.

The United States declared independence from Britain on July 2, 1776. Congress adopted the final text of the *Declaration of Independence* on July 4, 1776, and it was signed by the thirteen

States on August 2, 1776. The *Declaration of Independence* is a clearly stated philosophy of natural law. The *Declaration of Independence* also reflects American's belief in natural rights, equality, compact theory, the social contract, it is a clear statement that it is legitimate to resist despotic authority, and that government is derived from the consent of the governed — Lockean, Enlightenment, and Jeffersonian ideas that guided the American Revolution (1775-1783). Locke's *Second Treatise of Government* had an enormous influence on Thomas Jefferson's thinking and subsequent words, "We hold these truths to be self-evident, that all men are created equal, that they are endowed by their Creator with certain unalienable Rights, that among these are Life, Liberty, and the pursuit of Happiness."[15] This statement of rights — which men hold in the Lockean state of nature — is a statement of natural law. The wisdom of the self-evident truth of natural law is stated beautifully in the words of the *Declaration of Independence* where appeals are made to God our Creator and to natural law. It is a belief that was dominant and understood during the colonial era when the colonists were awakening to the moral and spiritual consciousness of independence from Britain.

The Continental Congress authored the Articles of Confederation for governing the nation which were approved by Congress in 1777 and ratified by the States in 1781. The Articles of Confederation lacked the power to regulate interstate commerce, trade, and the power of taxation. The Constitutional Convention (originally referred to as the Federal Convention, or the Grand Convention at Philadelphia, or the Philadelphia Convention in 1787), was called together to address the deficiencies of the Articles of Confederation, but the delegates soon realized that a new system of government was necessary to ensure that the States remain united.

A formative part of Constitutional history is discovered through a careful study of the delegates' debates during the Constitutional Convention. The Founding Fathers met in 1787 at the Constitutional Convention (Federal Convention) where they formulated a federal system of government that is a Republic. James Madison was instrumental in focusing the delegates' attention on the structure of the form of the government, and the practical operation of a complex central government that would have authority over the States, while the States retained their own areas of sovereignty that were not enumerated as a federal power in the Constitution.

The citizens of this Republic are sovereign and chose their president, congress members, and state governors along with state senators and representatives through elections. The debates during the Convention of 1787 demonstrate how the Founding Fathers used dialectic, deductive reasoning, inductive reasoning skills, the dialogue of natural rights, and a belief in natural law to write the United States Constitution. We will examine the formulation of the United States Constitution, and the analytical tools that were used by the Framers to write the Constitution.

The ratification debates and the arguments for the ratification of the Constitution by the Federalists, and the opposing arguments against the ratification of the Constitution by the Anti-Federalists gives us a clearer understanding of what was at stake in the Constitutional development of our new Nation. The debaters used reason and induction to formulate sound arguments for their position either for or against the ratification of the Constitution. A further examination of how liberty was codified through the written Bill of Rights strengthens this author's argument that the United States Constitution and the Bill of Rights are natural rights documents which have their foundation in natural law.

The key for understanding our American Republic is knowledge of the idea of natural law and what the Founders most often referred to as natural rights. Our United States Constitution and The Bill of Rights, along with Amendments XI through XXVII, are outgrowths of the Founders' understanding of natural law. As summarized in our venerable United States Constitution, and our glorious Bill of Rights, and subsequent Amendments, the idea of natural law is the criteria for judging all these areas: individual and collective freedom, freedom as a Nation, the rule of law which is equality before the law, justice, liberty, freedom to choose our President, freedom to choose our state and federal representatives, religious freedom, freedom of conscience, freedom of speech, freedom of the press, the right to assemble, the right to petition the government for a redress of grievances, the right to bear arms, autonomy, property rights, economic rights, the right to due process, right to a speedy and public trial, right to a jury trial in criminal cases, right to Counsel, right to be informed of the nature of the accusation, right to a jury trial in common law cases, fair bail, no cruel or unusual punishment, and in the ninth amendment, "the enumeration in the Constitution, of certain rights, shall not be construed to deny or disparage others retained by the people," among many other individual and human rights. We can make the case that the ninth amendment enumerates and protects the natural law which is the birthright of all American citizens. The idea of natural law is the criteria for judging all these aforementioned rights.

The United States of America was founded as a natural law and natural rights Republic. Natural law preexists positive law; and natural rights preexist the creation of government. Natural law was also a vital belief by the individuals known collectively as the American Founding Fathers who gathered in 1787 to write the United States Constitution. There were many influencing ideas on the Founders of our Republic, but natural law and natural rights were the foundational ideas. The Founders' arguments for the concept of natural law were the foundation for the Constitution that protects our natural rights and equality for all American citizens. The delegates to the Federal Convention of 1787 met to revise the existing form of government. During the years before the American Revolution popular leaders had relied on the concept of natural law to justify their right to petition for independence from Britain. Now that independence was won, the Convention delegates brought their belief in natural law with them to the Convention as a foundational concept. There was no need to define "natural law" — it was inherent in the beliefs of the delegates as demonstrated by Madison's notes of the Convention. The "natural rights of the people," "public liberty," and "republican liberty" are phrases and words that are used by the delegates to express "natural law".[16] Delegate Luther Marten, for example, used the theory of a "state of nature" when he argued in defense of state rights. The natural rights of individuals are protected by the state constitutions and therefore, the state's rights must also be protected in the national constitution.[17] Hamilton argued in a Lockean manner that just like individuals give up shares of their liberty to enter society; the state's also give up a part of their sovereign power in order that a union of states may be formed.[18]

James Madison, for example, believed in the existence of a higher law of reason and justice, and this belief was what generated the formation of a Constitution that placed structural and legal limitations on the powers of the federal government to give maximum freedom to the citizens in all areas of their own private lives, social lives, religious beliefs, conscience, and political endeavors. Although the Constitution does not mention politics or political parties, it is the success of the Constitution that maximizes our individual freedoms that subsequently will lay the fertile soil for the growth of successful politics and political parties. Nature's liberty as expressed in the compendium Bill of Rights ratified in 1791 further codifies American's belief in natural law and expresses the success story of the United States as a Nation of liberty.

The idea of natural law is the criteria for judging all these areas of freedom and liberty. Our spiritual inspection and actions based on natural law can lead to an enlightened age of human freedom. We can further flourish as a Nation under God's guidance with natural law. Natural law is known to us through the will of God, through our reasoning skills, and revealed to us through His Word and Grace. God commands us to love our families, neighbors, and others. Natural law keeps us mentally and spiritually situated in a spiritual perspective in relationship to God and to each other. Our religious ideas transform into our philosophical ideas, and these ideas influence our political ideas and the way in which we construct our Nation and our communities. Our ultimate goal in living in a free Nation is human happiness, and loving God and others brings us true happiness. We have the most fertile ground for the exercise of natural law within the United States where the Constitution is our guide for the rule of law, and the rule of law is where we find God's natural law; and, God's Will is, we pray, to preserve our Nation.

We are blessed that God has designed us so that we may understand natural law and discern morality to live a virtuous and happy life. Natural law can be regarded as the foundation for how the mind can lay out reasoning arguments and conclusions for morality, and how our practical reason is situated within our epistemology, and is the ordinance given to us by our Divine law giver — God. Philosophy of religion does not presuppose religious faith, however, as Christians there is nothing more urgent than following our Creator's governance for us. God created us in His image, and to live in harmony with natural law; and it is by obedience to His Divine will, that we will live in happiness. Everyone has beliefs before they set out to philosophize. I am a Christian philosopher and as a philosopher, I hold knowledge in high regard, and seek to know the truth of things. As a Christian, my highest purpose on earth is to live my life according to God-given natural law, and to return — with an open heart — the love of God to others as the highest goal that we can achieve; and love of God is also the basic presupposition of natural law. (Genesis 1: 26-27). I hold rational discourse in esteem and my personal profession of faith notwithstanding, I will defend natural law with the same rational approach that sheds light on the problems of natural law. Human beings who have a strong disposition to natural law carry their virtues with them as they solve daily problems — the solutions lay within an ethical realm.

This individual disposition toward natural law is the inherent quality of a virtuous mind and was the cohesive characterization of the Founding Fathers of the United States Constitution. American constitutional history demonstrates the relevance of the growth of our Republic within the concept of natural law. Natural law is the body of innate moral principles that guides us in our wisdom to govern ourselves. Our President of the United States, congress members, lawmakers, representatives, justices, and judges respect natural law, and legislation, judgments, and rulings are generally in harmony with natural law. Natural law is not a substitute for positive law, but it is the reasoning framework that guides our intellectual understanding of the rule of law. Constitutional scholar, Edward S. Corwin, demonstrates in *The "Higher Law" Background of American Constitutional Law*, how the laws by which we live are essentially the embodiment of natural law. Corwin writes, "in the American written Constitution, higher law at last attained a form which made possible the attribution of it of an entirely new sort of validity, the validity of a statute emanating from the sovereign."[19] Corwin teaches us that this statutory form has been backed up by judicial review. A current question that all the American citizens should be contemplating is, what happens to our individual sovereignty as citizens of a Nation whose congress members now relegate the creation of our laws to bureaucrats who are not elected by the citizens? Natural law provides the foundation for the Constitution and this foundation entails the natural rights and popular sovereignty of the people. Constitutional dialogue and reason are the instruments that keep the Constitution at the forefront of our focus to maintain our liberties. Judicial review is a key element of our natural law because the power of judicial review generates an understanding and clarity of the meaning of the Constitution and binds us as citizens to the Constitution.

The American Founding Fathers incorporated the idea of individual sovereignty into the *Declaration of Independence*, the United States Constitution, and the Bill of Rights. It is the sovereign individual who forms our government; each citizen is a sovereign individual who must consent to be governed, and then to utilize their consent by their vote for our leaders — President, federal and state congress members, governors, mayors, all elected office holders, and any additional civic or tax proposals on the ballots. The *Declaration of Independence* and the United States Constitution are inspiring documents: uplifting and energizing for the individual citizen — and if followed as a form of government and rule of law — they are a blessing for the improvement of everyone's quality of life within the United States. The beauty of both documents is not just the uplifting language and the virtuous ideas, but that they also affect the individual citizen's personal growth. The nature of the human being is that we desire freedom (spiritual, intellectual, mental, physical, and political) to fulfill our soul-yearnings. The nature of a human being is that which owes it quiddity (soul) to an intensive something (natural law), whose configuration is conformable to a specific composition or pattern. The soul possesses the matrix (pattern) for our personal development, and the intentional cast for the harmony between the soul, body, and the mind. The soul has the capacity to assist in the development of actions that are consistent and obedient to God's laws for us and to form all that one can be. We are blessed that God has formed us so beautifully — with a soul, a heart, a brain, and a body — and, He has given us the potential for an understanding and knowledge of natural law so that we may form a free government that allows the greatest number of citizens to fulfill their talents and capacities. This beauty is the universal truth of our Founding documents — the *Declaration of Independence*, the United States Constitution, and the Bill of Rights. The cumulative wisdom of our Founding Fathers has created the Founding documents — these documents are there for the benefit of all us and have illuminated a creative form of republican government that remains a national space for conscious and active citizens to exercise their freedoms.

The architectonic beauty of freedom is that it is both universal and particular and, therefore, pertains both to the community and to the individual. Freedom is universal as an ideal that has become workable as an idea in the United States Constitution, and individually it expresses our inner being. God has bequeathed to us all the universal concepts, for example, freedom, justice, liberty, and goodness. The seed that is planted within us which assists us in knowing these universal concepts is the seed of natural law. Through the beauty and grace of God's creation, the seeds of natural law will grow into the spiritually mature and active human being.

The fundamental and universal idea of freedom is easy to visualize if we think of freedom as freedom of self (width and length), freedom of the intellect (breadth), freedom of movement (temporal), and freedom of ratiocination (spatial). Our desire for freedom is our spiritual drive and represents the passions of a finite creature of God that is striving for immortality. Our freedom reveals itself to us as the movements of an autonomous being in time, and we utilize our reason to construct our ideas spatially. How can we feel secure in developing a relationship to perfect things in another dimension, that is, the universal ideas of freedom, justice, liberty, and goodness — (for our omnipotent and omniscient God is not bound by space or time), — when our classroom is situated in the here and now, and we are not perfect beings? The answer to this question is with an understanding of our Founding documents: The *Declaration of Independence*, The United States Constitution, and the Bill of Rights, and how the conceptual and legal boundaries for individual freedom within these documents have prescribed to us our freedoms.[20] We keep in mind that the socialism and Marxist ideology that is currently being propagated is being pushed by those within the United States who wish to take power, destroy our Nation, destroy our United States Constitution, banish our Bill of Rights, banish the rule of law, and enslave us. These Marxists falsely teach that the human being is perfectible, and malleable. The Marxist sociologists preach that we must have a socialist government with bureaucrats and "scientific" specialists in charge of all our freedoms to reach this "utopia" of perfection. The universal truth is that the human being is not perfect (we are born flawed), and that we rely on God's Grace to forgive us of our sins and bring us into God's Blessed family. God teaches us that all human beings are a blessed part of God's creation, and natural law is a gift to us to achieve this divine goal. Our freedoms are God's gift to us. Let us not squander our blessings by throwing them away for the false promises of a "utopia" that will enslave us. Let us be free!

What is good and beautiful is pleasing to the eye, and a better proportion of said good thing is intricately patterned — the seeing of which delights. Natural law was implanted within the Garden of Eden. Adam and Eve were given an unwritten law that was God's rule of law, and our first parents shared in divine governance. Adam and Eve understood natural law — instructing them to honor the divine Word and turn away from evil — but they did not obey natural law. The bitter fruit of modernity has been transplanted from the sweet fruit of the Garden of Eden. Even though Adam and Eve sinned and transgressed God's natural law, God — in His mercy and goodness — gave us natural law to spiritually connect us to Him. The natural law was then handed down to the patriarchs — Noah, Melchizedek, Enoch, and Abraham. The omnipotence of God and His infinite love includes us in His eternal plans. We can say that political life is a holy gift from God, who, after the flood, created political life through Noah.[21] God teaches us, "Whoever sheds the blood of man, by man shall his blood be shed; for in the image of God has God made man." (Genesis 9:6). The ban on homicide was one of God's natural laws given to us after the flood. In murdering another human being, the murderer is disobeying God's natural law, and showing a contemptuous and evil nature against God. One of the foundational laws for all civilized societies has been a legal ban on murder.

Natural law philosophy has its roots in Plato and his student Aristotle. It is an enlightening experience to read Plato, Aristotle, and St. Thomas, and a humble-hearted exercise to gain an understanding of natural law. The ancient Greeks demonstrated this natural law morality even though the ancient Greeks worshipped a pantheon of gods whose shrines, customs, sacrifices, and cults played a key role in the society and government of classical Athens. Socrates, Plato, and Aristotle emphasized the distinction between "nature" (*physis*), and "law," "custom," or "convention" (*nomos*). In the *Rhetoric*, Aristotle wrote that there are particular laws that people set up for themselves, and then there is a "higher law" that is according to nature. Aristotle writes, "We must urge that the principles of equity are permanent and changeless, and that the universal law does not change either, for it is the law of nature, whereas written laws often do change."[22] The Stoic philosophers formulated the doctrine of natural law teaching that natural law was an order that governed the activity of cosmic material. Natural law was further articulated in ancient Rome by Cicero, Seneca, and the Roman jurists.

After Christ's teaching, natural law found Christian expression by Saint Augustine (354-430) and was then spiritually formulated by St. Thomas. The traditional notion of a law that is an inner nature and turns us away from evil and assists us in honoring God was called *lex indita*. Later St. Thomas calls this law *synderesis*. Some authors refer to St. Thomas' *synderesis* as moral norms that are crystallized upon our hearts (combined with St. Thomas' notion of *prudentia*). The law of nature is *lex naturals* and defined at the Second Council of Arles (473 AD) as "the first grace of God."[23] In St. Thomas's *Summa Theologica*, we get a classification of law: *lex aeterna* (the eternal law), *lex nova* (the new law), *lex Mosaicae* (the Mosaic law), *lex membrorum* (the law of the members), *lex humana* (the human law), and *lex vetus* (the old law).[24]

Natural law is also expressed in English common law. In the sixteenth century, Hooker's *Laws of Ecclesiastical Policy* gives us a fresh look at natural law philosophy. The American Founders were communalist protestants influenced by moral philosophers, for example, Thomas Browne and Edmund Burke. The American Founders were influenced by the philosophy of natural law and valued this philosophy as a key to the development of the new Nation's Constitutional Republic. The American Founders shared a belief in natural law, Christian religion, philosophy, ideology, and the symbolism that bound them to a transcendent God. The early American settlers shared a belief in a redeemer Nation to be established in America along with the influence of the Biblical covenants and compacts for the colonists to covenant together for worship of God, and the good of the community. Along with this was their belief in natural law and that the Gospel was the source of all our moral principles. When we read the early colonial documents, we find evidence of the colonist's belief in God and natural law. (See

The Mayflower Compact). The first two paragraphs of the *Declaration of Independence* (1776) are statements about natural law and its importance in a free and just society. John Locke's natural law epistemology influenced the American Founders, especially James Madison and Alexander Hamilton.

The doctrine of natural law is not a substitute for positive law, but the moral foundations of natural law are necessary for positive law to give structure and pattern to the formulation of our written laws. The United States Constitution is based upon the doctrine of natural law and the Providential governance of God. The justification and legality of our national laws are ordained by the people, which is the citizens, who hold the truths of natural law to be sacred. The written Constitution was the outgrowth of the beliefs, laws, customs, and traditions that the citizens rationally discerned from the higher law. The right reason of all us is the intellectual and transcendental springboard that brings us to an understanding of higher law. The structure and form of natural law is validated through legal statute and confirmed through judicial review.[25] The principles of natural law are in harmony with our positive laws that guarantee our traditional rights, human freedom, and the advancement of our individual rights under the United States Constitution.

This natural law morality has a Christian heritage which gave birth to a new idea of freedom and a governing balance of democratic institutions. An examination of the ancient idea of natural law and democracy, counterpoised against the development of our modern republican democracy, will shed light on the problems of freedom and democracy that we are faced with today. As we meet these new challenges of individual freedom, we find that the early Christian belief in natural law was the bedrock from which our nation was built, and this moral foundation is refreshed today for a vigorous human flourishing. We can truly say that this is a rebirth because it was a faithful body of Christians that originally escaped from temporal tyranny to the shores of America for religious and spiritual freedom to worship their God.

The early Americans understood that they had a claim to the rights of natural law. As well as natural law, the authority for the early American rights were set by the British constitution, common law, colonial charters, and custom. Early state constitutional language reflected natural law principles along with natural equality. Fundamental state documents also reflect natural law language.[26] Natural law was a key concept for the early American settlers as well as a motivating concept during the American Revolution. Natural law has a timelessness and was the heritage of all Americans who brought their love of God with them to the New World, and they continued to live with an obedience to His precepts. God grants to each of us inalienable rights that no government can transgress. American history, religion, and philosophy teach us how we frame our reason in the service of the larger truths of God's natural law. Natural law is in the mind of God, and it is through God's love that He has created within us the capacity to reason using the precepts of natural law. We utilize the conclusions of our rational inquiries by willing that these insights be used for the common good. Our individual will to act marks us as moral creatures whose actions are in harmony with natural law.

The Founding philosophy is stated in the Preamble to the *Declaration of Independence*: "that all men are created equal, that they are endowed by their Creator with certain unalienable rights, that among these are life, liberty and the pursuit of happiness."[27] Christianity teaches us what the truths of God's natural law are and how we may adhere to these truths. These natural law truths are in harmony with the Founding documents of our Republic and are also in harmony with the religious beliefs of the majority of American citizens. The rights of individual freedom, moral freedom, religious freedom, liberty, security, justice, equality, equity, economic freedom, property rights, the right to just laws, the right to a jury trial, and self-defense are premises of natural law, and are also the basic freedoms that are protected under the Constitution. The colonial American's emphasis on property rights is a premise of natural law. Colonial Americans considered their personal rights as a portion of their personal property, and property rights were sanctioned by nature, natural law, birthright, and inheritance. Property rights are a key to individual happiness, and happiness and the good of each individual, as well as the good of the community as a whole are portions of natural law. The authority of rights in the Constitution are founded upon the law of God, and known to us through reason, and constituted by our nature as formed by God. All laws touch the periphery of natural law with at least a minimal content of natural law inhering in law if they are just laws. It is both symbolic and substantial that we search for the wisdom to order our relationship to God while, at the same time, being blessed to exercise our natural law while living in the American *Republic*. Our mastery (or at least an understanding) of the founding era, and the founding documents — the *Declaration of independence*, The Constitution of the United States, and the compendium Bill of Rights — are what qualifies and constitutes us as citizens.

Our heritage as Americans is to be blessed by God with freedom. I am writing as a philosopher, and because of my love for my Nation, I hold a reverence for the Constitution and natural law, and respect for the American Founders. I have immersed myself in the historical records and writings of the Founding era — an era that bears witness to God and natural law. A glimpse into philosophy is like a glimpse into history where you are left with a fuller view of life. We respond to Socrates who taught us to know ourselves first, and then our historical curiosity will be tempered by that which we are able to digest at the time. We are rooted in time insofar as we are grounded in existence as a human being, and life's landmarks are the patterns of those individuals whose lives are well-known to historians and now to us. The memory of a good person's deeds and accomplishments will live on whether the individual becomes a prominent figure in history or not. When we read about Socrates our knowledge is from secondary sources, primarily Plato, because Socrates did not write anything down. However, this historical knowledge has such force that he speaks to us out of the depth of time, that is, his thinking has as much relevance today as it did in ancient Greece when he walked the streets of Athens and questioned his fellow citizens. We can say the same thing about our Nation's Founders — that their ideas and thinking has had a profound effect on us today. If we look deeply into the historical record, we see the strength of a courageous Washingtonian soul, an intelligent and creative spark from the minds of both Jefferson and Madison, and the visional leadership of the Founders. From all points of this historical compass, we gather as citizens of this great Nation to preserve and enrich our American freedoms.

The undermining of our current democracy has taken place through our ethical failings, and although many of us are informed bystanders to this downfall, the absence of virtue in the citizen body has had a profound and damaging effect on all of us, as well as our nation as a whole. There are numerous negative ideological forces that are alive today that threaten our republican democracy. As we put on the mantle of natural law, we will fight back against the forces that are working to undermine the moral fabric of our democracy. We bring the capacity for an understanding of an innate natural law with us as our heritage, and the ability to exercise the virtues of an individual living by natural law can be readily acted upon if we have our Constitution as our keystone, and the structure of a republican democracy as our foundation stone to support and protect our individual freedoms.

The spirit of our modern American democratic age is a republican spirit. To understand and strengthen our Constitutional Republic, we will look back to the ancient Athenian philosopher's, Socrates, Plato, and Aristotle — who lived, philosophized, and taught during the historical period when the theory of democracy was first introduced and practiced. We look back to the creation of the *Declaration of Independence* and the historical setting of the United States during the founding era. We refresh our understanding of the creation of the United States Constitution, and the Founders who were instrumental in writing this seminal document. As citizens, we remind ourselves of the liberties and rights that are granted and guaranteed to us through the Bill of Rights. By reminding ourselves where we historically come from in theory, we will be better equipped to maintain our republican democracy and strengthen our civil society against the current detractors. Keeping in mind that our republican form of government is a unique governmental structure, the moral pattern of natural law that the ancient Greeks practiced is the same moral pattern that is recognized today — a virtuous citizen body constitutes a good government. God's "higher law" for us is natural law, and this natural law teaches us to practice stewardship of the United States Constitution.

Socrates

Chapter 2

Natural Law and the Ancient Greeks

"So Paul then stood up in the meeting of the Areopagus and said: 'Men of Athens! I see that in every way you are very religious. For as I walked around and looked carefully at your objects of worship, I even found an altar with this inscription: TO AN UNKNOWN GOD. Now what you worship as something unknown I am going to proclaim to you.'" (Acts 17:22-23).

The roots of natural law are very deep and extend back to the Old Testament in the Holy Bible. The Biblical accounts of the Creation and the Fall of Adam and Eve in Genesis are spiritual stories about natural law. "By wisdom the Lord laid the earth's foundations, by understanding he set the heavens in place." (Proverbs 3:19). The Old Testament teaches us about the learnedness of Moses, and Moses's role in Christianity was retold in the New Testament, "Moses was educated in all the wisdom of the Egyptians and was powerful in speech and action." (Acts 7:22). In the New Testament Bible, we find Paul's reference to natural law in Romans where God's natural law is written in our hearts. (Romans 2:14-15).

From the ancient Hellenes, we are the heirs of theoretical thinking that examined politics and man, virtues and morals, justice and laws, universals and particulars, nature and convention, and the gods and natural law. The Stoics meant by natural law that we live in accordance with nature, and nature is reasonable, as well as our reason is natural. Plato conceived of natural law as an idea of natural justice. Natural law ethics are found in Plato and Aristotle, where their realistic moral theories will lay the foundation for natural law. We will begin our search for natural law clarity with a study of the ancient Greek philosophers: Socrates, Plato, and Aristotle. We will continue our natural law exposition with an examination of the thirteenth century Catholic theologian and philosopher St. Thomas Aquinas — with a reading of the natural law passages in his book, The *Summa Theologica*. We will then examine the natural law doctrine of John Locke and his influence on eighteenth-century America, especially the constitutional period.

Natural law is spiritually necessary to us today: natural law assists us in following God's laws, and it is essential for the development of a Christian soul and our human character which will benefit us eternally with the blessedness of an immortal life lived with God. Natural law is also essential for the maintenance of our free Republican government because it promotes the moral character that is necessary for us to sustain our freedoms. As God's creatures, we follow natural law and seek to understand the wisdom and truth of His Word. "Wisdom is supreme; therefore, get wisdom." (Proverbs 4:7)

As we travel this road together, seeking the foundations of natural law, we must give some thought to the notion of teleology in the philosophy of Plato, Aristotle and St. Thomas. A quick definition of teleology will assist us for our knowledge; teleology is the reason or function for the end, purpose or goal of a thing or person. Teleology is derived from two Greek words: *telos* which means the end, goal, or purpose, and logos which means reason or explanation. These thinkers have taught us that we have the ability through reason to know the true natural end or natural *telos* of human life. We will discuss the teleology of each of these thinkers in depth later in this book, but a summary will get us on the way. Plato divided the world between the changeless world of the Forms, and the ever-changing world of ordinary objects. Plato postulated a hierarchy of Being, and the Form of the Good was the highest object of contemplation; the Good is so attractive that it draws all things to it. All things aim at the Good. Aristotle taught that all things are composed of form and matter, and the form of a thing is its core essence that unfolds so that each thing will realize its nature. For Aristotle, if we understand the essence of a thing, then we will understand the *telos* or end to which it aims. Aristotle influenced St. Thomas, and he argued that the universe is directed by God toward an end (*telos*), or purpose. St. Thomas also argued that the practical evidence of an intelligent design in the world implies the existence of an intelligent designer, i.e., God.

The ancient Greeks were part of a dynamic political culture that inherited an oral tradition that kept the culture alive without a dependence on the written word. There was a tradition and habit of reading aloud, and a verbal exchange of ideas and public discourse amongst the males in public areas like the marketplace (*agora*). The philosopher Socrates demonstrated this oral tradition via dialectic and public discourse; laws and political institutions were also keys in sustaining the Greek political culture and democracy.

The classical Greeks inherited this verbal tradition from their cultural ancestors who were the bards for a moral education. Traveling bards or storytellers would recite or sing the ancient myths, stories, and legends that gave a coherent and human-like nature to the pantheon of gods, goddesses and magical beings who appeared in these stories. For example, pre-political Greek society during the Dark Ages (1100-900 B.C.) did not benefit from texts, but what they did have were the Homeric epics. Homer's *The Iliad and the Odyssey* were written in the late eighth or early seventh century BC, where the adventures of the gods and extraordinary men are told in imaginative and beautiful poetry. The blind bard's remarkable epic, *The Iliad* is a poem about Ilium (Troy) that poetically narrates the attack on Troy by the Achaeans, and the rage of Achilles who was the son of a mortal father and an immortal mother. Achilles was described as a physically strong warrior, who was also as handsome as a god. He wrestled with the dilemma whether to lay siege to Troy to insure his glory or return home where his fame would surely die. The Greeks destroy Troy, and[28] *The Iliad* recounts the ten-year Trojan War.

The sequel, the *Odyssey*, begins after the end of the Trojan War and tells the story of the Greek hero Odysseus' journey back home to win back his kingdom in Ithaca.[29] The voyage home took ten years due to the wrath and trickery of the gods, monsters, mythical creatures, and sirens. Odysseus' cleverness and shrewdness to overcome these perils attracts the support of Athena, patron goddess of Athens. Athena (or Pallas Athena) was one of the most powerful goddesses of ancient Greece; she was always successful in her battles, and was the goddess of learning and wisdom, as well as human ingenuity, and skill in human relationships. Athena fought on the side of the Achaeans in the Trojan War, and she only fought for a reasonable cause, much preferring to use intuitive wisdom to settle a dispute, rather than force or violence. The ancient Greek myths were moral lessons for the ancient Athenians. The poets, Homer, and Hesiod gave the Greek gods their titles and assigned them a function, their honors, and identification with nature, as well as a human characteristic which the ancient Greeks could identify with when they honored the gods. Homer's pantheon of gods have anthropomorphic characteristics that serve as moral lessons for the behavior of mankind. Destiny was the most powerful and oldest of the Olympian gods, and impersonal Destiny set boundaries for both the gods and mankind that were not to be transgressed; and these landmarks served as the markers for assignments, distributions, duties, actions and punishments for any transgressions. Nature was self-sustaining and could restore balance, and the pantheon of gods were there to assist in keeping everything working in harmony. Zeus, for example, was the lawgiver in heaven, where Solon, Lycurgus, and Pericles were the lawgivers on earth who petitioned the gods in heaven for assistance and favor in their human endeavors.

Ancient Athenians worshipped a pantheon of gods, goddesses, and nature, and their culture intertwined the religious worship of the gods with the politics of the city. The ancient Greeks did not possess individual rights as citizens, but they did have a duty to the *polis* and could, however, petition for certain privileges; however, they were members of a moral community where they were duty-bound to participate in politics. The ancient Greek's civic life was inextricably linked with their devotion to the gods. The performance of religious rites was expected as part of the honor, duty, and recognition of the male citizen's obligations, as well as their expected participation in the city's government. The women also had an obligation to perform their civic duty through the performance of religious rites; unfortunately, any civic recognition of the Athenian women was only through the achievements of their husbands or the talents of their sons. In the classical period women were denied political and legal rights. We see a harsh contrast between the women's segregated life, and the active and full political life of the Athenian men who relished the exchange of ideas and conversation in the marketplace (*agora*).

As young men, the Greek educational (paideia) program included gymnastic exercise, athletic contests, military training, rhetoric, mathematics, dancing, music, and poetry. The men were also obligated to serve as soldiers in one of the many wars that preoccupied Athena's golden city. A soldier was expected to procure and maintain their own armaments, to fight for the honor of Athens. Socrates, for example, fought admirably as an armed infantryman (*hoplite*) in the Battle of Potidaea (432 BC), where he courageously saved the life of Alcibiades. Alcibiades was decorated for bravery during the Battle of Potidaea, but Alcibiades states that Socrates should have received the decoration because, "Socrates single-handedly saved my life, ... and he rescued my armor as well,"[30] Socrates would have received two years of military training while he was in his early twenties. Socrates' military service took place when Socrates was between the age of thirty-eight and forty-eight, making him one of the older soldiers to serve. As a *hoplite* soldier, Socrates' body was protected with a shield and body armor, and he would fight the battle with a spear (*doru, or dory*) as his weapon. Socrates also exhibited endurance, courage, self-discipline, and heroism during the Athenian assault on Delium (424 BC), and at the expedition to defend the Athenian colony of Amphipolis (422 BC). Socrates was already a renowned philosopher during his military campaigns, and he was well-known for his physical stamina on the battlefield, as well as his intellectual honesty in the *agora*. At all times, the Greeks displayed *sophrosune*, i.e., the self-restraint and moderation that was necessary to cooperate with other citizens.

The philosopher Archelaus, who taught Socrates, held that any right and wrong action were not part of nature but by law. In Greek philosophy, there is a distinction between nature (*physis*), and law (*nomos*). The Greeks taught that what was law or custom (*nomos*) would vary from place to place, or country to country, and as a general enactment the law remained valid for all time. A psephisma was a law that was specific in scope and applied for a limited time; but what was considered "nature" (*physis*) when the law was universally the same everywhere. The ancient Greek philosophers expressed natural law within their theories of natural justice or righteousness. They expressed natural law as telelogical (*telos*: the end, goal or purpose); where human activity is good, when it is purposeful, and aims at the fulfillment of the human good called *eudaimonia*. The origin of natural law exegesis written in the philosophical works of Plato and Aristotle bequeaths to us a realistic moral theory. These two ancient Greek philosophers taught that reason or intellect are developed to discover the universal moral commands and virtues. For both Plato and Aristotle, the city-state (*polis*) existed to help men to achieve an ethical life.

The school of philosophy known as Stoicism expressed the natural law when they taught the Greeks to live according to reason and nature. The Stoics taught that natural law is an expression of natural justice. They placed a premium on reason, and it was reason that produced the universal Design or Law of the universe. Zeno of Citium (334-262 BC) was the founder of the Stoic school in Athens (300 BC), his successor was Cleanthes of Assos (331-232 BC), followed by Chrysippas of Soli (280-206 BC), and then Zeno of Tarsus (200 BC) who was the fourth leader of the Stoic school. The Roman philosophers, for example, Marcus Tullius Cicero (106-43 BC), Lucius Annaeus Senecca (4-65 AD), Marcus Aurelius (121-180 AD, Roman Emperor from 161-180 AD), and Epictetus of Hierapolis (50-138 AD), and the jurists, for example, Gaius or Caius who wrote the Institutes (161 AD), Paulus, Ulpianus, Papinianus, Celsus and Marcianus, as well as the Emperor Justinian viewed natural law as natural right (that is, the dignity and autonomy of human nature).

Seventh century Athens had a king who ceded most of his power to civic and religious bodies. The oligarchic government was concerned about the unrest between the Athenians who lived in the city and those who lived in the countryside, and the increased attacks on the shore by privateers, and they appointed Draco to codify and fix the laws. Draco (650 BC-600 BC) was the first recorded legislator of Athens (7th century BC), and he replaced the oral law and blood feuds by a written code that was to be enforced by a court of law. The laws were posted on wooden tablets called axones — pivoted tablets of law that allowed the Athenians to read the law from any side. These laws were considered to be the first Athenian constitution. Draco's laws were known for their Draconian harshness due to the harsh punishment for even minor offenses. Draco invented the Council of Four Hundred, where free men elected the members from among themselves. Before the democratic system was born, archons or chief magistrates, and the Areopagus (religiously based governing council made up of ex-archons) ruled Athens. These members were primarily aristocrats who ruled for their own advantage and power.

We can benefit from studying ancient Greek history where we find similarities to launch a solution to the democratic problems that we are now facing. When the aristocrats were ruling ancient Athens, the political community was stultified and dull. When the middle-class citizens began to assume political power and governing abilities, we find a creative foundation for the city for philosophy, politics, history, literature, and art. Athens was increasingly being governed by laws instead of the patronage and good-will of aristocrats. (See, for example, Victor Davis Hanson, *The Dying Citizen: How Progressive Elites, Tribalism, and Globalization Are Destroying the Idea of America*, New York: Basic Books, 2021). Historian Victor Davis Hanson reawakens our consciousness to revitalize our citizenship virtues, because American citizenship draws on the talents, enterprising spirit, energy, creativity, and innovation of the American population – not the elite officials of big government who have created a government responsible today for only a multitude of crises due to their own inept policies.

Returning to ancient Athens, by the 6th century BC, the rich citizens were ruling Athens, and the common people called upon Solon (638-558 BC), the chief archon at that time, to liberate them. Solon was a lawgiver and a poet, and the Athenians considered him to be a wise (sophos) man. However, Solon was an oligarch who believed that rule was by the few, and the aristocrats still controlled the political life. The historian Herodotus described Solon as a sage, poet, and author of the Athenian Code of Law. Solon was an aristocrat, but he was also a merchant who was aware of the economic impact of trade and was familiar with the problems of the common people. Athens at this time was a society primarily made up of independent farmers who had lost their land holdings to creditors and had become enslaved in debt-bondage. This social crisis led to social and political unrest, and the people elected Solon as head archon in 594 BC to reform the Draconian laws that had forced debtors into slavery. Solon's reforms repealed Draco's harsh edicts (except for the homicide law), he cancelled all debts, passed a law that forbade debtor enslavement, limited the amount of land one person could own, healed the division between the rich and the poor, saved the family farm, allowed no exports other than olive oil (exported corn fetched high prices, however, the Athenians were starving and needed their own corn for consumption), introduced a native coin, established new courts, and created a *polis* where Athenians could rationally and peacefully settle their various conflicts. Solon created the Council of Four Hundred, one hundred members from each of the four tribes; the Council prepared the agendas for the Assembly. Solon divided the Athenians into property classes: *hippeis* (cavalry), *zeugitai* (owners of a yoke of oxen), and the poorest class (*thetes*) or day laborers who were excluded from any state offices. The most important state offices could only be chosen from the top property class (*pentakosiomedimnoi*) which was made up of men who produced a measurable amount of corn, wine, and olives. Solon's reforms shifted the power structure from the rule of the aristocrats or power because of birth status to the rule of wealth.[31]

The laws of Solon functioned as the foundation for Greek politics and culture for hundreds of years. Solon's laws contained private law, criminal law, and procedural law; after the restoration of democracy in 403 BC, provisions for state powers and administrative regulations were added to the laws. After successful reforms and aptly bringing about the just rule of law, Solon voluntarily left Athens for ten years, leaving a leadership vacuum that the Peisistratids family (Peisistratos and his two sons: Hippias who ruled from 527-510 BC, and his younger brother Hipparchus who was murdered in 514 BC, in a failed attempt to murder Hippias by Harmodios and his lover Aristogeiton) filled with a popular tyranny that continued from 561 until 510 BC.[32]

Thirty-three years after Solon's reign of compromise, Peisistratos (608-525 BC) made himself tyrant ruler over Athens in 561 BC by gaining support of his bodyguards and the poor. Our modern connotation of a tyrant is a single ruler, often repressive, violates the laws, lies, and is often violent or unpleasant to the citizens. For American citizens, a tyrant is an elected leader who violates The Constitution of the United States, violates the legislation passed by our elected congress members, violates the state and federal laws, does not protect the citizens or the nation, does not protect the nation's security, allows and encourages illegal aliens to cross our sovereign borders, mandates unconstitutional vaccines that corporations are required to enforce, and where citizens who object to the vaccine will lose their jobs, ignores voters' concerns, and whose unsound actions has led to a continuous on-going crises for the nation. Unlike our modern tyrant, Peisistratos ruled by personal ability although he took power through a coup in violation of the Greek tradition. He was an autocrat who seized power illegitimately. Peisistratos established a revolving loan for farmers and peasants, so that the lower and middle classes could keep possession of their property, and he established "deme-judges" who went on circuit and exercised their judicial powers. (A "deme" is a geographical unit of local government.) Peisistratos and his sons renovated the temple of Athena Polias on the Acropolis, ordered public building projects, expanded the Panathenaic Festival, and sponsored the tragic theatre that took place as part of the Festival of Dionysus. The tyrant and his sons maintained the constitutional reforms of Solon, the Assembly still met and was advised by the council of 400, and the courts still arbitrated any legal disputes. The elites in Athens appeared to hold less power, but the real power was in the hands of Peisistratos. After the death of Peisistratos in 525 BC, political conflict was heightened by the presence of Spartan military forces in Athens. Open civil war broke out between 510 and 508 BC, with a struggle between the Alcmaeonid family and Isagoras who was archon in 508/7 BC, and a Spartan group.

Athenian democracy flourished around the fifth century BC, and Solon (594), Cleisthenes (508/7), Ephialtes (462), and Pericles (461) contributed much to the development of Athenian democracy. The constitutional reforms of Cleisthenes in 508/7 BC removed the domination of the aristocratic families from the city's rule. Cleisthenes welcomed the hoi poloi (ordinary people) into his circle to obtain power, and the first direct democracy was born. The word "democracy" (democratia) combines demos, which means "people" and refers to the entire citizen body, with kratos, which means "force" or "power", "rule" or "authority." Cleisthenes set up 139 deme centers where each Athenian citizen was instructed to register, and the demesmen were responsible for determining the legitimacy of the registration of new citizens. Controlling citizenship registration was one of the means for the community to impose its will against an individual. Ancient Athens exercised a collective mentality in their politics and in their society, as we can see from the practice of ostracism where a majority of the citizens could ostracize a citizen to banishment from the city for ten years. The collective will of the people could ostracize a citizen who threatened the political society for any reason, and the ostracized individual was morally obliged to obey. These citizens from each deme then made up the new advisory council of 500, which Cleisthenes had changed from the Solonian council of 400. The council of 500 was responsible for stating the agenda for the Assembly, and for dealing with any matters of the state. The Athenian assembly and the Areopagus of ancient origin (made up of the old aristocracy), and the Areopagus Council that was made up of nine Archons whose membership was restricted to the wealthy property classes slowly became more democratic with the common citizen (instead of the aristocracy) now able to exercise a voice in the democracy.

Pericles (495-429 BC) was the son of the politician Xanthippus and was born into the powerful Alcmaeonid family on his mother's side. Pericles was an accomplished *rhetor* or orator, and general (*strategos*). Pericles' center of power was his military accomplishments where he gained Athenians' respect for his leadership skills, tactics, intellect, and incorruptible virtue. He led many naval military expeditions against the Peloponnesians. Pericles came to power in Athens in 461 BC, and his political longevity was known as the "Age of Pericles." Pericles shaped and promoted democracy, and under his reign Athens had a period of cultural and political growth: victory in battle, growth of wealth, laws, art, music, literature, and architecture. Pericles was the mastermind behind the building of the Acropolis with the Parthenon, the Propylaea, the temple to Hephaestus and Nemesis, and the golden statue of Athena which was sculpted by his friend Phidias.

Pericles' strategy was to protect the Athenian empire, not expansion, so he fortified the walls around the city to protect her from the Spartans, and he emphasized the cultural practices that honored those Athenians who had died in war. In 430 BC at the annual state funeral, Pericles gave a eulogy of the war-dead; he honored, praised, and glorified the bravery and acts of valor of the fallen soldiers, and their forefathers. Pericles praised Athen's achievements, the *polis*, and its constitution. Athenian commitment to democracy and freedom was demonstrated by a government made up of the majority, and each citizen has equal rights before the law, and has merit and respect. The *Funeral Oration* was designed to stir the spirits of the Athenians during war time and give the community a shared sense of purpose and cohesion.[33] From Pericles' *Funeral Oration* (Pericles' famous speech is from Thucydides' *History of the Peloponnesian War*), we can identify the goals of Athenian democracy: democracy (*demokratia*), freedom (, equality (*isonomia*), justice (*dike*), and free speech (*parrhesia*). These ancient Greek goals for Athenian democracy are the same goals that we strive for today in our American Constitutional Republic.

After Pericles death in 429 BC, Athens was ruled by a series of oligarchs who had gained their wealth from commerce or trade (*neoploutus*). Toward the end of the Peloponnesian War (431-404 BC), the Athenian democracy was interrupted twice by oligarchic revolutions. After the rule of the Thirty Tyrants (404 through 403 BC), democracy was restored in 403 BC. Fifth-century Athens was a potent time when direct democracy was discussed and debated, and the power of persuasion (*peitho*) was used successfully to stir men's minds for the collective freedom of the *polis*. Similarly, it is a potent time today in the United States, where Marxist criticism of our democracy is leading to powerful individual voices defending our democracy.

Democracy was abolished in Athens in 322/321 BC when the Macedonians overran the country. Prior to the end of democracy freedom had meant the rule of law, and the citizens themselves were a part of the decision-making process. The Greeks did not have the concept of individual rights or inalienable rights. The Greek notion of *politeia* contributed to the tradition of constitution-making for the Greeks. We shall discover how the ancient idea of virtue taught to us by the ancient Greek philosophers became a symbol for the politeness and civility of the eighteenth-century Americans.

The first republic — Athens — appeared in ancient Greece. Hellas bequeaths to us the philosophical writing of Plato who teaches us the philosophy of Socrates, and the written works of Aristotle, where we learn the language of politics, and where the political regime (*politeia*) animated the public spirit. Women or slaves were not allowed to vote in the ancient world, however by the fifth century BC citizenship of native-born Athenian males had increased, with the privileges of voting and speaking freely in the assembly. (See, Victor Davis Hanson, *The Dying Citizen: How Progressive Elites, Tribalism, and Globalization Are Destroying the Ideas of America*). The ancient Greek *polis* with its attendant customs, culture, habits, and laws is an excellent study for those of us who ask questions about natural law in reference to our own Constitutional Republic. All the ancient ideas about natural law are important for a modern understanding of natural law. The natural law ethics of ancient Greece are ethics that were pre-Christian philosophical ideas, but nevertheless the ethics were based upon individual and civic virtues, and the development of the human soul within a democracy — all ideas that are critical to an understanding of our modern American Republic.

Natural law ethics can also be identified with a theological theory where the sacred foundation is issued by a command of God. God is the source of natural law, and His creatures are endowed with a rational discernment to understand His moral law that is inscribed in nature. Philosopher John Wild writes, "It is implied that natural law is a theological rather than a philosophical conception, and that it was the idea of divine laws which led to that of natural laws."[34] Wild goes on to write, "The medieval Church stressed its dependence upon the theory of a supreme lawgiver and the arguments of natural theology. But even if there is such a connection, the theory of natural law depends on natural theology, not on revealed theology, a point which needs to be stressed."[35] Natural law theory states that the principles of law are inherent in the nature of things, and we can understand these laws through our ability to reason. Christians believe that we are rational beings, and our reason reflects the image of God. God's universally valid principles guide us as we work toward the perfection of what it means to be God's creature. As rational creatures, we have the ability to discern right from wrong, but it is only with Christ's guidance that we have the ability to develop a moral perspective and live a life of virtue in preparation for an eternal life. Christian wisdom inquires where are we today in the body of Christ?

Natural law is a universal concept that is applicable to everyone, everywhere and at all times, and is part of our human nature. This definition of natural law is adapted from the natural law definition by the philosopher John Wild.[36] As a Christian philosopher, I understand that natural law is given to us as beings created in the image of God, and we come to know God's precepts for us, and His moral expectations of us, through natural law. The ancient Greek philosophers were pre-Christians, but they believed in the existence of a universal goodness, virtue, morality, and truth. The ancient Greeks debated the concepts of nature versus convention in morals and law, and these debates took place in the fifth and fourth centuries in Athens. An understanding of the ancient Greek distinction between nature and convention is helpful to the modern student in understanding natural law. The ancient, fifth-century, philosophers known as the Sophists, for example, believed that morality and law were conventional, and they made their living teaching other prominent Athenians various skills to advance in life, including the art of politics, public speaking, rhetoric, and the management of personal affairs. *Protagoras*, for example, was a professional sophist who became famous as a character in Plato's dialogue the *Protagoras* where Socrates examines the usefulness of *Protagoras*' sophistic teaching. (Other famous sophists in Ancient Greece were Gorgias, Antiphon, Hippies, Prodicus, and Thrasymachus). *Protagoras* taught the young Athenian men the art of disputation and rhetoric for a fee. The argument in Plato's *Protagoras* revolves on whether virtue can be taught. *Protagoras* claimed to teach virtue, but his definition of virtue was that it was useful to advance one's position in life. *Protagoras* taught that "man is the measure of all things," which meant that man is the source of law, truth, and value, and that there is no final truth. This relativistic philosophy — which leaves God's role out of our lives — is widely taught today. Plato and Socrates, on the other hand, taught that truth was a universal quality, and that the usefulness of the virtues was to train the soul to recognize and understand virtue, so that we may apply this knowledge to daily living. Socrates claimed that virtue is knowledge, and therefore virtue can be taught. (See Plato's Dialogue *Protagoras*). Our beliefs in natural law can trace arguments back to the ancient Greeks where philosophers like Plato, Socrates and Aristotle believed in the innate and universal characteristics of natural law versus the conventional belief that the laws and values were contrived from social, political, and cultural teaching, and conventions, and not God. (See Plato's Dialogue *Protagoras*).

Socrates was a philosopher born in 469 BC in the deme Alopeke on the slopes of Mount Lycabettus — a short walk to Athens. We know Socrates through the words of Plato who presents his master as the main interlocutor in the philosophical inquiry that takes place in the Platonic *Dialogues*. Socrates' famous student Plato was born in 427 BC into an aristocratic family on both his mother and father's side. Plato met Socrates when he was twenty years old and became his disciple until Socrates' death by hemlock in 399 BC. Aristotle was born in 384 BC in the Macedonian city of Stagira on the peninsula of Chalcidice (on the northern perimeter of Classical Greece). Aristotle's father was the physician Nicomachus, and his mother was Phaestis — both parents were of aristocratic Greek descent. Aristotle joined Plato's Academy in 367 BC, at the age of seventeen, and spent twenty years in the program. Aristotle was deeply influenced by Platonism; however, he taught and wrote many of his objections to the complex Platonic ideas.

Socrates was the most interesting figure of antiquity, and it can easily be said that he was also the most controversial philosopher. Socrates was a philosopher and a lover of wisdom, but he did not teach in an ordinary way — he did not have a classroom, nor did he put anything in writing. Socrates walked through the streets of ancient Athens and questioned the townspeople because he believed that his questions could bring out knowledge that lay dormant in the interlocutor's mind, and that this knowledge would bear fruit. Today, we learn Socrates' philosophy through the pen of Plato and the Platonic *Dialogues*. Plato wrote his dialogues five centuries before the birth of Christ. Socrates was interested in questioning and examining concepts: beauty, justice, goodness, truth, and virtue. Socrates' political vision was an ethical pursuit, where he believed that the state should place ethics above power and wealth. Socrates practiced a systematic form of interrogation to discover if his interlocutors knew what they claimed to know, and whether they agreed with the Socratic moral position that takes virtue seriously. We follow Socrates in our quest for wisdom and truth and learn to utilize our reasoning powers to dialectically examine the nature of man and particular things.

Socrates awakens in us a quest for philosophical wisdom – we can picture him walking through the streets of ancient Athens and engaging others in the exercise of question and answer. Plato gives us our image of Socrates who is the main character in the Platonic dialogues. We see Socrates, the philosopher, who is an ethical man in search of moral and ethical principles. When we follow Socrates, we learn to trust in our reasoning power. We discover that the path to truth is discerned through dialectical question and answer, and reasoned arguments. Socrates held that there was a divine being higher than man, and that this divine being had wisdom that surpassed what we have.[37] Socrates believed that god ordered him to teach that the state of the soul was our chief concern, and that tending the soul was more important than tending the body.[38] In Socrates' closing statement to the Athenian jury in his trial for impiety, he said, "A good man cannot be harmed either in life or in death,..."[39] Virtue depends on knowledge.[40] The good for man is the complete realization of his nature.

Socrates sought natural law by subjecting the laws to a critical examination, to find the essential characteristic of the thing questioned. Socrates believed that it was his divine mission to discover what is good by nature, i.e., intrinsically good versus what is good by convention.[41] The legal codes in Ancient Greece came from numerous sources described as divine (oracles, dreams, and visions), tradition, and custom (ancestral customs).

During the height of Athenian democracy philosophers, military leaders, statesman, historians, dramatists, playwrights, sculptors, poets, architects, ship builders, farmers and talented artisans were the intellectual and cultural achievers of the city. Reading the ancient historians, Herodotus, and Thucydides (460-400 BC), we gain a more comprehensive insight into the history, politics, and culture of the ancient Greek world. The playwrights Aeschylus, Aristophanes, Sophocles, and Euripides entertained the ancient Greeks with their political, philosophical, and satiric dramatization of the *polis*. The creative advances of the Greek sculptors Praxiteles, and Polyclitus were so remarkable that their style was copied by the Romans. The artisans who created the Attican red-figure pottery are admired even today in the Greek museums and world-wide.

Democracy flourished in Athens for almost two centuries, while Rome at the time was debating the positive assets of republicanism. Democracy and republicanism were no longer a part of Greece and Rome during the time of Christ. During the mid-seventeenth century democratic ideas will resurface, and we can say that the freedom of speech that was important for citizens in ancient Athens becomes important once again in democratic nations. We can define a democratic nation as one that maintains the free nature of the human being and allows its citizens to participate in free and fair elections.

The free exercise of natural law is essential for any democratic nation. Natural law is that element that is essential to our particular mode of being something that is natural is what is fundamental to our existence. Natural law is fundamental to our existence. The concept of natural law is an axiological idea. Axiology is derived from two Greek words: axis (worth or value), and logos (logic, theory, or reasoning), and is considered to be a theory of value. As an axiological idea, natural law will enable us to identify the values that influence our beliefs, perceptions, decisions, actions, and deeds. Natural law is a fundamental framework for our patterns of thinking, and as we utilize natural law reasoning, we understand cognate notions, for example, democracy, freedom, liberty, and justice. There is a necessary and logical connection between the ideas of natural law, individual freedom, and democratic rule. Socrates teaches us that the methodology to understand natural law is through the utilization of dialectic, i.e., question and answer, cross-examination, refutation (*elenches*), and inductive reasoning. Socratic philosophy forces us to re-examine our beliefs, and to clarify our conceptual notions.

When Chaerephon, one of Socrates' friends, asked the Delphic Oracle to name the wisest person in Athens, the Oracle replied that it was Socrates. That inspired a life-long search by the philosopher to find the wisest person in Greece, and Socrates concluded that his own wisdom meant that he knew nothing, and he was conscious of his own ignorance. Socrates' search for the wisest person in Athens, led him to his life-long occupation of walking throughout the Athenian *Agora* and questioning his fellow Athenians. Socrates' mission was a rational inquiry and moral examination of his fellow Athenians. Socrates' philosophizing remained within the public sphere of the *polis*; but where he became intimate within the private sphere of the individual was with his elenchos of the doctrine of the soul. He examined each thing dialectically and asked the meaning of what a thing is. Socrates' philosophy is important for us today because he does not teach us what to think, but how to think.

Socrates' political vision was an ethical pursuit, where he believed that the state should place ethics above power and wealth. Socrates asked many questions: what justice (*dikeosyni*) is, virtue (*arete*), moderation (*sophrosune*), courage (*andreia*), good (*agathos*), and piety (*eusebeia*). Socrates' search for *arete*, excellence, had a moral purpose. The Socratic questions of how we ought to live, and how do we have knowledge of the virtue which leads to happiness as we live the right way, are questions that we continue to ask ourselves today. The natural law ethics of Socrates is the same natural law ethics that we use today to discover the truth and wisdom of the animating spiritual kernel of our souls.

Socrates examined the consistency of the beliefs of the person that he questioned. "The unexamined life is not worth living."[42] Although Socrates was born in an era of polytheism and superstition, he taught that virtue could assist us in becoming a better human being. For Socrates, virtue was found through the practice of philosophy. Virtue is without gender. Socrates hears a "divine voice."[43] This supernatural voice (*daimonion*) advised him on what course of action that he should not take.[44] Socrates did believe in a divine being of intelligence and power.[45] Both Plato and Xenophon refer to Socrates' religious dimension. Socrates' soul looks out to ancient Athens with wisdom's eye.

The Socratic virtues are courage, moderation, justice, and practical wisdom. (Also described today as prudence, temperance, justice, and fortitude). Socrates teaches us that the virtues are not just good in themselves, i.e., good characteristics, but are the means to the end for exemplifying the noble or beautiful (to *kalon*). Liberty is the means to express the acts of a virtuous man. Civic virtue is commendable but is not a complete virtue; the fuller excellence is moral or ethical virtue.[46] Great moral challenges are found in the actions of the leaders of the *polis*, for example, Solon, who exhibited courage, moderation, justice, and practical wisdom. Aristotle reminds us that, "Experience with regard to particular facts is also thought to be courage; this is indeed the reason why Socrates thought courage was knowledge."[47]

Plato and Aristotle taught us that virtue is consistent with justice — our Founding Fathers would agree with this assessment of virtue. Today, however, we have externalized our virtues where a person will describe himself or herself as a virtuous person, but their actions are not virtues actions. (Instead of internalizing our virtues as Socrates taught us to internalize our virtues, and he taught that virtue is knowledge). Knowing what the right thing to do is, will then lead us to make the right choices. We need to know what the higher natural law is and how we access it, because knowledge of natural law will provide us the knowledge of the right action in the situation. Socrates examined morality and religion to discover the higher natural law and the highest virtue. A republican civil society must have committed statesmen who exhibit leadership skills and among these skills are virtue and wisdom. Plato wrote that philosophers use their wisdom and intelligence to bring about virtue and happiness in the citizen body. This rule of reason also influenced Aristotle's philosophy where he wrote that intelligence will rule over desire, and that law is intelligence without desire.[48]

Plato speaks for Socrates in the early Platonic dialogues. Xenophon wrote about Socrates to clear Socrates' name of the charges of impiety, and he gives us an accurate account of Socrates' religious beliefs (See Xenophon's *Memorabilia*), and Socrates was satirized by the playwright Aristophanes in the Clouds.

Plato uses the linguistic term "the law of nature" infrequently[49] (See *Gorgias* 484 and *Timaeus* 83e); however, the concept of "natural law", (*nomos tes phuseos*), where the world is governed by a normative order for human beings who can access this intelligible structure through reason, emerges from Plato's works. The ancient Greeks viewed "nature" as a notion that represented what was not permanent. "Law" was viewed as something that was part of human agreement. Plato's dialogues analyze the concepts of the "natural", (*phusei*) and what is "according to nature" (*kata phusin*). Plato uses the word "nature" to refer to changing events, the general flux within the world, the motion of the stars, and the laws of change in nature.[50]

For the ancient Greeks, the role of government and laws was to make human beings good. The legislator's job is to legislate for the common good. For Plato, reason has the authority to rule, therefore, government should aim at virtue and reflect reason. Citizens will obey the law because it is a part of the rule of reason which has the aim and common interest of the individual good. Natural law is an expression of natural justice for the ancient Greeks.

For the ancient Romans, natural law is defined as natural right. (See Cicero, Senecca, and Epictetus). St. Thomas brought Greek learning, and Christian doctrine together in a remarkable examination of natural law. For St. Thomas, natural law derives from our human nature — a nature that follows the Aristotelian essentialist philosophy that is teleological in that it follows our various capacities toward final causes. For St. Thomas, for example, there is a correlation between what we desire and what nature intends for us as our end.

For the fifth-century Athenians, the idea of political power was evolving from the power that belonged to the privileged few by birth or wealth, to the promise for freedom, justice, and political rights (*isonomia*) for the *polis* as a whole community (*koinonia*). Cleisthenes (570-508 BC) was regarded as the founder of Athenian democracy, and he believed that political responsibility was based on Athenian citizenship, not on the membership in a clan. The constitution of Cleisthenes, for example, represented the idea of equality for Athenian citizens before the law.

Plato was the founder of natural law philosophy, however, as a pre-Christian philosopher, his philosophical theories did not include Christian revelation. (For an example of a natural law philosophy that is inclusive of Christian revelation see, for example, St. Thomas Aquinas). Plato's analysis of human nature, and essential rational characteristics that lead us toward the care of the soul and our human realization are pre-Christian notions. The pagans believed that god(s) were limited by the laws of nature, and they created an ordered cosmos out of chaos and unformed matter. Contrast this with the Christian beliefs (from the Holy Bible) that God is not bound by the laws of nature, and God created matter "out of nothing" by willing it. Plato taught that god is the cosmic order of nature and holds the norms of justice within this nature.[51] Both Plato and Aristotle identified natural law with natural justice and righteousness.

The Platonic dialogues are intelligent, entertaining, and creative dialogues that examine philosophic issues that are still relevant for each of us today: the meaning of wisdom, knowledge, virtue, justice, and happiness. The universal and inestimable value of wisdom was discussed frequently by the ancient Athenian philosophers. Socrates comes to mind as a seeker of the truth, and an example of a wisdom seeker, and for those who have studied Socrates' teaching; we can easily say that he was a sage. We know by studying philosophy that Socrates did indeed embody wisdom, compassion, and loving-kindness to others as he practiced the art of dialectic with others. In our current day, I cannot remember when I last read or heard of someone living today as being referred to as wise. The activity and thinking of a wise person, or a wisdom seeker cannot be surpassed in excellence. Plato taught that the natural law is contained within the existential structure of each entity. The human law is grounded in the structure of the universe and divine judgements. The outcome of studying Plato's philosophy, however, leads us to the harmony of the soul that is, today, also our gift as Christians, with the addition of our love for and belief in Jesus Christ.

The Republic is the most well-known of the Platonic dialogues and is the name of the city that Plato creates in his philosophical writings, but this city does not actually exist. Plato wrote the *Republic* approximately 380 BC, after the execution of his beloved teacher Socrates. We can imagine Plato walking in the olive groves of the Academy where he had retired to teach, and how he relived his Masters' words with the markings of his pen onto wax tablets where his words were later transcribed onto possibly papyrus.[52] The tragic loss of his teacher must have influenced Plato's criticism of democracy as a form of government. The *Republic*'s focus is on the rule of reason within the political realm, and on an individual's life, and how they are based on a divine foundation. In the *Republic*, Socrates considers a range of subjects to defend the just life: rival theories of justice, nature, competing views of human happiness, education, philosophy, the role of philosophers, virtues and vices, the good and bad souls, political regimes, the structure of reality, the Forms, the nature of the Good, the role of women, and the purpose of art in society. Socrates examines these questions within the context of the political communities, and in terms of the individual person or soul. Plato constructs a city to examine virtue, and then (through Socrates' personae) he illustrates it by the analogy of justice in the individual human soul.

There are diverse interpretations of the Platonic philosophy; this author ascribes to the cogent interpretations of John H. Hallowell, John Wild, and Paul Shorey — critical studies that demonstrate Plato's realistic ethics of natural law. John Wild defines natural or moral law as, "a universal pattern of action, applicable to all men everywhere, required by human nature.[53] Wild's examination of the incorrect interpretations of Platonic theory demonstrates that Plato's critics hold that norms are man-made constructions whose existence is legislated by arbitrary human interests.[54] Wild guides us in understanding the correct interpretation of Plato's natural law theory. The Platonic standard of justice is natural and known through reason, and the human laws will conform to this natural law. Natural justice is universal and eternal, whereas legal justice is particular and temporal. The Athenian city-state (*polis*) was a self-governing community that centered on a city, and in this case it was

Athens.[55] The *polis* was the appropriate place for the citizens to become better human beings, because the city-state promoted the good in all things by promoting justice; the *polis* included religion, politics, family, society, trade, and in the case of Socrates' teaching, philosophy. Socrates enjoyed gathering in the marketplace (*agora*) and engaging the Athenian youth in an exercise of dialectic where Socrates asks questions of the youth. When we read the Platonic *Dialogues*, we learn that the Socratic examination deepens the Athenians understanding of key natural law ideas and concepts and enlightens individual actions in response to the knowledge of these concepts.

Plato's natural law theory is founded on his ontological and epistemological principles. The Platonic epistemology (the study of the nature and validity of knowledge) and ontology (the study of the existence and methods of discovering these truths) are bound together. For Plato, true knowledge of changing sensible objects is impossible, for each person experiences their own reality and develops their own theories of the world and how they perceive it. However, if an individual is philosophically trained to utilize the mind, he/she will have intellectual knowledge regarding the world of Forms — perceived through a dialectical process of reasoning. Our soul is affected by a clarity and truth through the partaking of the Platonic Forms without the utilization of the senses. The Platonic Forms (mathematical, ethical, and physical ideals) subsist in a metaphysical realm and are eternal, uncreated, and immutable.

Essentially, natural law theory is a concept that Plato portrays through the utilization of the Theory of Forms. The Forms (*eidos*) are absolute patterns and standards of judgment for the individuals in the sensible world and are "seen" by the intellect. Justice, for example, subsists within the Form of the Good, and when one learns this, then he/she is in a state of true knowledge. The Platonic Forms are the true being or essence of things: justice, beauty, and goodness. These Forms are unchanging, indestructible, and incorruptible. Sensible things are copies of the unchanging Forms, and any change will tend toward corruption in proportion to the movement that leads away from participation in the Forms. Plato writes that only philosopher "kings" (those individuals who are wise enough to rule the community because they have knowledge of the Forms) are trained to understand the true Forms, moving intellectually from the sensible Forms that are viewed in the phenomenal world, to the Form of the Good where all the true Forms of knowledge, truth and beauty will emanate from.[56] As patterns for the individuals in the sensible world, the Forms are the absolute standards of judgment. Plato writes that the philosopher loves what is (the Forms), not what is becoming (the world of senses). For example, if one is asked to indicate "justice," and replies that justice is a set of laws, then this person is in a state of opinion regarding justice. However, after education, training, and the utilization of the dialectical process of reasoning, we can learn to comprehend the Form of justice itself.[57]

Platonic natural-law theory is critical for us to understand so that our modern ethical ideas can easily evolve to a moral reliance on natural law. This is the vision of moral citizens that will — hopefully in the future — participate in and animate our representative government. And it was Socrates' vision for those who ruled, and the rule of law in Athens, that those who governed, and the government would be founded upon the knowledge of the development of the soul of its citizens. In the *Apology*, Socrates also expresses basic convictions that are compatible with natural law theory. Socrates maintained that the evils of the soul are worse than evils of the body;[58] therefore, we can deduce that Socrates believed that we are a composite of body and soul, and the soul is more integral to our moral development than the body,[59] that tending to the soul is a key to our proper development, and that virtue depends upon knowledge.[60]

For Plato, the role of reason is a central theme in both ethics and politics. Plato's *Republic* offers the reader an understanding of the role of reason in the political realm that is based on a divine foundation. For Plato, the physical laws of nature exist as the organic principles of things, but it is the universal moral laws that are according to nature and will relate to the political life and our conduct in life. Plato's *Republic* offers us a city that is based upon a rational political order, with rational citizens who are striving to improve their souls.

Plato tells us that he was a devoted follower of Socrates (*Apology*), and we hear the voice of Socrates in the Platonic dialogues. Socrates subjected the laws of Athens to critical examination by seeking what is good by nature instead of convention. (*Republic* 538 d3-4; *Statesman* 296 e8-9). In the *Republic*, however, Socrates does teach us about the nature of political things, and, instead, we gain an understanding of the relationship of the philosopher (and the important role that the philosopher plays) to the political community. In Plato's *Republic* Book I, written in approximately 380 BC, the main character, Socrates, asks the question, what is justice? The question is answered in the *Republic* Book IV, as Socrates examines this query within the context of the political community, and in terms of the individual living within a political community. In the *Republic*, Socrates develops a position on justice and its relationship to human happiness (eudaemonia). Is the just person happier than the unjust person? Plato uses the concept of order or harmony to define justice; justice is a harmony in the *polis*; and justice is a harmony in our soul.

We have already noted that the *Republic* is one of Plato's most well-known dialogues, and it describes a city that Plato artistically creates but does not actually exist. Plato's *Republic* examines the nature of justice both within the city (political community) and within the individual soul. Today, in our study of natural law, we are learning that natural law addresses justice. In America, for example, our Constitutional Republic was designed to give maximum freedom to our citizens in all areas of their individual private and public lives, for example, their social, religious, and political endeavors. Our Constitution protects us from harm from others, or harm from the community, or harm from the government, and we have legal redress if there is a violation of that protection. Justice is a vital concept for natural law seekers; and it is a key concept for our legal system. We know that our God-given natural law protects us within justice; and the legal system is our communal and constitutional source for that justice. An example of the importance of justice for us today is the current crisis of the Corona virus pandemic that has caused 53,275 deaths so far (as of April 25, 2020) in the United States, and 201,502 related deaths in the world. "Why, O Lord, do you stand far off? Why do you hide yourself in times of trouble?" (Psalm 10:1). Senator Tom Cotton and Representative Dan Crenshaw have produced legislation that would allow Americans to sue China for virus damages to health, individuals, businesses, and the economy. The Bill would amend the Foreign Sovereignty Immunities Act to create a narrow exception to seek damages caused by China's dangerous mishandling of the Wuhan Virus outbreak. The communist regime of China maliciously lied and covered up the virus allowing it to spread faster and further than it otherwise would have, and so China's actions can be considered a tortious act. The American's loss of life, the loss of livelihood, and the economic disaster caused by the virus was further exacerbated when state governors began curtailing citizen's liberties and movements by mandating the closure of the public sphere – restaurants, bars, health clubs, small shops, libraries, movie theaters, bowling alleys, beauty and barber shops, -- preventing citizens from conducting their individual business affairs, and preventing citizens from exercising their religious liberty to worship in a church or synagogue. The overreaching of governmental authority and power is in stark contrast to our individual freedoms that are protected by our United States Constitution. It is important for us to study natural law and the Constitution of the United States of America so that we can push-back against these unconstitutional and illegal mandates; natural law is at the foundation of our natural rights and is the basis of the formation of our Constitution.

Socrates' questions lead us to examine our ideas of justice, liberty, equality, virtue, and freedom. These ideas are a rational outcome of natural law thinking, and a rational outcome of our laws based upon a common history, heritage, and American development of British common law. Our Constitutional laws are always in harmony with natural law to be considered just laws. The idea of justice was also a key concept for Socrates who also wanted to know if the just man (or woman) was happier than the unjust? It is important for us to study Socrates' ethics because he teaches us how to question everything, and to question in a dialectical (question and answer) and rational manner. God has created us as questioning and curious beings; to ask questions and to seek answers is the beginning of wisdom.

The events in the Republic Book I, take place on the festival day of the goddess Bendis (Artemis) at the Pireaus, and in the house of Cephalus. Socrates has a lively discussion with Cephalus (a wealthy merchant and businessman who is the father of Polemarchus), Polemarchus, and Thrasymachus on the subject of aging which brings the men around to discussing "justice." We know that Socrates was a charming and personable philosopher because of the crowds of men that would follow him and engage him in conversation. On this day, the men ask Socrates to accompany them for the pleasure of his company. When the men begin talking about the subject of aging, Cephalus tells Socrates that the loss of youthful vigor is pleasantly liberating. Socrates suggests that perhaps Cephalus' personal wealth brings about a level of comfort that attributes to his material well-being. Cephalus admits that wealth does give one peace of mind when facing the afterlife. Cephalus says that "when someone thinks that the end is near, he becomes frightened and concerned about things he didn't fear before. It's then that the stories about Hades, about how people who've been unjust here must pay the penalty there..."[61]

Cephalus' definition of justice (*dikaiosyne*) is that one speaks the truth and pays back debts, i.e., justice is defined as giving back what is owed."[62] Socrates and Cephalus agree that truth-telling and paying back one's debts is not a definition of justice. Cephalus leaves the discussion, and the conversation is then taken up by Polymarchus who clarifies Cephalus' position to define justice as to give a man what he deserves, i.e., "the art which gives goods to friends and evil to enemies."[63] Polemarchus reminds Socrates that the poet Simonides (considered to be wise) defined justice as giving to each what is due to him. Polemarchus stated that it is just to do good to your friends, and to harm your enemies. Socrates responded that we can be mistaken about who are friends, and who are our enemies, therefore, the just man could unintentionally harm his friends and help his enemies.

At this point in the conversation, Socrates brings in the notion of a craft (techne), which is any skill or activity that requires a specialized knowledge — to help clarify the idea of justice. For example, a physician is skilled at healing people and keeping them alive; however, he could also be proficient at killing people if he was inclined to do so. So, Socrates asks is the physician just? Polemarchus responded to Socrates question by stating that a just man is capable of benefitting friends and harming enemies, and in both waging war and in alliances. Socrates asks Polemarchus if one is not at war, how can he be helped by the just person? Polemarchus responded that justice helps one to use or acquire contracts. Socrates asks him if what he means by contracts is partnerships, and Polemarchus answered yes. Socrates then enquired what special skill does an ethical person have that is helpful in contracts. Polemarchus stated that they are excellent with keeping money and other valuable items safe by guarding them. Socrates asked if he is so good at guarding money, then will he be equally clever at stealing it?[64] Polemarchus has become confused under the critical examination and states that he no longer knows what he meant except that "I still believe that justice means to benefit one's friends and harm one's enemies." Socrates keeps pursuing the matter, "When someone is harmed do they become worse in human virtue (*arete*)?" Socrates defines justice as human virtue; therefore, he concluded that "people who are harmed must become more unjust." Socrates asked Polemarchus, "It isn't the function of a just person to harm a friend or anyone else; rather it is the function of his opposite, an unjust person?"[65]

The Platonic dialogues are full of colorful characters who are seeking justice and truth, and Socrates is the most charming and eccentric of the philosophers. Socrates drew his listeners to his philosophy, and to his teaching of the truth, in order for them to gain knowledge and wisdom. Socrates taught his fellow Athenians to care primarily for their souls. Socrates exhibited love toward his fellow Athenians, and he served as a lifelong teacher for the care of their virtue and spiritual nature. This love that Socrates held toward his fellow citizens is the same type of love that is needed today in America, where we must open our hearts to others to save our Republic and our Constitution that our Founders worked so hard to create. Today, with an alarming spread of Marxist ideology, it is crucial for us to continue to strive to understand and implement the constitutional concepts of individual freedom. We Americans are a spiritual and loving people, and our nation was founded upon a belief in God – we continue to hold that belief today. The assault on our religious freedoms and beliefs has strengthened us to fight back for our freedoms – God has furnished us with a shield and a sword for a purpose! We pledge our allegiance to the United States of America and our fidelity is to the Constitution of the United States of America.

In the *Republic*, Book I, Plato writes that Thrasymachus was agitated by the discussion with Socrates and soon he, "coiled himself up like a wild beast about to spring, and he hurled himself at us as if to tear us to pieces."[66] Thrasymachus yelled at Socrates, "Give an answer yourself, and tell us what you say the just is...tell me clearly and exactly what you mean; for I won't accept such nonsense from you."[67] Socrates responded that he never claimed to have the answer, and since an eminent man like Thrasymachus forbids him to express an opinion, then it is best to let Thrasymachus give his own thoughts on the subject.

Thrasymachus defines justice as the advantage of the stronger.[68] Socrates refutes all these positions on justice and confesses ignorance on the definition of justice.[69] Socrates concluded that he cannot know if justice is beneficial until he knows what the essence of justice is. Socrates argues that the just life is better than the unjust, and that a just person is good and clever where an unjust person is ignorant and bad.[70] Injustice causes disharmony and prevents effective action. Justice can be expressed as the virtue of the soul where the soul is performing its functions well, and this leads to a happier person.[71] If the soul's end is life, and the activity of that end is the fulfillment of life, then justice is the excellence of the soul, and the just man will enjoy a better quality of life.

In Book IV in the *Republic*, Socrates again sets out his belief that virtue promotes happiness, and that knowledge is necessary for virtue. Each man in the city is assigned an occupation that best suites his natural talents. (This assignment is given by the wise ruler who is a philosopher king because he knows the nature of what is essential and real, i.e., the Forms. The Forms are grasped after a strict regimen of dialectical thought and training, and after a preparation in mathematics). The city must contain justice, as well as wisdom, courage, and temperance, which are the corresponding virtues that are also found in the individual soul. The three classes of men found within this city are the guardians or rulers (wisdom), soldiers (courage), and producers or farmers and artisans (appetite) — temperance is found in all three classes. When these distinct classes perform their duties well, the result is a harmony that is called political justice. Then when the three parts of the human soul (the rational, the spirited, and the appetitive) are performing their tasks well, they are in harmony. This harmony is called individual justice. Justice is the virtue that allows all these characteristics to strive within the three classes of men, and within the individual soul. Virtue is the natural functioning of the soul; and vice is the disordered or corrupted nature of the soul.[72] Human nature is active, and natural law requires virtuous action, and this action is the same pattern for everyone. Our natural law goal is to complete our human nature. The primary goal for living well is to care for the soul.

The harmony within the soul produces justice within the *polis*, where all three classes of men will serve, and therefore we will find harmony within the whole state.[73]

The concept of liberty (*eleutheria*) included liberty in the public sphere and personal liberty in the private sphere. Liberty in the public sphere was the right of every citizen to participate individually in the institutions of the state. Personal liberty was every citizen's right to live his life without being oppressed by others. The ancient Greek notion of liberty was not individualistic as our modern notion of liberty is, for example, as contained in the *Declaration of Independence* where our life, liberty and pursuit of happiness are protected by our Constitution, and equality is asserted as a fact based upon the law of nature. That we are equal according to natural law, we then have equal opportunity to prosper in all things. Historian Mogens Herman Hansen teaches us that the Athenians had several terms for equality 1) *isonomia* which referred to equal political rights. *Isonomia* does not refer to equality under the law, which modern political equality refers to, but in ancient Athens it refers to the equal rights of the citizens to exercise their political rights; 2) *isegoria* which meant equal rights to address the political assemblies, and equal right of speech. Freedom of speech was a recognized freedom in ancient Athens, and one that was practiced by many of the Athenians, especially Socrates; 3) *isogonia* which was equality by birth; 4) isokratia which was equality of power. The reader will notice that the ancient Greek notion of equality was used in a political sense, and not used in any manner to refer to the social or economic spheres of the *polis*.[74]

Socrates was seventy years old in 399 BC when his beloved Athens indicted him for breaking the law for 'impiety,' for offending the Olympian gods by not recognizing the gods of the state and introducing new divinities, and corruption of the youth. Socrates was charged before the basileus by Meletus, and his accomplices Anytus and Lycan. Socrates defended himself by his claim that he followed the gods through his devotion to philosophy. We read in the Apology, "It is said that Socrates commits a crime by corruption of the young men and not recognizing the gods that the city recognizes, but some other new religion."[75] He told the jury of 501 male Athenians that he was a good person, and because he understood what to care about, he knew how to behave. The jury voted for conviction. Socrates tells the men of the jury, "Now the hour to part has come. I go to die, you go to live. Which of us goes to the better lot is known to no one except the god."[76] Death did not silence Socrates' wise tongue; Plato's pen kept Socrates' words alive and gave him immortality.

It saddens us to think that the ancient Athenians — who placed such a premium on every citizen's right to free speech (*parrhesia*) — put Socrates to death, when the philosopher spent his life teaching (without any monetary renumeration) the citizens about the nature of virtue, justice, goodness, and the care of the soul. We can suggest that Socrates was brought to trial because of his association with malfeasants during Athen's defeat in the Peloponnesian War, and his silence during the oligarchs' reign of terror (404 BC through 403 BC) had left him under suspicion. In the *Apology*, Socrates acknowledged that his only knowledge was ignorance, and that he was not competent to teach anyone about political things. When we study the *Dialogues* of Plato and learn about Socrates, we soon become aware that the Socratic virtues (justice, virtue, integrity, loyalty, honesty, and goodness) are the moral foundations for any political activity, and, although, Socrates denies any political involvement in political things, his philosophy is necessary for a moral political community. For the ancient Greeks, the city's soul was the essence of the political regime (*politeia*). When they executed Socrates, the city did damage to its soul. We take Socrates' words to heart when, on the eve of his death, he says, "The unexamined life is not worth living for men."[77]

Chapter 3

Natural Law and Aristotle

"We hold these truths to be self-evident, that all Men are created equal, that they are endowed by their Creator with certain unalienable Rights, that among these are Life, Liberty, and the Pursuit of Happiness." The precepts of natural law are expressed by Thomas Jefferson in this sentence in the *Declaration of Independence*. Jefferson's natural law declaration in the *Declaration of Independence* was the foundation for the right for Americans to revolt against the tyranny of King George III. These natural rights remain the foundation for our republican democracy: equality, equal rights, liberty, and individual freedom that are so crucial to our well-being today. Thomas Jefferson's words reflect an understanding of Aristotle's philosophy of happiness and how to pursue it. In a letter to Henry Lee, May 8, 1825, Jefferson writes that the ideas of the Declaration came from the ideas of Aristotle, Cicero, Locke, and Sidney. In Jefferson's correspondence, Aristotle is only mentioned four times; however, the Founders knew Aristotle's ideas primarily through the works of Machiavelli, Bacon, Sidney, Harrington, Locke, and Montesquieu. At the foundation of Aristotle's philosophy are natural law principles. Aristotle teaches the universal nature of the moral law, the normative grounding of nature, and that the ultimate good for human beings is the realization of human nature.[78] Aristotle discusses natural law in the *Nicomachaen Ethics*, the *Politics*, and in the *Rhetoric*. Understanding the history of natural law is important for our understanding of republicanism.

Aristotle (384-322 BC) was born in the Macedonia city of Stagira, on the peninsula of Chalcidice (on the northern perimeter of Classical Greece). Aristotle was the son of a doctor who provided the young

Aristotle with a private tutor. Aristotle was eighteen years old when he joined Plato's Academy (368/7 BC), (Plato's Academy was distinguished within the Greek world as a place for learning) where he remained until the age of thirty-seven -- after Plato's death (348/7 BC). After his departure from the Academy, Aristotle spent five years in Assos on the coast of Asia Minor and then on the island of Lesbos where he devoted some time to empirical research, scientific observation, and marine biology. It was while Aristotle was in Lesbos that he married Pythias, the niece of Hermeias (Aristotle's host and the former ruler of Assos). Aristotle and Pythias had one daughter together named Pythias.

In 343/2 BC, Philip, King of Macedon, invited Aristotle to Lesbos, the capital of Macedonia to tutor his thirteen-year-old son, Alexander (who would later be known in history as Alexander the Great. Alexander was a spirited and passionate youth who enjoyed taming wild horses). Aristotle remained as Alexander's tutor, until Alexander was appointed regent for his father in 340 BC.

When Aristotle returned to Athens, he established the Lyceum (or *Peripatos*) in 335 BC, a program of study for all branches of philosophical and scientific inquiry that included ethics, aesthetics, logic, physics, biology, zoology, metaphysics, poetry and poetics, theatre, music, rhetoric, linguistics, politics, government, and science. Whereas Plato's Academy had focused on mathematics, speculative and political philosophy, Aristotle's Lyceum favored the natural sciences and biology. Aristotle enjoyed walking along the Lykeios (the athletic fields) while he lectured his students — adjacent to the temple of Apollo where the Lyceum was located. The Walk was called *Peripatos* — therefore Aristotle's school is later referred to as the Peripatetic School. Aristotle has been described as slight of build with small eyes, thinning hair (or bald), a short beard, and was said to have spoken with a lisp. Aristotle left Athens when Athenian political sentiment became anti-Macedonian after the death of Alexander the Great in Babylon in 323 BC. (Where Alexander the Great had reigned for twelve years). Aristotle remarked that he left Athens so that the Athenians could not sin twice against philosophy (a reference made to the Athenian execution of Socrates by hemlock poisoning in 399 BC). Socrates accepted this judgment by Athens, rather than fleeing into exile away from the city that he loved. Aristotle died in 322 BC in Chalcis, on Euboea, an island off the Attic coast.

As well as Plato, Aristotle may be regarded as one of the founders of the natural law philosophy. Philosopher John Wild, writes in *Plato's Modern Enemies and the Theory of Natural Law*, that the three concepts of moral realism that represent the philosophy of natural law are the universality of moral law, norms that are grounded in nature, and the ultimate good for man is a realization of human nature.[79] These three basic natural law principles are taught by Aristotle, and taught by his master, Plato. Aristotle teaches that finite entities act in harmony with the laws of nature. Human beings have essential traits in common and act in accordance with a universal moral law called natural law. If an action fulfills the human beings' nature, then the act is right; if an action destroys or harms the human being's nature, then the action is wrong. The final good for the human being is the realization of his or her nature.

Plato and Aristotle developed an ontology that was teleological; but unlike Plato, Aristotle developed a philosophy that was empirical. The natural world that we live in is the real world, and the things that we experience are the real things. Both Plato and Aristotle aim at the universal, but unlike Plato, Aristotle finds the universal in particular things, which he calls the essence of things. Aristotle calls his metaphysics, "first philosophy," and he begins with a critique of Plato's Theory of Forms. Plato taught that objects are changeable and correspond to an ideal, immutable Form, which can be perceived by the intellect. Aristotle's epistemology begins with a study of particular phenomena which has a structure of its own, and intellectually rises to the knowledge of essences (the formal element of an object). The essence of the object is understood as the function for which the object is fitted for by its nature. Both Plato and Aristotle aim at the universal, but unlike Plato, Aristotle finds the universal in particular things, which he calls the essence of things.

Aristotle uses the word nature to refer to the changing universe as a whole. Nature will include the motions of material things, human beings and mental acts, and the unchanging source of change. Changes are subject to a cosmic order, and this order is never arbitrary, but tends toward the best of what is possible. Aristotle teaches us that "God" is an everlasting, unchanging, and perfect embodiment of what he calls the "Unmoved Mover," and is the source of all change. We can envision the Aristotelian Unmoved Mover as a god, but unlike our Christian God, Aristotle's God has no involvement in the individual human, gives no moral guidance, and is impersonal and remote without any emotion or love toward his creation. The whole universe is made up of individuals whose independent activities are ordered together to serve a common end.[80] The mature individuals will understand their role in the common end, and they will always obey and are bound by moral law.[81]

To understand any great thinker, we must first understand their metaphysics. Metaphysics is that branch of philosophy which examines the fundamental nature of truth and reality: the meaning of existence, the nature of the mind, the meaning and nature of time, space and casualty, and the relationship between mind and matter, substance and attributes, and potentiality and attributes. Plato postulated a distinction between appearance and reality. Plato utilizes dialectic, the logical theory of deductive logic, to take into account appearances, but to further seek the truth of reality through dialectic. Aristotle taught causality and substance, potentiality and actuality, and the study of being. Both Plato and Aristotle taught that nature was conceived as an ordered existence within an ordered universe. For Aristotle, the word nature refers to the changing universe, and means the definitive structure of a thing, and the active tendency of a thing to be something of a certain kind; and what is generated has a certain form.[82] A natural entity is always in the process of transformation and contains an essence (form).

Changes are subject to a cosmic order, and this order is not random or chaotic, but is an orderly process. Nature is comprised of individuals whose actions contribute to the good of the whole; mature individuals understand their acts and are bound by the moral law.[83] The idea of nature includes the first unchanging source of all change, human beings and their mental acts, and the motion of material things.

Philosophers pose many questions, and the philosophical structure of their inquiry is important in searching for the answers to their questions, and to our own questions. For both Plato and Aristotle, we can have knowledge of a thing only when we understand the cause. Plato, for example, in the *Phaedo* enquires into the nature of things, and searches for the causes of each thing. Aristotle postulates that each individual substance has a structure (form or *eidos*) of its own, and this structure will determine how the matter will be generated into a particular thing, and the powers and tendencies of each thing, which are our objects of knowledge. Matter is a necessary aspect of any changing entity, and this matter is called *nature*.[84]

Aristotle postulates a Theory of Causality to answer the 'why' for whenever we study nature and pose a question. For Aristotle, there are three basic principles of nature: matter, form, and privation. Four causes are used to explain everything: the formal cause, i.e., the essence, idea, or form (*eidos*) that is introduced by the efficient cause; the material cause, i.e., the stuff or matter out of which a thing comes to be the efficient cause, i.e., the agent which produces the effect; and the final cause, i.e., the purpose for which a thing exists. All four kinds of cause can enter the explanation of a thing, i.e., the explanation of natural change. For Aristotle, god was the ultimate final cause, i.e., the Unmoved Mover. Unlike our Christian God, the ancient Greek god(s) had no interest in the universe or mankind.[85]

Aristotle is a philosopher who focuses on change. What is the source of change? The source of change for something is its essence or form.[86] In Book V of the Metaphysics, Aristotle postulates that change is always on the way to something beyond itself, and so the potency for movement is contained in the form itself. Aristotle gives the human soul as an example of the essence or structure of the human body,[87] and the soul is also the source of movement and tendency[88], of locomotion[89], of growth[90], of nutrition and reproduction[91], and the source of all the vital powers.[92] For both Plato and Aristotle, similar entities act in similar ways; therefore scientific induction is made possible as well as the correct prediction of future events.[93] Although both Plato and Aristotle were philosophizing in a pre-Christian era, their philosophy on natural law, and the vital powers of the human soul are in harmony with the Christian beliefs, with the added truth of God as our Creator, and Jesus as our Savior.

In the *Nicomachean Ethics*, Aristotle examines the Socratic question: how men should best live a life as a virtuous character (*ethike arete*) to achieve happiness or fulfillment (*eudaimonia*) — the goal of life. Socrates believed that knowledge is virtue and knowing what the right thing to do will then lead one to make the correct choice. Aristotle believed that knowing what was right was not enough; one had to choose to act in the proper manner and form the habit of doing good. Aristotle taught that the good was happiness, which is an activity of the soul, which he divided into the rational and irrational parts. For Aristotle, ethics was not just theoretical (where we contemplate good living), but also practical (where we actively create it). Our use of reason alone is a theoretical activity, but with the help of the appetitive and irrational part of the soul, we will be led to the practical aim of good living — the most admirable human activity.

For Aristotle, there are two types of virtue, the intellectual and the moral, which correspond to the two parts of the soul. Every virtue has a mean between two extremes, and the extremes are considered vices; for example, courage was a mean between cowardice and rashness. For Aristotle, the Golden Mean was excellence in activity where the individual uses moderation in all things to avoid the extremes so that virtue in character is built by following the right habits. The virtue of anything is what brings it into well-being, and makes it perform its function well.[94]

Aristotle taught us that there is a distinction between what brings a thing into existence and what purpose a thing serves. As we will see in the next chapter, Aristotle influenced St. Thomas. For St. Thomas, knowledge and love of God are the basic presuppositions of natural law. St. Thomas' epistemology is an Aristotelian philosophy that maintains that if you want to know something, then you must know the matter, form, power (what brings a thing into existence), and the end or purpose of a thing. Natural law ethics seeks a purpose or end of human life. For Aristotle, the highest human good that is sought for its own sake is eudaemonia, which means "doing well and living well."[95] Eudaemonia is also translated as happiness, flourishing or fulfillment. Aristotle sought the essence of man within the physical, observable things themselves. Aristotle believed that we can use our reason to know our own essential nature, and the constituent parts, and relations of the human. Aristotle taught a teleological view of human nature where the end for mankind is "that for the sake of which a thing is done.[96]

In the *Nicomachean Ethics*, Chapter 7 of Book 5, Aristotle refers to three types of justice: political justice (*politikon dikaion*: what we would term civil law), natural justice (*physikon dikaion*: translated as 'natural justice' or 'natural law' (Leo Strauss uses the expression 'natural right' as a substitute for 'natural law.'), and legal or conventional justice, (*nomikon dikaion.*)[97] The Stoics divided justice or law into two categories; natural law or positive law. For Aristotle, conventional or legal justice was a part of political justice. If the principles of justice are unchangeable, then they are said to be natural. For Aristotle, to talk about the nature of justice, and natural justice are the same thing. Plato also believed that the nature of justice and natural justice are the same thing.

For Aristotle, the principles of justice will forbid actions that are morally wrong. There are some actions that are morally wrong by their nature and must always be wrong, and it is possible for us to know the "moral truths' of these acts, for example, the principles of justice forbidding murder, adultery, and theft must always be wrong and these principles are unchangeable. Because these principles are unchangeable, they can be called natural law (or natural justice) principles.[98] St. Thomas further develops the Aristotelian natural law principles and refers to these principles as secondary precepts of natural law.[99]

For Aristotle, there is another primary principle of natural justice under which these moral principles, for example, forbidding murder, adultery, and theft, will fall under. The supreme principle of natural justice, or the principles from which the actions like murder derive their status of necessarily wrong actions is related to the concept of equality. Aristotle believed that if we are equal, then we ought to be treated equal in similar circumstances. Aristotle does not give a name to the supreme principle of natural justice, but modern scholars have labeled it the principle of equity.

The principles of natural law (secondary principles) are necessarily related to the principle of equity (a primary principle), and we can deduce the secondary principles of natural law from the primary principles of equity by deductive reasoning. Natural equity is identical to natural justice. Aristotle defines the concept of justice by relating it to the notion of equity.[100] For those who are equal in all relevant aspects, then the principle of equity is an alternative formulation of the Golden Rule: "Do not do to another what you would not have done to you." Aristotelian philosophy of equity, natural justice, and the Golden Rule are taken up by St. Thomas, and of course are fundamental principles of Christian morality taught to us in the Bible.

The formal principles of natural law must be stated in a substantial way to account for which acts count as acts that violate natural law. For Aristotle, the substantial formulation of natural law is the task of legal or conventional justice. St. Thomas refers to this as 'specific determination' of certain generalities.[101] For Aristotle, the principles of justice that conduct the task of determination are changeable from a historical perspective: culture and society will play a role. Moral problems are solved by a combination of both natural justice and a determination of the principles of legal or conventional justice.[102] We can understand the historical significance of law and the universal nature of natural law when, for example, we study the Holy Bible. Paul was trained in Jewish law by the esteemed rabbinical scholar Gamaliel. St. Paul expressed his spiritual teaching of Christ in legal language.[103]

Aristotle believed that knowledge and knowing the right thing was not enough for virtue. For Aristotle, the good was fulfillment or *eudaimonia* (happiness or flourishing), and the good is an activity of the soul. He divided the soul into two aspects: the rational and irrational aspects of the soul. Aristotle also divided the soul into three major parts and taught that all three essential tendencies must be fulfilled for human life to flourish. The nutritive soul requires discipline to secure proper food, clothing, and shelter; the animal soul which has an appetite for sensible objects, and requires moral guidance; and finally, the rational soul, which requires education. Ethics was not just theoretical but also practical. Our use of reason alone was theoretical, but with the help of the appetite and irrational part of the soul we will be led to the practical aim of good living — the most admirable human activity. There are two types of virtue, the intellectual and the moral, which correspond to the two parts of the soul. Every virtue was a mean between two extremes, and the extremes are considered vices: for example, courage was a mean between cowardice and rashness. The Golden Mean was excellence in activity; the individual uses moderation in all things to avoid extremes so that virtue in character is built by following the right habits.

Aristotle examined how justice aims at what is good in the *Politics*, and begins with the statement, "man was by nature a political animal (*zoon politikon*)".[104] It is man that can make a communal community (*koinonia*) because he has the power of logos, i.e., speech, reason, and morality. The Greek *polis* was the highest form of the community because it denotes "an association of the men" where the ruled are the rulers of the city — they formulated their own law codes, maintained an army, had their own system of government, and worshipped their own Olympian gods. The political community is considered to be natural for Aristotle, because it is living within the political community that we can become fully developed as a human being. The city begins as a partnership between individuals and their households, and these associations enable us to flourish because we have a natural tendency to be social and interact with others. We need the thought and ideas of others to increase our wholeness and assist us on our way to happiness. Our natural purpose is to become as wholly human as possible, and the natural purpose of the state is to complete this process.

Aristotle's conception of justice was different from our modern idea of equality; for him justice was the 'right proportion' so it would sometimes involve inequality. He taught that ethics was a branch of politics, and the magnanimous (great-souled) man would have every virtue, and therefore the better man deserves more. Humility is a trait that he considered a vice — it was the man with proper pride, who did not underestimate his own talents, whom Aristotle considered fit for ruling in either a monarchy or an aristocracy (the ideal states). Aristotle wrote that economic self-sufficiency (*avutarkeia*) was the goal of each *polis*, self-supported by agriculture, hunting, and fishing. Aristotle taught that the constitution of a *polis* will give the citizens privileges and duties; he did not use the language of rights.

The Stoics, Plato, and Aristotle influenced Cicero (106-43 BC), and he taught that natural law was the command of a personal God who is the author and enforcer of natural law. Cicero wrote On The *Republic* (54-51 BC) a dialogue of Roman politics in six books, where he explains natural law, "True law is right reason in agreement with nature, universal, consistent, everlasting, whose nature is to advocate duty by prescription and to deter wrongdoing by prohibition. Its prescriptions and prohibitions are obeyed by good men, but evil men disobey them. God forbids us to alter this law, nor is it permissible to repeal any part of it, and it is impossible to abolish the whole of it. Neither the Senate nor the People can absolve us from obeying this law, and we do not need to look outside ourselves for an expounder or interpreter of this law. There will not be one law at Rome and another at Athens or different laws now and in the future. There is now and will be forever one law, valid for all peoples and all times. And there will be one master and ruler for all us in common — God, who is the author of this law, its promulgator, and its enforcing judge. Whoever does not obey this law is trying to escape himself and to deny his nature as a human being. By this very fact, he will suffer the greatest penalties, even if he should somehow escape conventional punishments."[105] Cicero claimed that if we disobey natural law, we are fleeing from ourselves because natural law is a part of our human nature. Cicero taught that natural law was immutable and unchangeable. Aristotle, before Cicero, taught that natural law is unchangeable and eternal in its first principles, and later St. Thomas agreed with Aristotle that the secondary principles of natural law may be changed in certain situations.[106] The meaning of Aristotle's and St. Thomas's changeable second principles and natural law is debated by many scholars, and I will address this question in the next chapter.

St. Thomas Aquinas (engraving), Boel, Cornelis (c.1576-1621) / © Bridgeman Images

Chapter 4

Natural Law and St. Thomas

"Who shall show us good things? The light of your countenance is sealed upon us, O Lord." Psalms 4:6-7

For those of us who seek God, His mystery is revealed through Biblical truths, and deepened by our study and dedication to theology and philosophy. We discover a spiritual God-given world view in the Bible, and a portrayal of natural law that directs us to love, live a moral life, and worship God. Our rights are not given to us by empirical data but are God-given rights since that we are spiritual beings created in the image of God, and our rights transcend our physical world within the realm of natural rights which are nestled in us by God. Our goal is a clear vision that will bring us back into the realm of knowledge of God's laws for us. Natural law ethics can be identified with a theological theory like St. Thomas's theory of natural law, where the sacred foundation is issued by a command of God. God is the source of natural law, and His creatures are endowed with a rational discernment to understand His moral law that is inscribed in nature.

Natural law theory states that the principles of law are inherent in the nature of things, and we can understand these laws through our ability to reason. Christians believe that human beings are rational, and our reason reflects the image of God. God's universally valid principles of natural law guide us as we work toward the perfection (or perfectibility) of what it means to be God's creature. As rational creatures with the gift of natural law, we have the ability to discern right from wrong, but it is only with Christ's guidance that we have the ability to develop a deeper moral perfection and live a life of virtue in preparation for an eternal life.

St. Thomas married philosophy to theology without corrupting sacred theology. St. Thomas called this revelation (*revelabilia*) where our knowledge and understanding of God's Holy Scripture is revealed to us in faith and beyond our grasp of human reason. St. Thomas drew upon Sacred Scripture, Catholic doctrine, canon law, Pre-Socratics, Socrates, Plato, Aristotle, Zeno the Stoic, Chrysippas, Cleanthes, Stoic Panaetius, the Epicureans, Dionysius, Philosopher Judaeus, Andronicus, Plotinust, Seneca, Proclus, Porphyry, Simplicius, Themistius, Cicero, Varro, the Roman Jurists, Boethius, St. Ambrose, St. Augustine, St. John Damascene, Maimonides, St. Albert the Great, Avicenna, and Averroes' philosophy to expound and defend Christian theology. This is not a complete list of scholarly names. St. Thomas mentioned more than two hundred authors in his texts, with an extensive reference to Cicero in the *Summa Theologica*. St. Thomas' philosophical examination of natural law is an important source of knowledge for our modern consideration of natural law. To understand the Thomistic terms of natural law an understanding of Aristotle's metaphysics is necessary as well as some understanding of the theological premises that concern the existence and will of God. For Christian believers, it is a delightful and humbling experience to read St. Thomas and understand more fully the submission of mankind to the divine governance of the world by a Holy God.[107]

The American colonists were suspicious of Catholicism, and of course, St. Thomas was a devout Catholic; however, it is important to understand him because his theology and philosophy influenced the Christian theologians and philosophers who also influenced the American colonial doctrine of natural law. It is also critical to keep in mind that natural law was not a theory for St. Thomas; natural law is the universal truth. I read many modern commentators on natural law, and many of these writers refer to it as 'a theory' or a theoretical idea. In an increasingly secular Nation that often publicly reflects the views of agnosticism and sometimes atheism, we must spiritually fight to hold on to God's universal truths — and natural law is one of the most important of these truths. St. Thomas synthesized Aristotelian philosophy, Christian theology, and natural law, and wrote genuine Christian views of his own about the Christian concept of God and human virtue. This is what St. Thomas teaches us, and why it is so important to include him in this book about our Nation's early understanding of natural law.

The colonist's knowledge of classical writers was apparent with their reference to the ancient authors in colonial literature, conversations, arguments, letters, sermons, political speeches, debates, dialogues, broadsides, pamphlets, and tracts. This novel Nation looked to the timeless truths in the Holy Bible as the pattern for our new Nation. Natural law was a profound idea known to the ancient Greek philosophers: Homer, Sophocles, Socrates, Plato, Euripides, Herodotus, Thucydides, Xenophon, and Aristotle. Among the Romans writing about the concept of natural law were Livy, Marcus Tullius Cicero (Tully), Horace, Vergil, Tacitus, Seneca, Ovid, Cato, Marcus Aurelius, Caesar, Ulpian, Gaius, and Justinian. All these men can be counted among some of those early natural law thinkers who influenced colonial thinking about it.

The Christian philosophers and theologians who influenced the new Nation's spiritual and theoretical thinking includes St. Augustine of Hippo (354-430), and St. Thomas, who reminds us about the importance of natural law. The list of influential philosophers and writers continues with Francesco de Vitoria (1483-1546), James Harrington (1611-1677), Sir Edward Coke (1552-1634), Sir William Blackstone (1723-1780), Jonathan Swift (1667-1745), Thomas Hobbes (1588-1679), David Hume (1711-1776), Jean-Jacques Rousseau (1712-1778), Francois-Marie Arouet, known as Voltaire (1694-1778), Hugo Grotius (1583-1645), Algernon Sidney (1623-1683), John Locke (1632-1704), Nicolo Machiavelli (1469-1527), Charles de Montesquieu (1689-1755), Thomas Paine (1736-1809), James Thompson, Emer de Vattel (1714-1767), Jean Jacque Burlamaqui (1694-1748), Francis Wollaston (1762-1823), Henry St. John, 1st Viscount Bolingbroke (1678-1751), Benjamin

Hoadley (1734-1761), Robert Bellarmine (1542-1621), Marquis Beccaria (1738-1794) and Francisco Suarez (1548-1617). We continue with the scientific theories of Isaac Newton (1643-1727), and the political tracts of John Trenchard and Thomas Gordon writing as Cato (1720-1723), as well as the ideological influence of the Glorius Revolution, Whig theory of politics, common law, English institutions, and the Renaissance.

St. Thomas was a Dominican Friar of the Order of Friar Preachers, scholar, philosopher, professor, theologian, and writer of an extensive oeuvre which includes two books that are widely considered to be his masterpieces — *Summa Contra Gentiles* and *Summa Theologica* (1266-1273). The *Summa Theologica* is a didactic synthesis of theology that was written for students to replace the conventional synthesis that was used at that time. St. Thomas's goal was to write a theology that would achieve the status of a science.[108]

St. Thomas was born in the castle of Roccasecca near Aquino — a small town located in the Kingdom of Italy. (Which is now in the Lazio region of Italy). He was born into an aristocratic family; his father was Count Landulf of Aquino (and a cousin of the Pope). St. Thomas was the youngest of seven brothers and they all lived in the castle called The Dry Rock — between Naples and Rome, and a few miles from the large and wealthy Benedictine Abbey of Monte Cassino (Founded by St. Benedict in 529, The Abbey was a citadel with a strategic location that was used for the advantage of either the Emperor or the Pope. Monte Cassino was later sacked by Frederick II and his imperial soldiers. St. Thomas's uncle was abbot of the original Benedictine monastery at Monte Cassino. St. Thomas's family had hoped that Thomas would follow in his uncle's footsteps.) St. Thomas's mother was Theodora, Countess of Theatre, and was related to the Hohenstaufen dynasty of the Holy Roman Emperors. Frederick II, called the Wonder of the World, was St. Thomas's second cousin, and was a brilliant and fierce Crusader who dabbled as a statesman and philosopher, struck out against religion and the Pope, and envisioned himself as head of the Holy Roman Empire. The Medieval era was a time of battle between the Crusades and religion, and blood bound allegiance, power, politics, intrigue, and religion. St. Thomas received his early education from the Benedictine monks. As a young boy he received an early education at the University of Naples, and it was there that he encountered the Dominicans — a popular mendicant preaching order. He was also introduced to Aristotle, and the Jewish and Muslim commentators on Aristotle. St. Thomas committed himself to the Dominican order in his late teens. The Dominicans were teachers and contemplatives who took a vow of poverty. We are reminded of Socrates who also lived in poverty and took no money for his teaching, denouncing material things to contemplate the truth. St. Thomas's family was not happy with his choice for a vocation (his family aspired for their son to become a Cardinal or possibly a Pope), so as he was traveling to Rome his family kidnapped him and kept him captive for two years hoping to persuade him to change his mind. The colorful story emerges that his brothers sent a courtesan into St. Thomas's room to tempt him into breaking his religious pledge to be a friar. His family finally allowed him to escape, and he was lowered from his window in a basket into the waiting arms of the Dominicans. After St. Thomas professed Dominican vows, he first studied in Paris, then in Cologne under Albertus Magnus (Albert the Great), who was influenced by the Neo-Platonic mystic, Dionysius Areopagita. St. Thomas was ordained priest in Cologne in 1250 and later received his doctorate in theology from the University of Paris. St. Thomas travelled widely to teach and preach. During his lifetime he produced over sixty major and minor works, including the *Summa Theologica*, and the *end*. After a revelation late in his life, Thomas stopped writing saying that what had been revealed to him made everything that he had written seem to be straw by comparison.[109]

St. Thomas was on foot on his way to Lyon, France to attend the Second Council of Lyons, when he fell ill. Thomas died at the Cistercian monastery of Fossa Nuova, Italy on March 7, 1274. He was canonized by Pope John XXII in 1323, and his remains were placed in the Church of the Jacobins in Toulouse in 1369. In 1567, Pope Pius ranked Saint Thomas St. Thomas with Ambrose, Augustine, Jerome, and Gregory.

St. Thomas's physical movements were slow (but he was certainly quick in intellect); he was not known to be sociable, even somewhat shy, peace-loving, a lover of poetry, simple and always humble wherein God's children show humility. He was described by contemporaries as a tall, heavy man with a large girth and head, dark complexion, receding hairline, and a great pondering spirit. Like the ancient Greek philosopher Socrates, St. Thomas's spiritual ecstasy and trances were carefully concealed from others. He loved books, and it was reported that he was thankful to God that he also understood what he had read. St. Thomas accomplished remarkable clarity of thought and reasoning power during a tumultuous age when war between the Catholic Church and the Holy Roman Empire was a perpetual duel between the Pope and the Emperors. When we struggle to understand St. Thomas's words, we envision a man who was intelligent, rational, solid, spiritual, and saintly, and we are reminded that the path to sainthood — for the godly — runs along the muddy and turbulent river of humanity.

St. Thomas wrote prodigiously and was influenced by the ancient Greek thinkers, especially Aristotle. "In the case of natural law, Thomas defines the law from the standpoint of its causal origin (that is, what makes it a law), not in terms of a secondary order of causality through which it is discovered (the human intellect)."[110] Scholar Russell Hittinger writes, "Natural law is never defined in terms of what is first in the human mind or first in nature in St. Thomas"[111] Do not confuse what is first in human cognition with what is first in being. For St. Thomas, natural law is *lex indita*, instilled in the human mind by God, moving the creature to its proper acts and ends. Natural law is a participation in the eternal law.

St. Thomas viewed philosophy to be the handmaiden of theology. We benefit from the Angelic Doctor's illumination in *Summa Theologica* for our understanding of natural law. St. Thomas defines law as, "an ordinance of reason for the common good, made by him who has care of the community, and promulgated."[112] In *Summa Theologica*, St. Thomas identifies four types of law: eternal, natural, human, and divine law. The temporal counterpart of eternal law is human law. St. Thomas introduces us to natural law by writing, "all things partake somewhat of the eternal law, insofar as, namely, from its being imprinted upon them, they derive their respective inclinations to their proper acts and ends. Now among all others, the rational creature is subject to divine providence in a more excellent way, insofar as it partakes of a share of providence, by being provident for itself and for others. Wherefore it has a share of the eternal reason, whereby it has a natural inclination to its proper act and end, and this participation of the eternal law in the rational creature is called the natural law."[113] To paraphrase, we can say that our participation in the eternal law is natural law, and we are rational creatures with the ability to participate in eternal law. The first principle of the natural law is that good is to be pursued and done, and evil is to be avoided.[114]

St. Thomas taught us that the natural law was rooted in our human constitution, and this patterned morality was placed in our constitution by God. St. Thomas also taught us that the world is real and rational. We study the wisdom of this thirteenth century thinker and compare this with the insight of the Founders of our Nation — while we also reflect upon our own relationship to our United States Constitution, government, politics, our polity, our community, family, morality, and our individual existence. We hold the doctrine of natural law to heart, and as we practice the morality and virtue that are the marks of our Christianity; we view the world in a Thomistic manner — holy, moral, realistic, and rational.

St. Thomas taught us that God's very essence is His existence, and we cannot know God because He is outside of space and time. However, God is a personal God whose image we share, and we seek to glorify and love God as our end. St. Thomas writes about the virtue of the whole person and the goodness of our souls, and we learn about the moral, theological, and intellectual virtues from his *Summa Theologica*.

St. Thomas teaches us that we can discover God through reason and understanding nature; and when we align our ends with God's ends or purpose for us, then we are following natural law. St. Thomas gives us instructions for understanding God by teaching us five logical arguments for the existence of God. The first argument is the argument from motion. We all know that we can perceive motion of things through our senses, and whenever there is movement there is something which has acted upon the thing that is moved. The sequence of things that are moved cannot continue into infinity; therefore, God is the First Mover who sets all thing into motion. The second argument for the existence of God is the argument from efficient cause where St. Thomas teaches that nothing causes or creates itself without the First Cause, i.e., God. The third argument for the existence of God is that God is a necessary Being. St. Thomas writes that God is a necessary Being; where we come into the world and pass out of the world at a particular time; God is the necessary Being that must exist at all times. The argument from gradation states that there are different degrees of goodness in things, and different degrees of biological complexity. God is the highest form of Good, and God is a perfect Being. The final argument for the existence of God is the argument from design. We are in awe when we see the designs and purposes that are at work in the universe. God is the divine intelligence, and the divine Designer.[115]

St. Thomas teaches us that there are three categories of goods found inherent in our nature. The first category of goods are the ones that we all share and have in common with all living creatures; for example, our desire to preserve our own existence. The second category of goods are those that are common to all animals; for example, our desire for procreation and our child-rearing activities. The third category of goods are unique to us as rational animals; for example, our desire to know the truth about God. All St. Thomas's goods are arranged in a hierarchy that correspond to the hierarchy of living things, i.e., vegetative, sensory, and rational souls, where the higher goods presuppose the lower goods, for example, we cannot avoid ignorance (a good in the third category that is unique to us as rational animals) without fulfilling the desire to preserve our own existence.[116] We will fulfill the vegetative and sensory aspects of our nature to fulfill the rational aspects of our nature. The highest, ultimate, and necessary good for us follows from our human nature, and this human good is knowing the truth about God, and the good of living in companionship with other persons who share in these goods. Thomistic ethics is an ethics of human happiness, and knowledge of God constitutes man's happiness.[117]

St. Thomas held that, "good is to be done and pursued, and evil is to be avoided. All other precepts of the natural law are based upon this."[118] It is self-evident that whenever we act in accord with reason we do so because we take the action to be good in some way and avoid that which we take to be evil.[119] The goal is to fulfill the ends set for us by nature and to avoid the frustration of these ends. Saint Thomas's first principle of practical reason is: bonum set faciendum et prosequendum. All the other principles of natural law depend on this self-evident principle that we should pursue, support, and do the good, and avoid evil. This first principle of practical reason is our moral guidance; our moral end can be pursued consciously.

St. Thomas's ontology is based upon structured natural kinds. For St. Thomas, it is by knowing the material thing that the soul has knowledge of its object, unlike the Platonic theory where we turn away from material things to discover the doctrine of innate ideas. We can know the end of things by using our reason. There is a natural end or *telos* of human life. St. Thomas's epistemology teaches us how this realist structure might be known. The Aristotelian categories of matter and form, and essences are a foundation for St. Thomas's natural law theorizing. St. Thomas's metaphysical theory is the existence of natural kinds or essences. All human beings share a common nature or essence. St. Thomas uses the Aristotelian metaphysics to maintain that certain objects are natural and serve to man's end (To know God is our ultimate end!), and our desire to reach that end is natural. So, the laws of nature regulate our behavior as we attain our natural end.

Remember from the last chapter, Aristotle presented us with his theory of four causes: formal cause (idea), material cause (matter), efficient cause (agent), and final cause (purpose). St. Thomas teaches that the rule for the good is substantial form or first matter. There are two kinds of change: substantial change and accidental change. St. Thomas also teaches that there is a final cause at work in our natural processes. Form, essence, and nature are concepts that are essential to St. Thomas's ethics. The world of sensible experience is what we must deal with, and substance, change, and casualty are the concepts that we utilize to understand this reality. In Aristotelian terminology, the capacity for something to change is its potency or potential. The present state of being for a thing is its actuality or act. A completely perfect being is completely in act, (with no potential to act), and such a being is God who is infinite. A finite being always has some potential to act.

St. Thomas's metaphysical realism serves as the foundation for his moral philosophy. St. Thomas teaches that there are two aspects to any matter: substantial form, which make a thing what it is, and first matter, which does not have a quality but makes the form to be of a certain kind. And there are two kinds of change: substantial change and accidental change. St. Thomas's metaphysics relies on the Aristotelian doctrine in the *Posterior Analytics*, and Aristotle's systematic conception of logic in the *Prior Analytics*. Aristotle believed that we obtained information through induction, deduction, and inference. Aristotle used inductive reasoning to create a universal process of reasoning where we can learn everything conceivable about reality. Reasoning for St. Thomas, as well as for Aristotle, is syllogistic, a logical form that is Aristotle's invention: if a=b and b=c, then a=c. Aristotle also pointed out the difference between a *priori* knowledge (knowledge that is independent of experience), and a *posteriori* knowledge (knowledge that is dependent on experience). We can demonstrate knowledge by proceeding from necessarily true propositions to a necessarily true conclusion — a procedure that science and logic uses for the demonstration of true propositions. We can also gain probable knowledge by using dialectical skills, that is, question and answer — a method that Socrates had mastered. St. Thomas also used induction, the discovery of knowledge by reasoning from all the particular attributes to the general conclusion.[120] For St. Thomas, when we search for demonstrable knowledge, we come to know first principles by induction and intuition (intellectus) where we will see a rule that is embedded in a series of particular examples.

The universal moral law is the natural law that is written in our hearts. "I will praise the Lord, who counsels me; even at night my heart instructs me." (Psalm 16:7). To know our objective reality, we utilize our human way of knowing that allows us to know our being, we can then know the good toward which we aim which is in harmony with reality. This good which we aim at (*telos*) leads us to know the reality of our own nature and an understanding of universal moral knowledge. All our knowledge begins with the senses where we can know the essence of a thing from our knowledge of all the particular things known.

Our knowledge of things begins with the world of experience where substance, change, and casualty are the concepts that we use to understand our world as it really is; although, St. Thomas tells us that there is much more to know about the world than we can ascertain through our senses. For St. Thomas, closely related concepts are form, essence, and nature. The actuality of a thing exists in its present state, but all finite things have the potential for change. Change is the progress from potency to act. There are two kinds of change: substantial change and accidental change. There are also two aspects of any material substance: substantial form, and its first matter. The substantial forms are the qualities and organization that make something what it is – the stuff out of which something is made. While first matter is a quality-less and indeterminate component that has the function of giving the form its individualization -- first matter is signified by the organization of matter.

In the *Summa Theologica*, St. Thomas studies the voluntary moral acts of mankind — a study which is influenced by Aristotle's philosophy of the soul. For St. Thomas, man will use the intellect and the will to work toward the fruition of a moral act. The progression that takes us to the end of the act is the intellect which apprehends the end to the act and presents this to the will. The will then wishes this end. A judgment is made by the intellect that this is a proper end for us. Finally, the will then leads the act toward the end. The intellect will then deliberate the various possible means to this end. Our will then consents to the judgment, and then judges which is the preferable means to use toward the end. The will then selects the means to be used. To execute the act, the intellect along with the will orders the means to be used, then the will actively initiates the means toward the act. The fittingness of the act performed is judged by intellect, and the will rejoices in the performance of a good job. Therefore, we can see that the moral agent combines both the intellect and the will when performing a moral act.[121] Dr. Bourke reminds us to remember that, according to St. Thomas, it is the moral agent who is acting through the intellect or will.

The good moral act is in conformity with right reason which is the rule of human morality. This faculty of reason is a principle that we have as part of who we are created and governed by God, and part of His Divine Providence. Reason conforms to what is right in our voluntary acts. Speculative reason conforms to the nature of real objects. Practical reasons will be ruled by the judgements of speculative reason. A practical judgment leading to a moral act is a right act if practical reasoning conforms with speculative reasoning (not by a comparison of the act with the nature of things).[122]

All our genuine knowledge derives from self-evident and necessary true propositions that St. Thomas calls the first principles of speculative reason. Our practical reason has first principles that can be said to be the content of *synderesis*. The law of non-contradiction is a first principle of speculative reason. The law of non-contraction says that the same thing cannot be affirmed and denied at the same time. The first principle of practical reason is that good is to be done and evil is to be avoided.[123] We have a natural inclination toward self-preservation, marriage, family life, social interaction, a desire for knowledge, and a desire for knowledge of God. St. Thomas teaches us that we also have a natural inclination for a political organization. This author maintains that we also have a natural inclination for individual freedom. Freedom is a consequence of the natural law. We are morally good when we seek that which God also wants us to seek. Our love for God is the basic presupposition for natural law. We are rational beings, and it is proper for us to act according to reason.[124]

What is the difference between theoretical or speculative and practical reason, and the consequences for morals? Does God have theoretical or practical knowledge of His creatures? Theoretical knowledge aims at the perfection of the knowing process, and the goal is truth. We aim to have our knowledge align with the way things are. When we aim at the perfection of some activity, for example in choosing something, we are using our practical reason. The theoretical intellect is aimed at the consideration of truth, and the practical intellect is aimed at the end of an operation. When we think theoretically the first thing that we think about is being, and it follows from this thinking that the regulative principle of all our thinking, i.e., the principle of contradiction, i.e., a thing cannot be and not be at the same time, will be applied. We aim at the good, and the first perceptive judgment of our practical reason tells us that we should pursue that which is good and avoid that which is bad. Our natural inclinations are also our natural impulses that lead us to the good. The natural inclination that belongs to man is according to reason. These truths of the general precepts of practical reason are the same for everyone and are equally known by everyone.

St. Thomas teaches us that there are four cardinal virtues — prudence (or practical wisdom), justice, temperance, and fortitude — that are acquired by human effort, and that all moral virtues depend on these four virtues. Acquiring prudence, for example, is an individual activity that we get through self-awareness and practical reason. We practice the acts which correspond to the cardinal's virtue until the virtue is habitual. Aristotle taught that moral virtues were a means between the two opposite extremes. The general principles of natural law apply to everyone, but, like the cardinal virtues, we must exert the effort to perfect our knowledge of natural law.[125] The end toward which we strive is the good, and happiness. The human being has seven basic goods or fundamental desires that draw us toward our end: we seek self-preservation, we wish to reproduce and educate our offspring, and we desire to know the truth about God and live in society, we avoid offense, and shun ignorance.[126] The ultimate and end of our desire is to have perfect union and contemplation of God.[127] Happiness consists in the total perfection of ourselves and our souls, and in keeping our will fixed on our end. Our instincts show us our basic goods and our right actions are in accordance with natural law. Instinct and reason point to natural law. Instinct (or disposition) are the formal cause that will lead to our final cause. If we are mistaken it is either out of ignorance or emotion; we are rational beings, but our emotions can overpower reason. A vicious disposition, unhealthy habits, or the corruption of our culture can all lead to a distorted moral development. St. Thomas would have much to say if he were living in our turbulent times within the United States where left-wing extremists and Marxists are irrationally destroying our nation's monuments, looting, rioting, distorting our Nation's history, murdering, and feverishly attempting to "cancel culture." The United States has reached an advanced culture with more citizens living comfortably, educated, and with more free time to pursue their passions of art, music, theatre, movies, dance, reading, sports, and a talent or hobby of one's own choice. For this author, as for many other citizens, this advanced culture includes our constitutionally protected freedoms, natural rights, and natural law, and especially our freedom to worship God. As St. Paul reminds us in 2 Corinthians 11: 2, "But I am afraid that just as Eve was deceived by the serpent's cunning, your minds may somehow be led astray from your sincere and pure devotion to Christ."

Plato, Aristotle, and later Christian thinkers like St. Thomas recognized four cardinal virtues: prudence, justice, fortitude, and temperance. In addition to these acquired virtues Christians added three spiritual virtues — faith, hope and charity or love. The moral part of the Summa in the Second Part expressed practical knowledge, for example, the definition of virtue, and the parts of justice. St. Thomas teaches us that a completely perfect being is completely in act so that no potency exists. This perfect and infinite being is God. What are the basic principles of morality supplied by *synderesis*? This is an interesting question, however, the examples that St. Thomas gives us are scanty.

We are taught what belongs to natural law through the teaching of the Old and New Testaments. God gave us His "Divine Law' in the Old Testament, and He lovingly added The New Law of the Holy Spirit in the New Testament giving us mercy, grace, and love. St. Thomas's cardinal virtues are a counterpart to the Aristotelian virtues in the *Nicomachean Ethics*, except humility, which Aristotle does not mention.

As we have discovered with our study of Plato and Aristotle, the natural law tradition goes back to the ancient Greek philosophers and continues to be developed by numerous thinkers prior to St. Thomas. His synthesis and analyses of natural law guides us both in faith and reason.

St. Thomas defines law as, "Law of its very nature is an ordinance of reason for the common good, which is made by the person who has care of the community, and this rule is promulgated"[128] So in general, law is a rational rule aimed at the common good. The common good is happiness which refers to living a good life while we are on this earth and our final goal is eternal happiness with God in heaven. We use our reason to guide our actions to act or not act, and to act in certain ways. St. Thomas distinguishes four kinds of law: eternal law (*lex asterna*), natural law (*lex naturalis*), positive or human law, (*lex humana vet positiva*; the human application of natural law), and divine law. (*lex divina*; the written revelation of God in the Scripture). God's eternal law is the most comprehensive law. The divine mind of God has archetypes which God utilizes to create and govern the world.[129] This divine plan in the mind of God pre-exists and is manifested as the eternal law that directs our movements and actions in the appropriate ways that conform to God's wisdom. The eternal law is God's divine reasoning power that governs the world and includes timeless truths. God's eternal law includes physical laws, moral laws, and religious laws that are revealed to us. We are rational beings who are subject to God's eternal laws by knowing what it is, and acting according to our internal principle that moves us to action, i.e., by following our natural inclinations.[130] St. Thomas writes, "The Natural Law is nothing else but the rational creature's participation of the eternal law."[131] We cannot know God as He is, and so that means we cannot know eternal law as it is (with the exception of those blessed individuals who have a direct vision of God). But eternal law is known intuitively or innately so that we have a reflection or participation of the eternal law.[132]

Natural law is the goodness that we have, our instincts and intuition, and our consciousness of God. We participate in natural law in two ways which can overlap: first, we recognize and understand the first principles of practical reason, i.e., that good should be done and evil avoided, and secondly, we are inclined to the good. God creates us with reason and appetite, and we participate in the natural law through both means. To know which goods to pursue and how to pursue them, we depend on the virtues that are under the direction of prudence. St. Thomas defines prudence as right reason about how to act.[133]

Natural law is both prescriptive, that is designed to bring about a certain conduct, and descriptive, that is a law that is a regularity of nature. *Synderesis* is our capacity to know the moral principles that are contained within natural law precepts.[134] The principles of speculative reason are self-evident and necessarily true propositions wherein all our knowledge comes from (see the principles of non-contradiction). The first principle of practical reason is good is to be done and pursued and evil is to be avoided. Our happiness is achieved in living a life in harmony with virtue; and our supernatural end is finally achieved in unity with God. Universal freedom is natural law. Human beings hold natural law in common, and practical reason forms the content of *synderesis*.

St. Thomas teaches us that we obey the eternal law by following our natural inclinations (*inclinations naturales*).[135] Our natural inclination is our tendency to act and respond in accordance with our human nature. St. Thomas uses the term *synderesis* to describe our innate God-given capacity to know the basic moral principles, and this infallible spark enables us to understand the precepts of the natural law.[136] The concept of *synderesis* was an important idea for thinkers in the thirteenth century; see, for example, St. Jerome, Bonaventure, and St. Albert the Great.[137] Some philosophers describe *synderesis* as the conscience, but St. Thomas describes *synderesis* as the innate habit of the first principles of practical reason. *Synderesis* is our inextinguishable source for our knowledge of the first principles of thinking.[138] It is a natural habit of thinking where we have an innate grasp of what is right and wrong. St. Thomas does not claim that we are born with complete knowledge of moral truths, but he would say that we have an inborn ability to grasp ethical truths, and he calls this ability *synderesis*. (*Synderesis* is also the major premise of a logical syllogism and is used to tie his theory of natural law with his theory of virtue). *Synderesis* means the knowledge of moral principles, where the major premise of the practical syllogism is that which the actual drawing of the conclusion is the work of conscience. St. Thomas -- along with Aristotle -- held that the moral situation is represented by the practical syllogism. The precepts of natural law must be rational propositions. Our mind is embedded with the necessary patterns for reasoning about what to do and what not to do. The act of judgment that applies to our deliberation is conscientia. God designed us as rational beings, and we recognize Him as the source for our innate, patterned intellect. We obey God. We confirm God's Word from Biblical revelation and Divine Law. We recognize that there are consequences for our actions. The morality that is embedded within our nature is the source of Natural Law. We think about our human potential for an understanding of ethical truths and how this special gift from God guides us in our morality and actions. We refresh our memory of the philosopher John Locke and the empirical philosophy, and we are certain that we were not born with a Lockean tabula rasa. Natural law precepts follow the order of our natural inclinations; however, St. Thomas does teach us that education, reflection, and forming the habits of good behavior are all part of learning to live in harmony with natural law.[139]

God governs the whole of His creation, and this governance is called providence. Our soul comes to know divine providence in a general way by starting from the things themselves.[140] The rational creature comes to know this natural order and freely chooses to act in accordance with this natural order, and this is called natural law. St. Thomas writes, "The natural law is nothing other than a participation of the eternal law in the rational creature."[141] There is a relationship that we have as creatures created by God and this relationship is one of participation. God gives us His principles of governance and the human mind grasps this divinely given law, and we participate in this divine law through our practical activity. This practical activity includes individual, social and political judgments. The natural law provides us with the general principles whereby individuals and societies ought to be governed. Natural law is inscribed in our nature, and we know natural law through our nature. We obey natural law because of our love for God. When we use our understanding of nature, our reason, and our purpose to align ourselves with God's ends, then we are following natural law. Love is always accompanied by desire, and it is this longing for union with God that inspires us to work in harmony with His natural laws.

Human action is deliberate action based upon volition and consciousness of our direction. Reason examines our choices for pros and cons, and reason discovers the good courses of action. We desire happiness and are free to choose as we reason toward happiness; however, the end is God's providence. We use reason to find our way to the good, but there is also a deeper understanding that God has instilled in our hearts where we can discern good acts from evil acts. When we think about natural law and our desire to conform to the actions of natural law, then let us remember that God also moves our actions through His internal love for us. Our expression of God's agape love is to move toward the Good, to understand the Good, and the ultimate *telos* for us is union with our Creator — the source of love.

"For when Gentiles who do not have the law do instinctively the things of the Law, they, not having the Law, are a law to themselves, in that they show the work of the Law written in their hearts,..." (Romans 2:14-15).

"You are our letter, written in our hearts, known and read by all men; being manifested that you are a letter of Christ, cared for by us, written not with ink but with Spirit of the living God, not on table of stone but on tablets of human hearts." (2 Corinthians 3: 2-3). "Such confidence we have through Christ toward God." (2 Corinthians 3:4). The eternal laws that apply to our choices and can be known by our reason are natural laws. St. Thomas was influenced by Aristotle's theory of natural law. Aristotle defines law as, "a rule proceeding from a sort of practical wisdom and reason."[142]

We have discussed how Thomas defines the first principle of practical reason: that good is to be done and evil is to be avoided.[143] The moral part of the Summa in the Second Part expresses practical knowledge as, for example, the definition of virtue, and the parts of justice. The first principle of practical reason is a self- evident principle that is a command that God has implanted in us. It is a necessary thing, and we reason from the necessary thing (that is characterized by the general principles of natural law), to the contingent commands of human law.

The human laws are the conventional principles that govern human societies based upon the general precepts and requirements of natural law. Human law is devised by human reason and is contingent instead of necessary and unchanging like natural law. Human beings are voluntary and free beings, and our morality is autonomous. We know the difference between what is right and wrong, and we have the free will to follow good or evil. Human law is part of God's plan for us, and it should promote the common good, and assist us in our goal of happiness with God. We derive the human law from natural law where we construct laws to promote the common good, or we can also determine the punishment of transgressors, while protecting the rights of individuals by providing a guide to morality, and principles of virtue. The general objectives of a community can be outlined with a reasonable set of human laws.

Divine law is given directly by God through divine revelation and is infallible, for example, the historical laws of Scripture. Divine law is a moral imperative justified by divine authority, for example the Ten Commandments. "The Lord God commanded the man saying, 'From any tree of the garden you may eat freely; but from the tree of the knowledge of good and evil you shall not eat, for in the day that you eat from it you will surely die.'"[144] As demonstrated from Genesis, we can know God's moral imperatives through the statements found in biblical texts. God is the author of our moral laws, and these truths affect our actions and understanding of what we can and cannot do to be in obedience to God's morality. St. Thomas's eternal law is God's Divine Wisdom that moves all created things to their natural end. (Remember that Plato teaches an ontological principle that is like St. Thomas, where the Platonic theory explained the world through the theory of the Forms).

St. Thomas defines natural law as the rational creature's, "share of the Eternal Reason, whereby it has a natural inclination to its proper act and end; and this participation of the eternal law in the rational creature is called the natural law...the light of natural reason whereby we discern what is good and what is evil, which is the function of the natural law, is nothing else than an imprint on us of the Divine light. It is therefore evident that natural law is nothing else than the rational creature's participation of the eternal law."[145]

It is important to repeat in summary, the first principle of natural law is to do good and avoid evil. The first self-evident principle of practical reason is that "good is that which all things seek after."[146] The basis of natural law is, "good is to be done and pursued, and evil is to be avoided."[147] *Synderesis* means the knowledge of moral principles, where the major premise of the practical syllogism and the actual drawing of the conclusion is the work of conscience. St. Thomas along with Aristotle hold that a moral situation will be represented by the practical syllogism. The precepts of natural law must be rational propositions. St. Thomas teaches that universal principles of moral obligation are identical with natural law, and that natural law is unchanging in its first principles.

To guide us in the truth we use our reason, rational arguments, an understanding of the limits of reason, and the process of reasoning. We support our faith by logic and evidence. For St. Thomas, as well as Aristotle, the moral problem is represented by the practical syllogism. The syllogism can be scientific with necessarily true propositions, and a necessarily true conclusion, or probable or dialectical conclusion. Socrates used dialectic in his reasoning to teach truth. We have a facility with logic and know the limits and nature of a logical argument. We know the proper evidence for the logical argument. We can support our faith by both logic and evidence. The primary percept of law for St. Thomas is that good is to be done, and evil is to be avoided.

The first principles of natural law are unchangeable. The secondary principles may in certain cases be modified. To have the binding force of law, and to be a universal authority over us ordered by a Divine lawgiver, the law must be promulgated. St. Thomas teaches us that, "The natural law is promulgated by the very fact that God instilled it into man's mind so as to be known by him natural."[148]

St. Thomas contrasted The Old Law with The New Law: The Old Law focused on fear and earthly rewards taught to us in the Old Testament. The Old Law foreshadowed The New Law where we learn about the love and heavenly rewards taught to us by Jesus Christ in the New Testament. Our Christian living and morality are necessary, but we also need grace to have knowledge of God.

The good is in accord with the essential nature of man which reflects the divine essence that is unchangeable. We have a natural inclination toward some things that are apprehended by reason, and these things include: to seek the highest good which is living eternally happy with God, self-preservation and preservation of the species, communal living with others, and to use our intellect and will.

Socrates analyzes the sophist teaching that justice was either in the interest of the stronger or entered for expediency. Aristotle, in the Ethics, advanced the concept of natural justice.[149] Of political justice he said that part is natural, and part is legal the natural is that which has the same force and does not exist by people thinking this or that. The legal is that which is originally indifferent. The essential ingredient of justice which is enforced by the state is not its own contrivance; it is a discovery from natural and a transcript of its constancy.

St. Thomas taught that God's very essence is His existence. There are two realms of reality: the material realm and the spiritual realm. The material realm contains material things that are composed of tangible parts. The spiritual realm contains things that are simple, with no parts, no shape, no size, and no dimension. There are five proofs for the existence of God: the proof from motion, the proof from cause, the proof from necessary being, the proof from the degrees of being, and the proof from the final cause.

For St. Thomas, the question of moral standards, and morality is part of God's essence. Plato raised the question of the source of moral values in the Euthyphro. Good and bad acts are by their nature good and bad; good and evil acts are fixed as good and evil acts, and God commands us to do good and not evil because of the intrinsic nature of good and evil. God's commands do not make the acts themselves good or evil, and we can reason about these acts because of the universal nature of good and evil. Moral voluntarists hold that certain acts are good or bad because God wills these acts to be good or bad. John Calvin and John Locke hold voluntarism moral positions. Moral standards are based on the will of God. This is a difficult position to maintain because it implies that moral standards are not fixed, and God could change these standards by changing His mind, and this would make God's essence changeable. Voluntarism gives us an easy answer to our question as to why we should behave, because God has commanded us so (which itself is not a bad thing!); we will ourselves to obedience of God's moral commands. However, moral rationalism (Plato and St. Thomas) teaches us that good and evil are intrinsic qualities or that there are inherently good or evil actions. God has created us and nature as a reflection of His own essence and the divine essence is not changeable. Morality is part of the essence of God so that moral standards are not prior to God's existence, nor do these moral standards exist independently of God. We do good and avoid evil because we can rationally discern (a perception that God has graced us with) the nature of good or evil, and our end purpose is to do good and avoid evil, which brings us happiness as a member of the community of God's children. St. Thomas reminds us that God's reason is the divine Logos, and we can participate in this divine Logos through natural law.

St. Thomas' theory of natural law is built upon a philosophically and spiritually sound theory of metaphysics which includes essences, *telos* or end for us, happiness, virtue, knowledge, and final causes. The new natural law theory (for, example, Germain Grisez, Joseph Boyle, and John Finnis) removes metaphysics from natural law. Socrates, of course, would object to the removal of metaphysics from any moral theory; he taught, for example, that knowledge is virtue. St. Thomas's intricate metaphysics is replaced with a discussion (for example in John Finnis) about basic goods that are intuitively known, desired and pursued for human fulfillment, and make our actions intelligible. An example of the Finnian phenomenological approach to natural law is the idea that basic goods are knowledge, our living, for example, our family life, children and health, and a plan for living that harmonizes with the moral good, our friendships, aesthetic experiences, social interactions, and religion. Natural law terminology is replaced with the language of natural rights.[150]

St. Thomas taught us that all governments are under God's rule, and we are bond to God under the laws of nature and obedience to natural law. We are commissioned to follow God's natural law, and reason, equity and the law of nature are concepts that assist us in our understanding of natural law. Is law an expression of divine order? The colonial Americans shared a vision of a spiritual and law-abiding nation, and a belief in a transcendent God bound them together as a people who believed in the principle of natural law. The American Republic was built on the foundation of a morality whose basic principle was natural law that was known by the individual's reasoning power. Virtue, justice, liberty, goodness and, indeed, human happiness stem from the principle of natural law. Our clear and precise understanding of the concept of natural law is a fundamental need for our human intellect; and the concept of justice within natural law helps to fulfill this basic need for us. We seek an absolute standard of justice, and natural law provides this essential need for us. Natural law theory teaches us that natural law is universal; the Word of God teaches us that natural law is universal. Our human purpose is to do good, and these good acts are discovered by reasoning, and the moral principles are universal and objective, and discovered through reason. If we are a good person who strives to perform activities that are for the good of everyone, then we also strive to be good citizens of our community. There are limitations in our ability to recognize and apply natural law; St. Thomas teaches us that God's grace fills in this insufficiency in our natures.

Chapter 5

Our Allegiance Is To God and The Constitution of the United States of America

"The tongue of the righteous is as choice silver" (Proverbs 10:20).

"The law of the Lord is perfect, restoring the soul" (Psalm 19:7).

We band together as citizens of the United States in the humble and vigorous search for God's truth, and to use our freedom to exercise this truth as we actively participate as moral citizens within our Nation. Our actions are in harmony with God's natural law — a law that He has instilled in our hearts. The idea of natural law reaches back in time to the original religious sources found in the Word of God as documented in the Bible, to the secular philosophers of ancient Greece and Rome, to the Catholic formulation by St. Thomas, then to Thomas Hobbes, Hugo Grotius, and, of course, to John Locke. The concept of natural law influenced our Founding Fathers and is important for us today as a key to our Nation's future. The American Founders believed in a society that was ordered in harmony with natural law, that is, a society that was in harmony with God's laws for us. Our Founders' belief in natural law was the moral compass that guided our new Nation to develop as a Nation under God, which gave birth to liberty, justice, equality, rule of law, inalienable rights, virtue, freedom, and the creation of our United States Constitution.

Natural law has taught us that to have wisdom is to know our sacred relationship to God, and to order our actions toward that end. In this modern age we bear witness to the Truth of God and live our lives in harmony with God's Word, and work to protect our religious liberty. We were born to lovingly serve God, and to bear witness to the mystery of God. The founders knew that the Supreme power behind the Constitution was God's providence for America, and this ordination entailed a religious belief and trust in God's natural law. All human beings have inherent dignity, innate reason, and are endowed with natural law. Today, we have forgotten our duties (duties that are mentioned and documented during our Nation's founding), and neglect our sacred bond with God, i.e., our government was created by God, formed by God's will, lawful under God, successful by God's blessings, fulfilled through His providence, and safe by God's protection and guidance for our Nation. We reach across the current material gulf that has separated us from our Creator, and as spiritual, God-filled beings, we now actively seek the transcendent truth of God's natural law.

We are not born with a tabula rasa or "blank slate consciousness" where our experiences alone dictate how we will view the world as the progressives claim, but we are born with the deep spiritual and innate ability of natural law to morally guide us, and to distinguish good from evil, and good acts from evil acts. We are not born with a full spiritual consciousness and mature knowledge of God's deep moral and ethical truths, but we have the human spiritual propensity to grow, mature, and to learn to know and exercise the innate natural law principles. Knowledge, reason, religion, habituation, education, family, society, reflection, wisdom, natural inclinations toward the good — all these qualities work toward the goal of our harmony with God's natural law. We have the innate pattern of what is good built into us by God, and the capacity to recognize this good, the reasoning power to understand the good, the will to pursue that which is good, and the inclination to achieve the good. It is not smooth sailing for everyone, because bad habits, faulty reasoning, misunderstanding, a darkening of our spiritual understanding, unruly dispositions, corruption, and corrupt social influences may all lead us astray.[151]

St. Thomas teaches us that, "The order of the percepts of natural law accords with the order of natural inclinations."[152] We have discussed St. Thomas' treatises on natural law and our study concludes that the essence of St. Thomas' natural law theory can be found centuries later in many of the philosopher's works: for example, Thomas Hobbes (1588-1679), John Locke (1632-1704), and David Hume (1711-1776) — philosophers whose theories influenced the thinking of the American Founders. John Locke, for example, presented a demonstrative science of morality where men are innately equipped with rational faculties where we can understand natural law and the ideas related to natural law.

The Holy Bible is the written testament to God's Holy arc, and the written Word of God is the spiritual teaching of natural law and morality. The mystery of natural law is deepened by the self-evident truths that God has revealed to us in His Word; and the wisdom of these truths are brought to light by our practice of natural law. God has commissioned each of us as Generals in His army of natural law. St. Thomas has taught us that our natural capacity to discern the general principles in the order of nature allows us to thrive as a species. Our human flourishing brings us together within communities that learn to live together in political associations that are governed by laws. All our political associations under our government are under God's rule, and our human laws are the living source and reflection of natural law. God's natural laws will always reinforce and demonstrate the truth of man-made law, if man-made law is a just law, then it is in harmony with God's natural laws for us. "Love and faithfulness meet together; righteousness and peace kiss each other." (Psalm 85:10). Our Lord's world is an orderly world, and to live our lives fully in this world, we follow natural law. Our dispositions are orderly and rational and will lead to our happiness (eudaemonia). God has created an orderly universe for our benefit. Following God's commandments, we can say that our purpose is to maintain ourselves as moral human beings who worship, and obey God, and the fulfillment of this purpose will bring us happiness. God is the light and the salt of the universe; we are blessed to live in His Holy light; and to be nourished with His life-sustaining spiritual salt. Jesus taught us, "You are the salt of the earth. But if the salt loses its saltiness, how can it be made salty again? It is no longer good for anything, except to be thrown out and trampled by men." (Matthew 5:13).

Our heritage as Americans is to be blessed by God with the capacity for understanding natural law, and to live under the canopy of the freedom that the natural law structure provides for us. I am writing as a philosopher, and because of my love for my Nation, reverence and allegiance to The Constitution of the United States of America and natural law, and respect for the American Founders, I have immersed myself in the historical records and writings of the Founding era — an era that bears witness to God and natural law. A glimpse into philosophy is like a glimpse into history where you are left with a fuller view of life, and a greater understanding of our Constitutional Republic. We remember that Socrates taught us to know ourselves first, and then our historical curiosity will be tempered by that which we are able to understand at the time. We are rooted in time insofar as we are grounded in our nation's history and the reality of our personal existence. Our life is a spiritual and a constitutional life — a life of respect for the law and the Constitution, but also a meaningful spiritual life where the individual worships and has reverence for God. Life's landmarks for us are formed partially by the patterns of those individuals whose intellectual activity helped to shape our Constitutional Republic — those whose lives are well-known to historians and now to us, like Thomas Jefferson, James Madison, and George Washington. But these well-known historical patterns of prominent characters that shaped our Nation's Founding are eclipsed by our belief in the reality of our patterns of natural law. Natural law is the moral precept that encourages us all to do better than our best; and to seek the Lord in all our daily thinking, activities and communication with others. The memory of a good person's deeds and accomplishments will live on whether the individual becomes a prominent figure in history or not. We believe in history; history is God's clothing that enables us to view a portion of His majesty working in the world. Marxists do not believe in history; they want to remove the witness to the glorious activity of the Lord. The Marxists want everyone to believe in the state, and to depend entirely on the state and government. Unfortunately, we are witnessing these Marxist attempts today within the United States government in their attempt to try to discredit, dilute and destroy our belief in God. We believe in The Constitution of the United States of America, and that we have not yet activated the full freedoms guaranteed to us by this document; we believe in the history of the formation of our Nation, and we see God's guidance in our good decisions; we study American history in order that we may be wiser citizens who can continue to live free in a Nation under God.

For those Americans who have a deep love and respect for our Nation, The United States Constitution, and our Founders — and a belief in God's Word and natural law to improve our Republic with the rule of law, innovative ideas and patriot actions — there is the painful knowledge that dark forces have been steadily at work to overthrow our Republic for the end goal of personal power, elite rule over us, control, and money. Many politicians and businesses have sold out their ethical principles and allegiance to our Nation for power and money to the Chinese Communist Party. For example, concrete evidence has shown that Hunter Biden (the son of President Joe Biden) has engaged in influence peddling for access to Vice President Joe Biden in exchange for money. There is no more crucial time than now to turn our face to God, to place a firm belief in His power and Rule of Law. We pray that the Mighty and Powerful arm of God, with His loyal Army of servants, will expose and strike down this sinister move to overthrow the United States of America.

The United States has recently been besieged by violent protests and mob-movements: Black Lives Matter, ANTIFA, CAIR, and other leftist groups who target cities governed by liberal democrats and are financed by those whose aim is to overthrow the United States. These Marxist groups falsely claim that the United States is a racist nation founded by evil men, and slaveholders; therefore, our institutions should be burned down, the statues of our historical figures should be torn down, our historical sites should be defaced, the businesses of others should be looted and destroyed, and that our police force should be defunded because these groups claim that the police force represents racists who should be disrespected and attacked. Many historians, writers, rational politicians, reporters, and reputable commentators have analyzed these individuals and the violent activity of these "revolutionaries," and trace the movement to radical socialism and Marxist ideology that is being taught to our youth in the universities and in our public schools. Added to these youthful agitators — who are ignorant of the history of the United States — are professional agitators who are being paid to spread anarchy by those financiers who plan to reap a windfall if the United States crumbles and China becomes the leader of their desired "new world-order". The agitators are framed and fueled and funded by the democratic party who remain silent about the destruction of personal property, murders (including innocent children, -- most recently a one-year-old child in New York City on July 12, 2020), innocent citizens, and police officers who are doing their job to regain control of the communities. The left-wing media (who remain a mouthpiece for the democratic party) spin a false narrative calling the looters "peaceful protesters" while businesses and personal property are being burned, looted, and destroyed. The democratic party's leadership are using this violence to control their narrative to try to get President Trump out of office — the democrats cannot win an election fairly on principles and ideas, and putting forth a plan for what they will do to improve our Nation, the economy, safety, security, and quality of life for citizens; instead hatred toward President Trump and their desire to regain political power in Washington keeps them silent and stops them from speaking out against this violence. Democrat Speaker of the House, Nancy Pelosi, for example, has been silent on the murders, violence and destruction of statutes stating that she never did like statutes and that "people will do what people will do." Instead of taking a leadership role in denouncing the violence, murders, and destruction of personal property and statutes, the democrats are fanning the fires of violence hoping that the democrats can retake the White House in November 2020. The common denominator for the protesters is that they are acting on a false narrative propped up by historical falsehoods, the falsehoods are then buttressed by the media; they have a disrespect for the rule of law, and God is totally absent from their violent narrative. The final goal for these haters of our democracy and our Nation is political power and control. The real end game is that their rage and atheism is directed against God and Christianity. While they spew evil hatred against God, they also attack the Nation and everything good that our Nation stands for: the Office of the President, Congress, the Supreme Court, The *Declaration of Independence*, the Constitution of the United States, the rule of law, natural law, individual freedom, democracy, republicanism, conservatism, the American family, American virtue, our police force, ICE, and American goodness. For those of us who believe in God, worship God, and follow God, and obey the rule of law, especially natural law, our daily prayer is for peace and prosperity to be restored to our Nation. We also fervently pray that God does not withdraw His Almighty and Holy protection from our Nation due to our transgressions and sins against His laws.

The disrespect shown by the violent mob-protesters toward our Nation's Founders, and historical figures illuminates a level of ignorance and dishonesty toward reality and reason held by these mob-protesters. This cultural dishonesty is mirrored by a political dishonesty that attempts to reframe American history to fit the political narrative of the radical left within the democratic party. The New York Times Project 2016, for example, is a false narrative of America's history claiming that the American Founders wrote slaves into the United States Constitution as property! Political elites who want the publicity to remain personally relevant have jumped on the false narrative bandwagon to push Project 2016. A false narrative labeled "critical race theory" has seeped into our university and secondary education curricula that teaches a racist doctrine that the United States is an inherently racist nation, and that our current social institutions are racist. There is no dialectical discussion for dissenting opinions for these Marxist carriers of propaganda, falsehood, and intolerance — anyone who corrects the record (based on fact, history, culture, reason, and reality) are labeled toxic and racist. Truth is not a concept known to these Marxist spreaders of hatred and discord – truth is a relative concept, individuals do not have any rights, and only groups have rights, they use force to cancel culture, work to overturn our Constitution and the Bill of Rights, overturn our legal system, interfere with capitalism and the free-market economy, and ban religion. Critical race theory teaches students that revolution and activism are the means to be liberated from the "oppressor;" and instead of successfully educating our youth for the future, they are indoctrinating our children with an ideology based on hatred. (See, Newt Gingrich, *Beyond Biden: Rebuilding the America We Love*, (New York: Center Street, Hachette Book Group, 2021).

The majority of Americans love our Nation, and enjoy American history, and for many of us, countless hours are spent reading to discover the truth about American history and our constitutional republic. The search for truth has always been an admirable characteristic. In ancient Athens, Socrates, for example, spent his entire life searching for the truth of a matter, and his greatest joy was in sharing this search for truth with the youth of Athens. Contrast Socrates' peaceful search for truth with the actors of our modern "mob-protesters" who have performed acts that have terrorized American cities and citizens, destroyed property, injured innocent bystanders, and they are even guilty of the murder of innocent victims. Of course, these criminals only target cities that are governed by liberal democrats because they know that the democrats will run cover for their atrocious acts. Let these agitators show up in the conservative towns of rural America — where the ideas of God, family and Nation are still practiced and very much alive today— and there will be a far different outcome!

When we read about Socrates in the Platonic *Dialogues*, we learn that Socrates spent his entire life seeking the truth and sharing his knowledge with others. Our knowledge about Socrates is primarily from the writings of Plato (The *Dialogues* of Plato). However, this historical knowledge has such force that Socrates speaks to us out of the depth of time; that is, his thinking has as much relevance today as it did in ancient Greece when he walked the streets of Athens and questioned his fellow citizens about the nature of their souls, the polity, and the nature of the Good. We can say the same thing about our Nation's Founders, that is, if we look deeply into the historical record, we see, for example, the strength of a courageous Washingtonian soul, the learning, analytical power, exceptional writing ability, and curiosity of Thomas Jefferson, and the intelligence, reasoning skills, creative mind, organizational skills, and visional leadership of James Madison. George Washington and James Madison were among two of the fifty-five colonial thinkers who gathered in the summer of 1787 to create, formulate, and write the United States Constitution. Thomas Jefferson was absent from the Constitutional Convention because he was serving as America's Ambassador to France during that time.

James Madison's belief in natural law and natural rights was the stimulus to the religious freedom, liberties, and the free acts of an individual conscience that are promoted and protected by the United States Constitution. A few of the highlights of Madison's life-long political career include: a delegate to the Virginia Convention when the Constitution of Virginia, 1776, and the Virginia Bill of Rights, June 12, 1776, were written, author of *Memorial and Remonstrance*, in 1785, which argued against Patrick Henry's Bill for a General Assessment in Virginia where Madison argued that state-enforced religion had never worked, the organization of the Annapolis Convention in September 1786, a leader in the Constitutional Convention that led to the Philadelphia Convention in May, 1787, an energetic leader with rational and creative ideas about the structure of the new government during the Constitutional debates in the summer of 1787, a leader in the ratification of the Constitution, a co-author (along with Alexander

Hamilton and John Jay) of *The Federalist* to generate support and answer questions about the novel Constitution, he served in the United States House of Representatives from 1789 through 1797, founded the Democratic-Republican Party in 1792 (along with Thomas Jefferson), and the initiator and author of the Bill of Rights in the First Congress, (The first ten amendments to the United States Constitution; at that time the amendments were numbered 3 through 12, and were adopted by the states to become the United States Bill of Rights effective December 15, 1791), he served as Secretary of State from 1801-1809, and Madison served as the Nation's fourth President from 1809 through 1817. These are a few of the accomplishments of just one of the Founding Fathers, and the illustrative careers of many of the other Founding Fathers will be discussed. (A detailed biography of each of the Founding Fathers is beyond the scope of this book. There are excellent historical biographies written about each of these creative and accomplished men; the reader will find book references in the Bibliography for Natural Law and the Constitution, published in this author's website: socratesplace.com). From all points of the American historical compass, the Convention delegates gathered as citizens of this great Nation to give form and structure to the new government, and in doing so, they created, clarified, enriched, and preserved our American freedoms.

Natural law was the Archimedean point from which our statesmen-founders viewed the fundamental principles of government including the political, domestic, and foreign policies, governmental balance of powers, federal and state balance of powers, equality, freedoms, justice, liberty, individual rights, the social compact, and the duties of the citizens. In referring to the concept of natural law, the founders often used the expressions "law" or "laws of nature". The concept of natural law is used extensively in early American political thought, however, the concept itself was not always fully analyzed. Natural law is a philosophical idea known to the colonists from the Bible, the Magna Carta (June 15, 1215), English constitutionalism, English common law, custom, the writings of Plato (428/427 -348/347 BC), the writings of Aristotle (384-322 BC),

Marcus Tullius Cicero (106-43 BC), St. Thomas, and John Locke (1632-1704). For the American colonists, the timeless truths of natural law were found in the Holy Bible. The list of philosophers and theologians who influenced the thinking of the colonists on natural law is extensive, and some of these wise thinkers will be discussed in this book.[153]

For example, the early Pilgrims took advantage of the covenant tradition of the Old Testament, the Church covenants of 1550s to the 1600s, the Pilgrim Code of Law the Mayflower Compact, New England Puritanism, American Protestantism, and covenant theology were ideational influences for the early Americans. Many colonists believed that they had a special place in God's plan — a plan not yet fully realized but Americans were part of the Christian destiny in following God's covenant plan to the new land.[154]

The Puritans wrote the Mayflower Compact on November 11, 1620, which would bind the community with rules based upon their familiarity with the Bible and religious covenants for forming communities. The first colonists pledged loyalty to the crown, however — due to the distance from the mother country, London's grant to the colonists of local control, and the preoccupation of London with their own Civil War — the colonists were granted autonomy for governance. Over a period, the colonists built strong religious communities that developed into their own sense of political communities, and their religious covenants became written constitutions.

The colonist's knowledge of classical writers was apparent with their reference to the ancient authors in colonial literature, conversations, arguments, letters, sermons, political speeches, debates, dialogues, and tracts. This novel nation looked to the timeless truths in the Holy Bible as the pattern for our new nation. Natural law had been a profound idea known to the ancient Greek philosophers: Homer, Sophocles, Socrates, Plato, Euripides, Herodotus, Thucydides, Xenophon, and Aristotle. Among the Romans writing about the concept of natural law were Livy, Marcus

Tullius Cicero (Tully), Horace, Vergil, Tacitus, Seneca, Ovid, Cato, Marcus Aurelius, Caesar, Ulpian, Gaius, and Justinian. All these men can be counted among some of those who influenced colonial thinking about natural law.

The Christian philosophers and theologians who influenced the new nations theoretical thinking includes St. Augustine of Hippo (354-430), and St. Thomas, both remind us about the importance of natural law. The list of influential philosophers and writers continues with Francesco de Vitoria (1483-1546), James Harrington (1611-1677), barrister, politician and judge, Sir Edward Coke (1552/1553-1634), jurist, judge and Tory politician, Sir William Blackstone (1723-1780), Jonathan Swift (1667-1745), Thomas Hobbes (1588-1679), David Hume (1711-1776), Jean-Jacques Rousseau (1712-1778), Francois-Marie Arouet, known as Voltaire (1694-1778), Hugo Grotius (1583-1645), Algernon Sidney (1623-1683), John Locke (1632-1704), Nicolo Machiavelli (1469-1527), Charles de Montesquieu (1689-1755), Thomas Paine (1736-1809), James Thompson (1700-1748), Emer de Vattel (1714-1767), Jean Jacque Burlamaqui (1694-1748), Francis Wollaston (1762-1823), Henry St. John, 1st Viscount Bolingbroke (1678-1751), Benjamin Hoadley (1734-1761), Robert Bellarmine (1542-1621), Marquis Cesare Beccaria (1738-1794) and Francisco Suarez (1548-1617). We continue with the natural law influence on the scientific theories of Isaac Newton (1643-1727), and the political tracts of John Trenchard and Thomas Gordon writing as CATO (1720-1723), as well as the ideological influence of the Glorious Revolution, Whig theory of politics, common law, English institutions, and the Renaissance.

Also influential was the Enlightenment, for example the Scottish Enlightenment (1730-1790s), and the philosophy of Francis Hutcheson, John Witherspoon, Thomas Reid, James Harrington, Adam Smith, and William Small.[155] The Enlightenment encompassed English, French, Scottish, American, German, Italian, and Spanish ideas. Enlightenment ideas first appeared in England with the publication of Newton's *Principia Mathematica* (1687), the *Glorious*

Revolution (1688), and Locke's *Letters on Toleration* (1689).[156] Francis Hutcheson philosophized about how our morality is an essential part of our human nature. Adam Smith theorized in *The Wealth of Nations* that our economic activity is an essential part of our moral and social nature. Covenant theories of the Magna Carta, American's newly founded covenants with the thirteen original states, and the Old Testament Covenant were also significant for the ideas that stimulated the creative thinking that would become the powerful words of the *Declaration of Independence* that outlined the dissatisfaction and grievances toward Great Britain. God as witness in the last paragraph of the *Declaration of Independence* states our basic moral values and defines the United States and its people as a "Nation Under God." These words would become the triumph of our constitutional republic.

The American Enlightenment ideas taught that human reason was the guide to human conduct, but that it must be grounded in morality. Some of the leading thinkers of the American Enlightenment were Adam Smith, Thomas Paine, and Thomas Jefferson — all these men were influenced by John Locke who believed that kings should not rule. The intellectual ideas of the American Enlightenment, (eighteenth to nineteenth century thinkers in America), taxation and over-bearing abuses by Britain against the colonies led to the American Revolution.

The colonists also absorbed the ideas of the seventeenth-century legal scholars as the Americans developed their own concepts of equity, justice, and rights. American eighteenth-century pamphlets referred to the authors of the history of English law: Henry Spelman, Thomas Made, Robert Brady, and William Petyt.[157] The ideas of the prominent European thinkers were used by the colonists to form their own arguments, develop the clarity of constitutional thought, and to make their ideas practical and relevant. For example, Montesquieu, Blackstone, Locke, and Hume were cited frequently during the debates in the Constitutional Convention. The delegates to the Constitutional Convention in 1787 discussed checks and balances from Blackstone, separation of powers from Montesquieu, and the analysis of factions within the government from the writings of Hume. The delegates to the Constitutional Convention adopted the political thought and patterns of the remarkable European philosophers to create a Constitutional document that was unique and workable for the new Nation.

The French Enlightenment (1715-1789) minimized the importance of faith and tradition and focused on human reason (see Rousseau). The Scottish Enlightenment (1730-1790s) and common-sense philosophy centered on God-given natural rights. James Madison and James Wilson brought pivotal intellectual ideas to the Constitutional Convention and their ideas were shaped by Scottish philosophical assumptions. Madison's legal theories were influenced by the moral epistemology of Thomas Reid who founded common sense realism. Reid, in turn, was influenced by Isaac Newton. The philosophers, John Witherspoon and William Small, influenced both Madison and Jefferson. Witherspoon's students included five who became delegates at the Constitutional Convention. Witherspoon's course in moral philosophy was influenced by Francis Hutcheson's *A System of Moral Philosophy*. Hutcheson taught that our morality is an endowment of our human nature, and it is what makes us the creatures that we are. Adam Smith, influenced by common sense philosophy, wrote that our economic activity is founded on our moral and social nature. Benjamin Rush travelled to Scotland to study at a time when European universities were considered superior to America universities, and Scottish universities, the best. William Small taught at William and Mary College from 1754-1764, and he influenced the young Thomas Jefferson. One of Madison's early teachers was Donald Robertson who established a secondary school in King and Queen County, Virginia; an elderly Madison wrote a note saying that he owed much of his abilities to Robertson's instruction as his teacher.

Some European Enlightenment philosophers rejected God as the author of natural law, thus, deifying nature or man. However, for the majority of Enlightenment thinkers, God is the center and source of natural law, and human reason is the faculty that we use to access our God-given natural law. Natural law is a universal law of nature, eternal, and a self-evident proposition that is accessible to us through our reason. It is the law upon which we build our morality to conform to God's Holy Word, His commandments, and His expectations for us. The American Founders used the principle of Natural Law as the foundation for the *Declaration of Independence*, and the Constitution has its philosophical roots in the concepts of the *Declaration of Independence* and natural law. The Constitution affirms our belief in God while maintaining a neutral position on differing religious sects. Unfortunately, today some citizens of our Nation suspend their belief in God, and even maintain agnosticism or atheism as a personal religious belief or point of view. The Supreme Court has also now maintained a neutral position on not only religious sects but also on the Nation's belief in God.[158]

Natural law is one of the oldest philosophical concepts known to us and its usage was a key concept in the formation of America. Natural law was examined in essays, pamphlets, and state constitutions during the period that colonial self-government was debated and discussed. The writings of Grotius, Pufendorf, and Burlamaqui emphasized natural law and God as the architect of natural law, and our ability to understand natural law through reason. The aspect of natural law that frequently referred to "natural rights" was generated from the English lawyers, for example Edward Coke, and Sir William Blackstone. The English poet John Milton, the philosophers Thomas Hobbes and John Locke, and the eighteenth-century revolutionary writer Thomas Paine wrote about the principles of natural law and taught the American colonists about the natural rights of men which cannot be taken away by government. Writing in *Common Sense*, Thomas Paine envisioned an America that was united with a shared sense of a common destiny defined by their social and cultural identities. Prior to the American Revolution, Americans shared a common identity of being British subjects.

Independence from Britain was declared on July 2, 1776. Congress approved the final text of the *Declaration of Independence* on July 4, 1776, and it was signed on August 2, 1776. What Americans held in common during the creation of the colonies, during and after the American Revolution, and throughout the Constitutional Convention where the Founders had framed the United States Constitution, is a belief in God and in natural law. The laws of nature express God's will and the true nature of the human being, and we can know these laws and the constitution of the universe using our reason. Early Americans held a deep religious belief in God as the Creator and the spiritual guide that had led them to cross the vast ocean to seek freedom for their religious beliefs. The laws of nature are an essential part of natural law.

The miracle of the creation of this Nation is that God's people and citizens of the United States of American are strong believers in God, Jesus as the son of God, and our faith in natural law is just as strong today. The current theft of our Nation's governance has caused fear, confusion, sadness, lack of faith, a lack of truth, evil policies, and a darkness upon our Land. God is a God of liberty and freedom, justice and righteousness, truth, and light: We pray that God again shows us His Almighty Power and Glory and stretches His mighty Hand over our Nation and strikes the evil out of our Land and restores our Nation through the intervention of the Holy Spirit.

Chapter 6

The Fruitful Tree of Natural Law

"The law of the Lord is perfect, reviving the soul. The statutes of the Lord are trustworthy, making wise the simple." Psalm 19:7.

The Biblical Book of Psalm goes on to teach us that the ordinances of the Lord are pure and altogether righteous — more precious than gold, and sweeter than honey. (Psalm 19:9-10). Philosophers often seek the essence of our nature, that characteristic that makes us who we are, and without this characteristic we would not be who we are. Natural law is the essential part of our nature and constitutes our essential being as a human. We are not isolated individuals, but are part of a family, a community, a state, and a Nation; therefore, we participate in activities that are compatible with our natural law. These intrinsic natural law norms guide us in our daily activities. Our purposeful action that is based upon natural law is a learned activity gained through our knowledge of what God desires of us, our obedience to divine percepts, God's rule of law, our wisdom, rational inquiry, attentiveness to the Divine Word, common law, and revelation.

Our American Republic was created through the Founding Father's understanding of natural law. Our defense of the principles of our American Republic, and our obedience to our United States Constitution are strengthened with an understanding of God's natural law. Freedom, equality before the law, a just legal system, justice, liberty, freedom to choose our state and federal representatives, freedom to choose the President of the United

States, freedom to choose our judges, freedom to choose our local representatives, autonomy as a Nation, autonomy as an individual, and human rights are all the outgrowth and Blessings of God's natural law. The idea of natural law is a criterion for judging all these areas. Our spiritual inspection of nature is taught to us through natural law. We pray for an enlightened age of human freedom, and for this to occur, natural law must come back into the consciousness of God-loving, and God-fearing Americans. We can flourish as a nation under God's guidance with natural law. Natural law is revealed to us as the will of God and revealed through His Holy Word. Our ultimate purpose is to love God with our whole heart. We are also commanded to love our neighbors. There is no more important time than now — with our Nation and our Constitution, and the integrity of our national elections under assault by enemies both domestic and foreign — to pray for God's guidance and wisdom for our leaders and for ourselves.

The United States was founded as a natural rights Republic. There were many influencing ideas on the Founders of our Republic, but natural law and natural rights were the foundational ideas. The historical role of the governments of classical Greece and ancient Rome are also considered to be strong influences on the thoughts of the Founders. Democracy was discussed as early as the pre-Socratic philosophers in ancient Greece to refer to a society where citizens control the policies and procedures of the state. The form of democracy was considered to be an unstable government by Plato and Aristotle; these important ancient Greek philosophers believed that democracy was a form of government that will degenerate into anarchy. It was not until the seventeenth century during the English civil war that democratic forms of government are discussed in a more favorable light by the Levellers, for example Gerrard Winstanley (1609-1676). Winstanley published a pamphlet called *The New Law of Righteousness*" based on the Biblical teaching from the Book of Acts, chapter two, verses 44 and 45. Winstanley reasoned that God created all men from a common stock, there should be no masters or slaves, no kingship, no aristocracy, and no property (land) ownership. The philosopher Jean-Jacques Rousseau

(1712-1778) joined the notion of democracy to the notion of society in the social contract. English common law and Whiggish thought also had a key influence on republican ideas. We have taken all these ideas into consideration and maintain that the keystone for our Republic was founded upon natural law and what the Founders most often referred to as natural rights.

Prior to independence the Crown appointed the governor, and the colonists elected their legislatures. (The exception was Connecticut and Rhode Island who had a charter that allowed them to elect their governors). Overall, the colonists had a distrust of any executive power, so the governor remained a figurehead with status and the British navy to be their only tools for power.

The Constitutional delegates looked for political thought and patterns that they could successfully adopt for the creation of the Constitution and the English Constitution was useful for their debate.[159] The English constitution was an informal constitution with laws, legal precedents, customs, and with a ruling aristocracy and a king. Thomas Paine's writing in *Common Sense* was critical of hereditary monarchy.

After independence, the Crown was no longer the sovereign power, so the colonists became the sovereign who created and constituted both national and state governments. The legal fiction of dual citizenship (Article IV, Section 2; Article I, Section 8, 9, and 10), is the mode of government of federalism. Federalism is the delineation of the power of state and national governments. (See: The Constitution of the United States, The Tenth and Fourteenth Amendments). Lutz states that "the concept of federalism—the creation of a new entity that is indissoluble yet preserves the freedom and integrity of its constituent parts—derives from the biblical notion of covenant, which the dissenting Protestant colonists understood so well."[160]

The Founders' belief in republican government was defined by the morality and virtue that was practiced within the citizen body. The philosopher John Locke divides moral law into four categories:

divinely revealed law, the law of nature, civil law, and the law of public censure or opinion. Some of the Constitutional virtues were defined by natural rights expressed as life, liberty, and the pursuit of happiness in the *Declaration of Independence*. Locke had defined natural rights as what people have under natural law: life, liberty, and property. In the *Second Treatise of Government*, Locke wrote that the duty of the government is to protect the natural rights of the people. The basis of a legitimate government is that the consent of the governed gives the ruler the authority to rule.

The Constitution has a strong moral background of republicanism, consent of the governed, liberty, freedom, and deliberative principles. The Americans created a community of values through their own authority and ability to choose their leaders and deliberate on the principles of government. John Locke's *Second Treatise on Civil Government* (1690) antedates the idea of popular sovereignty that was put into constitutional practice by the Americans. Historian Donald S. Lutz in *The Origins of American Constitutionalism* teaches us that we must examine a wide range of texts to determine the core of American constitutionalism, for example, John Locke was an important influence, but he was not the single influencer of a document that was so historically unique.[161]

The American colonies break with Britain (which we will discuss later) was the impetus and justification for creating and writing the Constitution. The early connotation of the word "constitution" meant the arrangement of existing laws, institutions and practices of the government, and customs along with the principles and goals that animate this arrangement. An example would be the common law and statute laws of early England. The Founders were modeling our Constitution after numerous models of the English constitution — not a written document, but a tradition and custom, previous laws and statutes, decrees, and arrangements of power. The Founders also relied on the natural law, and natural right concepts within the thirteen state constitutions and their respective state bill of rights.

The Lockean idea of a compact between the people and the rulers was an English Whig idea that did not apply to the Americans.[162] In Britain, The Crown, and the governors that it appointed were the government, and the legislature represented the people. After American independence, the Crown was no longer the sovereign authority, the American people were. The colonists had practiced a form of popular sovereignty under the Crown, after independence the people became sovereign, and this popular sovereignty rested on the agreement among the people on how they are to be governed.

The idea of the separation of powers came from Montesquieu, a prominent philosopher during the 1760s and 1770s, as was Locke. They were among the most frequently cited authors of this era including Blackstone and Hume.[163] Their names are featured at the top of Donald S. Lutz's two interesting charts that demonstrate the most-cited secular thinkers of their time. The Bible was quoted most frequently in the public political literature between 1760 and 1805.[164]

A large influence on the thinking of the Founders was also the state constitutions where James Madison and the participants at the Constitutional Convention in 1787 examined the strengths and weaknesses of the state constitutions. The delegates had experience to some degree in the drafting and implementation of their own respective state constitutions. Many of the delegates had experience in politics and had participated in the debates for the approval of the Articles of Confederation.

The Founders brought their knowledge of history, politics, and practical experience with them to the Constitutional Convention. They had knowledge of history and politics of the past: ancient Greece and Rome, and they read the historians, for example, Tacitus, and the philosopher's David Hume (1711-1776), and Samuel von Pufendorf (1632-1694). American documents, for example, the Massachusetts Constitution of 1780, state constitutions, and colonial documents were a source of reference for the delegates. The delegates personal experience in colonial politics, and their wisdom to know what would work, and the wisdom to compromise their own positions for a workable constitution for the whole Nation are important to keep in mind. Putting American's natural rights on paper did not create the right, but only affirmed the existence of such rights.

The concept of virtue was a foundational idea for 17th and 18th century Americans. The colonial concept of virtue was based on the Word written in the Bible and followed God's law. The American colonial concept of virtue was also a connotation from the ancient Greek notion of *arete*. The Greek notion of *arete* meant the accomplished abilities that we must achieve, e.g., excellence on a job or in a task. Socrates' search for *arete* had a moral purpose — the Socratic dialectic was a process of thinking and searching for ways for the improvement of the individual soul. Socrates even described politics as the care of the soul. The Socratic questions about virtue, justice, moderation, courage, goodness, and piety are all questions that we continue to ask ourselves today. Socratic virtue was to cause good to others, never evil, even if provoked. How do we have knowledge about virtue and how do we lead a good life that will lead to happiness? It is difficult for us, today, to understand any individuals' actions that have deliberately harmed other individual citizens (especially murdering others!), destroying property, and creating riots, destruction, and injury and harm to people, property or to the community.

Natural law and our belief in our Almighty God are at the foundation of our inquiries and gives us the courage to hold to our faith during these dark times. Americans are not able to exercise their freedoms during the prevalent lock-downs of communities by overreaching and despotic governors. There is no community spirit when individuals find their freedoms and their physical movements restricted by the government. We are not able to pursue a common good when all our freedoms are being stripped away. The inclination to pursue a common good was always important to the early American settlers as they sought and created self-government. Virtue meant that the citizens desiring self-government would pursue the common good. The desire to pursue a common good is also important today for those citizens who practice natural law. What is taking place today, instead, is an indoctrination of identity politics that is ideationally opposed to the politics of a common good for the whole citizen-body of politics.

Original political thought in America began in 1775 and 1776 when the states were constructing their state constitutions. Leading up to the Constitutional Convention in 1787 there was much constructive political thinking especially by John Adams and Thomas Jefferson. Later, ideological differences and preferences were defined with the establishment of the Republican and Federalist parties in 1795. Today in 2020, the progressive and far-left politicians want to destroy all the Constitutional gains for individual and collective freedom that we have made and everything that we have learned from our Founding Fathers, and lock-down our freedoms and liberty. Alarming censorship is taking place by Silicon Valley technocrats who are blocking conservative thought, and even blocking the messages of our President, Donald J. Trump, and the unprecedented action of closing the President's account on Twitter, Facebook, and You Tube. The technology giants have even conspired to "pull-down" a popular social media site called Parler that was used by many conservative republicans and independents to communicate with each other, and post important political news that was not being reported by the biased mainstream media. Social media sites are necessary means of communication for conservatives because we have had a liberal and biased press that has acted as a mouthpiece and arm of the Democratic Party for many years. The trampling on the First Amendment freedoms of over eighty million Americans is at a crisis level.

The current Administration has declared it mandatory that businesses with 100 or more employees make it mandatory that their employees receive the Corona virus vaccination by January 4, 2022, or the companies will be fined. Texas Attorney General Ken Paxton (along with Louisiana, Mississippi, South Carolina, and Utah) sued the Biden Administration to fight back against the mandate.

Attorney General Paxton stated, "The Biden Administration's new vaccine mandate on private businesses is a breathtaking abuse of federal power. OSHA has only limited power and specific responsibilities. This latest move goes way outside those bounds. This 'standard' is flatly unconstitutional. Biden's new mandate is bad policy and bad law, and I'm asking the Court to strike it down." (texasattorneygeneral.gov)

On November 5, 2021, the United States Court of Appeals for the Fifth Circuit ruled to temporarily halt the Administration's vaccine mandate (administered through the Occupational Safety and Health Administration (OSHA). We can expect copious litigation against the Biden Administration as a result of their unconstitutional mandates against the American citizens and American businesses.

The current state government lock-downs by democratic governors are also an unconstitutional ban on our individual and economic freedoms, and economic freedoms (as well as our fundamental Bill of Rights' freedoms) are protected by our Constitution. Where is God's Hand of Protection during this deliberate ruination of our great Nation? Where is the Power of Almighty God when our 2020 Presidential election has been rift with alleged fraud — where the democrats used every available fraudulent activity to achieve a stolen victory for Vice-President Joe Biden.[165] God is the Truth; God is Light; God and natural law teach us that our behavior should always be an ethical and honest behavior. The truth will be revealed, and we will prevail; we are a Nation founded upon the Rule of Law. Our voting rights and our elections are defined and regulated by our Constitution. We are a Constitutional Republic and voting integrity and our freedom to choose our leaders are part of our Constitutional rights. Those leaders in power who want to hollow out all our fundamental Constitutional rights must be held accountable! The truth of the 2020 election fraud will be revealed! God's powerful Hand will lift the veil of secrecy to expose everyone that was active in this election fraud. We are a Nation founded upon our allegiance to the Constitution of the United States of America, and the freedoms guaranteed to American citizens by this document. We are a Nation founded upon a belief in God. What are the enduring patterns in American's consciousness of God and religion? What are the enduring patterns of consciousness for Americans regarding their freedoms? What do Americans feel about our current political leaders that have created humanitarian crises at our southern border? What do Americans think of an Administration that has allowed COVID positive illegal aliens, and criminals to enter the United States and then allowed to stay? Why hasn't the Administration visited the border to see the humanitarian crises first-hand, and take an action to close our border? Why did the Biden Administration halt construction on the Border Wall when the building materials had already been paid for and were ready for construction?

We remember our discussion about Socrates and his lifelong search for the truth. Socrates' concerns about Athens and her citizens were always for the care of the individual soul, to question everything, and for a moral reliance on the rule of law. Socrates' vision of individualism is the same vision that has animated our representative government and the rule of law. As American citizens we should always be allowed to question our leaders about their leadership role, their vision for our Nation, and the implementation of any executive orders or laws, our own security and safety, and America's diplomacy with other nations. Although we are living in an era of Big Tech censorship of any ideas or opinions that Big Tech do not agree with, we have a responsibility to continue to question our leaders and politicians, and to remain informed citizens. Five years ago I wrote, "Our blessing as a Nation is that we already possess a workable form in the Constitution, and the guardianship of government is the responsibility of each citizen, so that our protection and freedom under the Constitution for our rights, individually and collectively, does not degenerate into an autocratic regime."[166] What do Americans think of our current political leaders who have deliberately stopped oil and gas production thus taking us from energy independence to dependence on other nations for our oil and gas? What do Americans think of our current political Administration's policies that are putting millions of Americans out of work? What do Americans think of an Administration's overly regulating industries and raising taxes thereby forcing companies to relocate outside of the United States, taking American jobs with them? What do Americans think of an Administration that has allowed our nation's borders to remain open and has not vetted anyone who is illegally entering our sovereign soil. What do Americans think of an administration whose policies are veiled in secrecy and that have a lack of transparency? What do Americans think of being led by a President who is apparently cognitively impaired? What is the current American understanding of our republic?[167]

Underlying Americans' search for justice and equality — and maintaining and formulating legal rights — is a written Constitution; and natural law — a law that we are born with and know through our reason and justice. Colonists believed natural law to be the law of God that is eternal and immutable. Some colonial Americans described the law of nature to be the will of God. (See, for example, James Otis). The commands of God's higher law were found in the Scriptures in the Bible. Colonial thinkers like Thomas Jefferson and John Adams believed that God had set the laws of nature in motion, and these laws followed cause and effect without God's interference. We discover the laws of nature through right reason. Blackstone, Locke, Pufendorf, Vattel and Burlamaqui offered natural law theories that the colonists used as examples to define the law of nature. The laws of nature were applied as moral imperatives for our human conduct which was discovered by reason, experience and revelation and could be summed up as the golden rule. Jesus teaches us, "So in everything, do to others what you would have them do to you, for this sums up the Law and the Prophets." (Matthew 7:12). The American cult of virtue meant the natural life for colonial Americans, and good government was natural government. Good laws were founded upon the law of nature. The State Constitutions were written replicas of the colonial understanding of natural law. Americans regarded natural law as the prohibition on Parliament's power to tax or govern the colonies. Natural law was equated with natural rights, and at times the two expressions were used interchangeability. The United States Constitution based its foundational ideas upon natural law: justice, freedom, equality, liberty, virtue, goodness, equity, and the freedom to pursue happiness for all the citizens of the United States.

We have forgotten our sacred bond with God, i.e., our government is a government created by God, formed by God's will, lawful under God, successful by God's blessings and His providence. We reach across the material gulf that has separated us from our Creator, and as spiritual, God- filled beings, we now seek the transcendent truth of God's natural law.

Chapter 7

Natural Law and John Locke

Thinkers on natural law have always searched the philosophers and theologians from the past to the schools of Plato, Aristotle, the Stoics, the Roman Jurists, and St. Thomas to understand natural law and to assemble new methods to describe the natural law doctrines. An understanding of natural law is generated not just by studying our philosophers and theologians but is most importantly and spiritually revealed to us through the study of the Holy Bible where we are strengthened by our individual faith in God's Providence and Rule for us. Our prayer while we are studying natural law is that God may enlighten us with wisdom and discernment so that we may better understand His natural law. Our modern culture is consistently attempting to severe the silver chords that connect our minds to God's natural law. Marxism and atheism are proclaimed with the loudest voices while believers in "socialism" bully and try to silence us by claiming, for example, that "a list" of conservatives must be kept to identify those who supported President Trump — a President who has proclaimed a belief in God and has (in his speeches) often invoked "God Bless America."[168]

There is no more important moment than now for an understanding of natural law. The natural law thinkers of the past assist us in our current understanding of natural law. Hugo Grotius (1583-1645), for example, laid a political foundation for international law that was based on natural law. Grotius' thinking on rights became important when he wrote that rights are not attached solely to objects, but that rights also belong to individuals in their ability to act. Grotius narrowed natural law thinking to thinking about the sphere of rights. Grotius' believed that natural law can be independent of God.[169]

Grotius' philosophy was followed by John Locke (1632-1704) who builds his moral and political theory on a foundation of natural law in his famous *Two Treatises of Government*.[170] Lockean philosophy and the doctrine of natural law laid the foundation for the novel American republicanism. Eighteenth-century Americans also relied on Lockean philosophy during the debates over the ratification of the Constitution of the United States of America.

John Locke's philosophy lies within the Christian tradition of natural law as represented by St. Thomas; however, Locke's natural law is different from St. Thomas' natural law thinking. The Founders were primarily influenced by Locke, and many other philosophers, for example, Hugo Grotius, Samuel von Pufendorf, Burlamaqui, and Vattel. Grotius wrote that the law of nature which "is a dictate of right reason" exists even if there were no God; Locke maintained that God is necessary for the law of nature which we discover through reason. Locke defines the law of nature as "the command of the divine will, notable by the light of nature, indicating what is and what is not consonant with a rational nature, and by that very fact commanding or prohibiting."[171] The Lockean individual rights are also the rights that we gain through God's moral order. The state is not our source of rights; the state is the institution or framework for the arrangement of individual rights.

There was a resurgence of Thomasism in England at the time that Locke was writing. Locke's *Two Treatises of Government* (published anonymously in 1690) can be read as an Exclusion tract meant to urge a constitutional constraint on the powers held by the monarchs. Locke and his patron Lord Shaftsbury (1621-1683) campaigned in Parliament (1679) to prevent James, the Duke of York, from succeeding his brother Charles II to the English throne because James was a practicing Catholic. Locke's theory of civil society penned in his *Two Treatises of Government* meant to accomplish a unification of the nation under God and sovereign using the tools of reason and tolerance. In Locke's *An Essay Concerning Human Understanding* (1689),[172] Locke developed his epistemology (theory of knowledge), and a theory of human nature based on natural law teaching and the corresponding moral virtues. Locke also taught that all knowledge is based upon experience, and therefore, there is no innate knowledge.[173]

An example of the political tracts that condemned corruption, abuse of power, and lack of morality in the British political system is Cato's *Letters* written by John Trenchard and Thomas Gordon around 1720.[174] The eighteenth-century Americans initially learned their Locke through the writings of Cato's Letters, who combined the English Whig political thinking with Lockean political philosophy.

Sir Edward Coke (1552-1634) set forth (in his, *Institutes* especially the *Second Institutes*) statutes that were validated since the Magna Carta, and the Americans, who knew the principles of Coke, viewed the Colonial Charter as a document that placed liberties beyond the legal reach of Parliament.[175] The colonists were well-read, and the political tracts in circulation were abundant — outlining the opposition to the corruption of princes and ministers with their endless quest for power to be cured by liberty.

The colonists had confidence in natural law and reason, as well as the beneficial belief in an individual's industrious nature for self-improvement. There were numerous opportunities for the early Americans to exercise their industry, talents, professions and character within the city or country; and for the adventurous soul, there was also a vast wilderness at their disposal for expansion westward. American colonists had ample opportunity to seek spiritual fulfillment and personal happiness for themselves and their families.

The independent-minded colonists rebelled when Britain began imposing new fiscal and regulatory controls that impacted the colonial sovereignty: Britain issued writs of assistance, restricted settlement west of the Alleghenies in 1763, passed the Currency Act in 1764, the Sugar Act in 1764 (also known as the American Revenue

Act of 1764 or the American Duties Act), and the Stamp Act in 1765. (I will discuss these Acts in the next chapter).

America's successful struggle for independence was a Lockean commitment to natural rights, natural law, and the social contract. The Lockean political philosophy from the *Second Treatise on Government* is reflected in the words of The *Declaration of Independence*. Thomas Jefferson departed from Locke's trinity of life, liberty, and estate and instead he substituted the concepts of life, liberty, and the pursuit of happiness in The *Declaration of Independence*. (Socrates, Plato, Aristotle, and St. Thomas believed in the pursuit of happiness as the end goal for the human being). The natural and inherent rights of man are affirmed in The *Declaration of Independence*.

Locke's natural law epistemology influenced the American founders and the principles of government. Locke's political doctrines can be read in the *Second Treatise* where he writes that we are creatures of the same species and rank, and can use the same faculties, therefore we should all be equal to one another.[176] We are all servants of a sovereign God, and are God's property, therefore, we may not harm each other.[177] For Locke, natural rights can be traced to obligations upon individuals brought about by the laws of nature, and natural rights are always the fulfillment of our duties to God.

Locke believed that our world of sensory experience is real and is as we perceive it to be. God is our Creator, and is a divine, immaterial being, and we do not have the ability to perceive the Creator. Locke, however, does not doubt His existence. God is necessary for the law of nature which we discover through reason. In his *Essays on the Laws of Nature*, Locke uses the "argument from design" as a sound argument for God's existence.[178] Our world is constructed so artfully and with such regularity, and, therefore, could not have been created by chance; but it is evident that a wise and powerful creator is responsible for the universe and us. Locke's philosophy is a

Christian philosophy that holds a faith in Jesus as Messiah. Locke's rational faith is a belief in the Christian revelations, prophecies of the Messiah, witnesses to Jesus, and Jesus's miracles.[179]

In *An Essay Concerning Human Understanding* (1663-1664), Locke writes about the concept of natural law. Locke defines the law of nature as, "the decree of the divine will discernable by the light of nature and indicating what is and what is not in conformity with rational nature, and for this reason commanding or prohibiting.[180] The law of nature is a law because it is a decree of a superior will prescribing an action that should be done or refrained from, and we are all obligated by the law of nature to perform. For Locke, we are (naturally through our human constitution) endowed with a conscience which judges our actions, which is only possible because of the laws of nature. The world is also constituted or created in such a manner where it is bound by physical laws. In the same respect, we are bound by a set of moral laws. We use our reason, mind, and intellect to understand how to use the natural laws in a specific way. We are by nature social creatures who enter society to interact with others, and this union is only possible due to the laws of nature. Without the law of nature there would be no virtue nor vice, nor distinction between good and evil.

Pleasure and pain are motivational influences for us; pleasure is called good, and pain is called evil. Locke writes about the varieties of pleasure and pain that we can experience ranging from joy to anger, and how the power of pleasure and pain cause us to desire the pleasure and avoid the pain. These innate practical principles indicate that we have an appetite for the good, but these passions are not impressions of truth on the understanding.[181] The mind has the power to will so that we will not be ruled by our passions. In *An Essay Concerning Human Understanding*, Locke states that there can be an inequality in the understanding of some men. If we are living in a political society then our awareness and understanding of the laws, and living within the laws, are a prerequisite to our right to liberty.

Locke draws a distinction between natural right (*jus naturale*) and natural law (*lex naturale*): natural right is the free use of something, and natural law is what will either command or forbid an action. In the Lockean state of nature, there is an absence of government and organized political society. All men are free and equal in a state of nature, where men are free to act, dispose of their possessions and persons, without asking the permission of anyone else, and within the bounds of the Law of Nature.[182] The state of nature is not necessarily good or bad, but it is chaotic. Men give up their perfect freedom living in a state of nature for security and to live together in a civilized society. Government is formed to protect our lives, liberty, and property.

The people form a social contract for the legitimacy of government. The authority of the government takes its legitimacy from the citizens who have created the government to protect their liberty. If the government trespasses against our liberty, then we have the right to overthrow that government. For Locke, natural law is hidden to the majority, but is known to the few that can utilize rational proof. If we do not know the natural law it is because we either prefer not to know it, or our own nature has become so corrupt that we cannot know it.

The Constitution presupposes that there is sufficient virtue in the citizens to achieve the goal of government — and that goal is justice. Some virtue in the citizens (hopefully there are more virtuous citizens than we hear about in our biased news broadcasts and social networks), an insistence on liberty, and the goal of justice for a free people are the hallmarks of the American body of citizens.

The United States is the Nation whose citizens have a fundamental relationship to the truths of God. These truths about God are discovered in our relationship to God; the relationship of our thinking to God; the relationship of our resigning powers to God; the relationship of our soul to God; the relationship of our heart to God; the relationship of our actions to God; the relationship of our family to God; the relationship of our work to God; the relationship of our political society to God; the relationship of our government to God; the relationship of our political leaders to God; the relationship of our day to day business of government to God; the relationship of our leaders to God; and the relationship of our fundamental truths to God.

Today, the radical progressives are taking our fundamental rights of freedom, equality, life, liberty, the pursuit of happiness, and they have exaggerated and widened the concept of rights to be so inclusive of everyone, even non-citizens, and hyper-inflated the notion of freedom to be awarded to non-citizens, so that the recognition of freedom for citizens has weakened over the inflated expanse of liberties to be awarded to non-citizens. The radical progressives are setting up idols of god made in their own image; the radical progressives are setting up idols of god made in the image of power; the radical progressives are setting up idols of god made in the image of money; instead of glorifying God as the Creator of our equal laws through natural law. God teaches us not to set up any idols of god before Him.

The premises of natural law are as true and sound today as they were in the thirteenth century when St. Thomas set out a scientific and religious theory based upon the theory of natural law. The premises of natural law are that we do have a universal nature created by God, our purpose is to act in accordance with God's purpose, and we seek our good in Him, our purpose is discovered through reason, and moral principles are universal and discovered by reason.

Natural law is the marker for our human place, where we recognize our humanness, and accept God and His commandments. With our belief in God, we thrive as a polity and a holy people of God. Natural law serves as a key for us to obtain the common good. Madison writes in *The Federalist* No. 49, "It is the reason and not the passions of the public that ought to control and regulate the government."[183] *The Federalist* papers taught us, then and now, a philosophy and morality of conciliation in dealing with others, moderation in actions, and deliberation on topics that are important to our personal well-being and the polity at large.

Progressives demand that all men and women be made equal even if it is at a heavier cost to some individuals than the equality that it incurs to others. Progressives attempt to remove God from the individual, from the state, from the government, and from the Nation. Progressives manipulate the polity to conform to their politics of remaking human nature as divorced from God. The government (and of course those progressives that are in power) wants to take the place of God.

The Thomasism and natural law thinking of Francisco Suarez and Roberto Bellarmine was a Christian natural law thinking. Of the late sixteenth and early seventeenth century philosophers, Hugo Grotius' new natural law thinking narrowed natural law to natural rights, but he also removed God from the founding of natural law. Grotius applied Aristotle's philosophy to the problems of the seventeenth century.

Locke broke with Grotius and his new rights theorizing and laid the foundation for the new republicanism in America. Americans learned their Locke from the writings of Cato (John Trenchard and Thomas Gordon). For Locke, all right is understood in terms of property which is natural. Locke taught that all rights are an obligation of human beings traced to the law of nature. Natural rights are our fulfillment to the duties of God. (See: Hugo Grotius (1583-1645); Thomas Hobbes 1588-1679); John Locke (1632-1704); Montesquieu 1689-1755); and Jean-Jacques Rousseau (1712-1778). Locke defines natural right (*jus naturale*) as "the free use of something", and natural law (*lex naturale*) as "that which either commands or forbids some action."[184]

Locke's idea of natural law is within the tradition of classical natural law as represented by St. Thomas; however, Locke's version of natural law is different from the other thinkers on natural law. For example, for St. Thomas, the natural law is written on the human heart. Our knowledge of the objective reality of who we are directs us to the knowledge of our essence or our being, and the end (*telos*) toward which we strive, and this achievement is guided by our universal moral knowledge that we gain through natural law. In the same mode of metaphysical realism, we know objective realty by the nature of the thing and by our human way of knowing which abstracts the essence of a thing from all the particulars. An example is that we see all the particular men: Plato, Socrates and Aristotle, and our intellect abstracts the essence of "man" from all the particular men.

Locke maintains that we cannot know the law of nature through the natural inclinations of mankind.[185] Locke believes that the natural law is hidden to the majority of us but known to a few through rational proof.[186] For Locke, natural law is transcendent and dependent on our rational knowledge of the transcendence of God. The precepts of natural law are known through Lockean rational proof.

Locke believed in equality and that men are equal in their rights and that they are not subjected to the will of another man in respect to their perfect freedom. Men are equal with respect to their property. Men exist in the state of nature which is a state that is not necessarily good or bad but is chaotic. In the state of nature men are free to do what they want, but men give up this perfect freedom to live together in civilized society. The purpose of government is to secure our natural rights, which means our property and liberty.

Historically, adherents to the principles of natural law are individuals whose thinking is creative, individualistic, imaginative, often visionary, and at times groundbreaking. Created in God's image, one of our unique characteristics is our creativity. The Founders demonstrated this God-given creativity when they created the Constitution of the United States of America.

A principle of natural law that we are very familiar with is that God is to be loved. Another principle of natural law is that we are to seek God's truth. We know from God's sacred instructions to us that He seeks individual freedom for us. The Founders were practicing natural law when they deliberated and formed a sound republic where individuals can maximize their freedom. The Founders were exercising that natural law disposition when they created a Republic where we can live freely and attune ourselves to God's law. God's law for us is rooted in our nature. Natural law directs us toward those activities which will lead us forward toward the achievement of human virtue and justice.

Natural law is not just a theory or an abstract idea, it is the moral guidance of rules and principles that considers facts, experience, and moral values. We are blessed to receive natural law from God to participate in His divine plan for us. Law and morality are inseparable; just as our conscience is devoted to the Spirit of God, we are conscious of deep moral truths that are ingrained in us by the fact that we are human. The deep moral truths of natural law are a force of nature and are in harmony with natural law. The conscious natural law morality is something that is built right into us, and it is what St. Thomas called *synderesis*. Another natural law marker is the meaningful order of the universe, i.e., the design of things. Of our human design. we are lovingly made in God's image, and our purpose — living within God's creation — allows us to flourish as human beings in His image. God's sovereignty is the divine Will that moves us toward completion of our human nature. God's sovereignty is the Holiness that spells the spiritual grammar of natural law. God's love is present in natural law. Natural law is the controlling force and creativity in nature and in the human soul.

Natural law confirms our individual sovereignty, a sovereignty that is rooted deeply in God's love, and is obedient only to God's Will. What we call our "spiritual sovereignty" is an activity of the soul that is in harmony with the universal truth of God. Spiritual sovereignty is anchored in the soul, and the soul's creative and controlling force in nature secures itself to God for its design and scope. Our Christian home for our Nation is "as an anchor of the soul." (Hebrews 6:19). The details of our human design and the soul allows us to flourish. Our brains have an enormous capacity for reasoning, deduction, induction, critical thinking, curiosity, questioning, and most critically for worshipping. Our hands are made for holding utensils, projects, writing, conducting, building and most importantly for praying. Our legs are made for mobility, for leisure, and to traverse space. Our eyes are made for vision, for guidance, and most importantly to bear witness to natural law and God's glory. Our hearts are made to sustain our life's blood, and most importantly made for the love of spouse, family, neighbors, others, and for spiritual love for God. God's spirit upon our hearts seals our inheritance as children of Christ. Our souls are a unique configuration for each individual which enables us to function within our spiritual growth as we seek God within earthly beauty, which will bring us comfort, peace, joy, and happiness.[187] Historian and scholar J. Budziszewski summarizes St. Thomas' classical considerations of natural law as "(1)The deep structure of practical reason, classically called *synderesis*, which I have sometimes called deep conscience; (2) the sheer designedness of human beings, along with what follows from this fact; (3) the details of this design, along with the purposes and markings embedded in it; and (4) the natural consequences of doing wrong, always recognizing that an intrinsically evil act would still be evil even if no evil consequences ensued."[188] Natural law leads us to our purposive action where we can fulfill our commitment to God as an essential being who obeys God's sovereign and intrinsic law, while at the same time we work to achieve just laws for the good of the community, and the nation where we reside. Justice is one of the main themes of God's holy Word, and justice is one of the main themes of the United States Constitutional history. Natural law provides guidelines for a just government. The criteria for a just government are consent of the governed, individual freedom (including religious freedom), and a secure platform for natural rights. Our conventional laws are always in harmony with natural law, otherwise they cannot be considered just laws or justice-bearing laws.

Eighteenth-century Americans did not have a national consciousness of the American states as a unified nation. This national consciousness would come slowly and later when Americans could envision a common purpose as citizens united under the rule of law in the Constitution. What early Americans did possess was a religious consciousness and a strong belief in God as Creator. Along with their religious belief was a common belief in natural law. This united belief in natural law brought the colonists together as spiritual God-fearing citizens. The colonists were divided, however, by states, by local laws, by territory, and by local economies; and historically, after the American Revolution, they were divided again by their different visions of a central governing authority after their relationship to the British Empire was displaced with independence. The colonists were suspicious of each other, of other states, and of any central power. They were united, however, in their religious beliefs, and their belief in natural law; and this religious belief in God's spiritual Sovereignty was the archetype for the expanding economic, social, and legal freedoms that were slowly gaining ascendancy after the framing of the Constitution. The belief in natural law was the root that grew the fruitful tree of an American identity. Without a thriving individual spiritual sovereignty, that is, the individual citizen's belief in the divine guidance of a Sovereign God, we would quickly find that politics, culture, economic security, and national identity are without substance, and subsequently will lack a form for growth and harmony. Liberty is freedom because it is liberty in love with God.

Spiritual sovereignty is still a deeply held belief in America today. We are believers in God, the Almighty God who has given us a Nation of Just Laws and a Constitution that frames our laws. We believe in the Truth and Holiness of God. We are thankful and praise God for our Nation. Today, our belief in God has been publicly silenced by the modern political bullies who seek power, money, and aggrandizement for themselves at the expense of the good of the country and the community. We will not be silenced. We pray that God does not withdraw His Blessings from our Nation due to our spiritual failings.

Plato has taught us (through the voice of Socrates) that the art of politics is the business to care for the soul. As Christians, we believe in the soul, and we believe in natural law. All freedom flows from our conception of natural law. Natural law principles have an energy of their own which can “push or pull” a moral decision into the right action or direction. This spiritual energy is consonant with the ways of the Lord; His ways are not always discernible by the non-believer; however, the believer follows wherever the spiritual trail leads. The United States is a spiritual nation, and the citizens are united not only in custom, manners, language, economy, culture, common interests, politics, ideas, democracy, freedom, and the Constitution, but also through the patterns of natural law.

Both our national and state governments hold areas that are considered to be sovereign powers according to their constitutional parameters. The states retain their sovereignty in the areas that are not enumerated in the Constitution as a federal power. The people, as a deliberative body, hold sovereign power when they give their consent to be governed. Individuals hold spiritual sovereignty when they act in accordance with natural law. The ultimate spiritual sovereignty resides in the body of Christ.

The moral light of spiritual sovereignty is a brilliant illumination that blocks out any lesser light. We cannot be illuminated by the sun and the moon at the same time. Natural law has banished the iron-age paganism; vanquished the silver-age agnosticism; and it will banish the modern atheism to lead us to a golden-age of spiritual sovereignty. Natural law leads us to a personal identification and reliance on that which is Holy. Spiritual truths do not change; what does change is the historical period, and whether we live in an era of religious light, so that the earnest soul seeking the truth can see and understand the truth uninhibited by society and social pressure from agnostics and atheists.

Chapter 8

Natural Law and American Independence

"But the man who looks intently into the perfect law that gives freedom, and continues to do this, not forgetting what he has heard, but doing it—he will be blessed in what he does." (James 1:25)

As American citizens our birthright is individual freedom, and our natural endowment is to live in a free republic. We have discussed many of the religious, political, and philosophical influences on the early Americans. The doctrine of natural rights and natural law came into colonial focus from 1710 through 1760 when Americans believed that they had a natural right to be free. The Revolution in England (1765-1776) influenced Americans, and they witnessed the struggles of the English citizens to reform government in the days of the reign of the Stuarts. Constitutional historian Andrew C. McLaughlin writes in *A Constitutional History of the United States*, that, "Americans saw the execution of one king and the dethronement of another because the king had broken the original contract between the king and the people."[189] Historians trace the religious thinking of the early Americans and demonstrate how the preachers used their ecclesiastical authority to also preach a political doctrine. McLaughlin, for example, writes that religious thought in New England intertwined with political thought. McLaughlin gives us four examples: 1) there is a divine law that is superior to all other laws, and this divine law binds everyone, both the ruler and the ruled. 2) An individual is a separate and distinct human being prior to entering any relationship with the church.

3) Churches are formed by the consent of their members, and this consent is a covenant between the church and its members so that the people create the churches. 4) God, the Ruler of the universe is the source of justice and duty and binds Himself by covenants and promises. McLaughlin notes that political thought in the struggles for liberty in America was enlivened not only by the formation of churches, but also by the sermons of the preachers.[190]

We have discussed John Locke and the influence that his writing had on the early American Republic. It is important to keep in mind that Locke's philosophy was not considered to be mere abstract principles; he was considered to be an authority on constitutional law, and an expert on English constitutionalism.[191] Colonial Americans believed in natural law, and equality, and their theory of natural rights was entailed by the contract theory, and consent of the governed that gave birth to the United States constitutional government. The theoretical problems encountered by the early Americans took on practical solutions, wherein the colonists did not have the sharp intellectual separation of theory from practice which we adhere to today. Colonial Americans were close to the source of natural law in practicing their Christian beliefs, and studying the Word of God, and their religious beliefs and practices overlapped their practical every-day living, and their political decisions.

Our Biblical Covenant with God is still very much in force; however, our modern society — with its technological and digital culture — has hidden some of the most important truths from our clear understanding, which has darkened our belief in the Almighty God. Truth lies in the nature of things, and in the essence of natural law. Natural law foreshadows the spiritual law of God. God's truth gives us spiritual sovereignty to worship Him, and a citizen exercising freedom in our democratic republic is a demonstration of an exaltation of our Constitution and our form of government. This individual freedom also gives praise to the workmanship of God, whose universal principles of law are reflected in the United States Constitution, whose structure upholds the greatest amount of freedom and liberty for the greatest number of citizens. "For we are

God's workmanship, created in Christ Jesus to do good works, which God prepared in advance for us to do." (Ephesians 2:10). The workmanship of God is taught to us through natural law, and natural law is demonstrated in our just laws, that is, in our United States Constitution, our Bill of Rights, our justice-bearing federal and state laws, the adjudication of these laws on the federal and state level, and the review and adjudication of federal and state laws by the Supreme Court of the United States. Where we have justice, we have the working of natural law, and where natural law is operating is where we find the form of the workmanship of God.

God is sovereign over all things and is the creator of natural law. The light of God shines through the eternal interstices of natural law — where we begin our belief in the universal nature and essence of God. Natural law is an essential reality for our existence; and Christians take a realist approach to maintain their spiritual perspective in relationship to the Nation. Our essential realities — through color, shape, position in space and time, sense, taste, touch — are the foreshadows of natural law. It is through natural law that we can respond to God's commands and follow Him to ready ourselves for a loving communion with God. We have learned to exercise our free-will to position ourselves for a loving relationship with God. This lovingly fettered by God free-will was the same force that bound colonists to one another for safety and security and legitimized in covenant terminology, and the same religious belief that was turned into a political philosophy within the historical accounts of the consent of the governed.

For colonial Americans, the strong and secure historical ladder of experience to God was erected in America, where the ideals, ideas and concepts of liberty were Biblical ideas — God created us free with a free-will to make choices and to live our lives blessed and in freedom. Colonists firmly believed that America was a nation blessed by God! Politics was a reliable sister to religion because she brought the reality of republican ideas to the forefront where everyone could examine these ideas for their practical worth in the new nation. Men of honesty and common sense were called upon to help write the new state constitutions.[192]

Americans, colonials believed, are God's chosen people, and bound to Him by a spiritual covenant. The covenant had also bound Americans in their loyalty to the mother country as citizens of the British Empire who exercised all their rights as Englishmen. Britain's violation of the consent of the governed — passing laws from Imperial London that the colonists had no say in — were a violation of the American's belief in the consent of the governed. Colonists believed that the English Constitution guaranteed natural rights to them, and that a free government was one that was limited by the British constitution and by common law. Natural rights, the colonists believed, were embedded in their British citizenship, and confirmed by the philosophers, politicians, thinkers, and religious leaders at that time, and confirmed by the Glorious Revolution of 1688.[193] Natural law thinking played an essential part in the American Revolution where Americans believed that they had a natural right to oppose the acts of tyranny leveled against them by King George III. Americans believed that they had a moral obligation to oppose acts that were contrary to natural justice and the law of God.

The passing of numerous revenue-raising and restrictive acts on the colonies by Parliament is an important series of events leading up to the Revolutionary War. The Parliamentary Acts passed to raise revenue for Great Britain through taxing the colonies were especially disliked by the colonies; along with the writs of assistance and placing the colonial courts of justice under the control of the Crown. I do not intend to do an extensive analysis of these acts — historians have written excellent accounts of this era; my intent is to demonstrate how a natural law consciousness by the colonists provided the necessary framework and foundation for the self-confidence necessary to move forward in seeking independence from the mother country. The colonists' spiritual self-confidence was based upon their natural law consciousness, and this consciousness assisted in forming citizens who were intelligent, energetic, determined, fearless, proud, and sensitive to God's will.

Today, we have forgotten God's greatest gift to us — the consciousness of His gift of natural law. It is my hope that this reminder of God's natural law will cause us to do an intellectual somersault flip which will land our souls back into the lap of God.

Colonial Americans had managed their own internal affairs since the creation of the colonies. Colonial Americans had developed the habit of colonial self-government and a political adeptness that was uniquely their own. Parliament exercised direction over the colonial external affairs, where the Crown had an interest in appointment of the royal governors, and instructions for the governors, disallowance of some statutes, and review of the decisions by the colonial courts. The Crown had an interest in the regulation of trade and commerce and provided protection of British interests through the defense of her colonies.[194] In general, the Crown had responsibility for the post offices, the army and navy, Indian affairs, and founding and organizing new settlements.[195]

Boston was home for many early leaders of the movement toward American Independence. The liberty men included: James Otis, Jr., Samuel Adams and his cousin John Adams, John Hancock, and Paul Revere. James Otis, Jr. (1725-1783) was a Harvard-trained lawyer, a political activist, pamphleteer, and a legislator as a member of the Massachusetts legislature. The colonists' belief in natural law is understood, for example, when James Otis, Jr. challenged the legality of "writs of assistance" before the Superior Court in 1761 in Massachusetts. The "writs of assistance" gave the British the general authority to search for smuggled goods in comprehensive and sweeping actions, to enter any home without notice, with no probable cause, and for no given reason.[196] Otis, an orator of excellence and power, argued that this "writs" threatened the dwelling and personal property of the colonists.[197] Otis used the words of Lord Coke to demonstrate that when an Act of Parliament is contrary to common law and reason, then the Act is to be void. The unchanging principles of reason and justice demonstrated that there were legal limits that Parliament cannot transgress, and that natural law has established natural equity which has been long-established in English constitutionalism.[198] James Otis did not win the case against the Crown, but his words inspired the fervor of American revolutionists to seriously consider independence from Britain.

In 1763 Britain reached a zenith of power and strength when they won the French and Indian War against France. (In America, this war was called the Seven Years' War.) Free from the physical and monetary constraints of War, Britain took a closer look at Her colonies and decided to tax and regulate them to pay for their financially burdened administration in London. King George III signed The Proclamation of 1763 which prohibited any English settlement west of the Appalachian Mountains. The Proclamation also required that any settlers who were already settled west of the Appalachians should return to the east to relieve tensions with the Native Americans.

Parliament passed a series of revenue raising acts: The Sugar Act of 1764 to enforce acts of trade and navigation and for raising revenue from the colonies — the first statute that directly taxed the colonies. The Sugar Act of 1764 increased the duty on imported sugar, textiles, wine, and dye. It doubled the duty on any goods that were reshipped from England. The Sugar Act of 1764 also prohibited the colonists from importing any foreign rum or French wine. In 1764, the English Parliament established a court to reorganize and enforce customs and have jurisdiction over the colonies, and the court was located in Halifax, Nova Scotia. The Currency Act was also passed by Parliament in 1764, and it prohibited the colonies from issuing their own legal tender paper money. The Currency Act threatened to destabilize the industrial economy of the north, as well as the agriculture economy of the south. The Stamp Act was passed on March 22, 1765, and required that all printed materials were to be taxed: for example, newspapers, legal documents, advertisements, diplomas, certificates, bills, pamphlets, maps, licenses, and playing cards. The colonists responded with protests — the secret organization "The Sons of Liberty", was organized — where they intimidated the stamp agents who collected Parliament's taxes. The

Quartering Act required the colonies to provide barracks for the British troops, as well as supplies. Parliament exerted additional power over the colonists and maintained that it was the colonist's duty to obey as British subjects. Americans were ever awakening to the fact that they had innumerable rights, and they demanded the recognition of these rights. American colonists began practicing nonimportation where they refused to use any imported English goods.

One rallying call was from colonists like James Otis, Jr., a loyal British subject, who argued that "taxation without representation is tyranny." (1761). James Otis, Jr. argued against the British "writs of assistance" in court; the "writs of assistance" allowed the authorities to enter any house without any advanced notice or probable cause, and no reason needed to be given to do so. When Otis published the pamphlet, "Considerations on Behalf of the Colonists," he argued that the "writs of assistance" violated British constitutionalism. Otis hearkened back to the Great Charter, the Magna Carta (June 15, 1215), which established a body of rights for Englishmen that Americans also claimed as their own. Otis expanded the idea of natural rights by linking natural rights to representation.[199]

Again, his argument did not win the case, but his rhetoric was important for the beginning of rational arguments for independence from British rule. Colonists believed that they had the right to manage their own internal affairs and govern without the interference of Parliament, and the colonists were quickly sharpening their natural law tools, and rational arguments to define their independence from Britain.

In 1762, James Otis, Jr. wrote "A Vindication of the Conduct of the House of Representatives," where he argued that taxes can only be charged by a representative government. In May 1764, during a Boston town meeting, he stated that without representation there could be no taxation, and he urged a united response to resist the acts imposed by the English Parliament. In 1764, he wrote and published the pamphlet, "The Rights of the British Colonies Asserted and Proved," where he argued that rights are not derived from human institutions, but from God and nature. Otis's pamphlet, "Considerations on Behalf of the Colonists," 1765, defined his philosophy of rights and linked these rights to the theory of equal representation.

Otis praised the balanced government of Great Britain that was structured with the king, lord, and commons who shared power. Otis maintained that rights are not derived from institutions or from monarchs, but that rights are derived from nature and God. Government is limited by the laws of nature, and therefore, by God. Governments exist to promote the good of the entire society. A just government will never exercise unlimited power. Otis wanted the colonists to send representatives to Parliament, and he hoped that Britain would respect the rights of colonial legislation.[200] In 1764, he stated, "The colonists are by the law of nature freeborn, as indeed all men are, white or black."[201]

Unfortunately, Otis recanted his earlier views later in life when he wrote his last pamphlet, "Vindication of the British Colonies and Brief Remarks on the Defense of the Halifax Libel." In this pamphlet Otis grants Parliament complete authority over the colonies. Many scholars have theorized that his change of philosophy was due to either mental illness, or his desire to defend himself against the charges of treason.

John Adams was also strongly opposed to the British taxation of the American colonies. He was born in Braintree, Massachusetts (1735-1826), and was a Christian, and a moral man who also believed in the concept of natural law and virtue. He was an accomplished American leader in the Revolutionary War, a public servant, the nation's first vice-president, and second President of the United States (1797-1801). Adams was an attorney (he attended Harvard University, and was admitted into the bar on November 6, 1759), statesman, writer, and diplomat to both France and England. His marriage to Abigail Smith Adams on October 25, 1764, was an important event, as Abigail proved to be as diligent, industrious, politically astute, and articulate as her husband. Abigail was a close advisor and confidant to her husband throughout their marriage. She was a strong voice in the American Revolution, an advocate for the education of both boys and girls, and an early leader for women's rights. Abigail was an articulate and prolific letter writer, and her correspondence gives us an insight into the thinking of one of the early American pioneers in the fight for equal rights for women. Both John and Abigail were devout Christians, believed in natural law, and God's providence and guidance over the new nation. John Adams maintained that "rights are derived from the great legislator of the universe and are antecedent to governments."[202]

We noted earlier that in March 1765, Parliament passed The Stamp Act, one of the first direct tax on the American colonies. In July 1765, the Sons of Liberty forced all the British stamp agents to resign, and they urged colonists to stop ordering British goods. Congress assembled in New York, 1765, to protest the Stamp Act.[203] The colonists accepted that Parliament had the right to make acts that were for the general good of all the colonists, but Parliament exceeded its power when it used an unlimited power of taxation without allowing the colonists representation; and Parliament, therefore, acted illegally. Following the passage of The Stamp Act there was a proliferation of colonial pamphlets, essays, state papers and state constitutions. This colonial literature demonstrated the development of the philosophy of natural law within the colonies that was so important as a strengthening resolve for independence from Great Britain; and is also evidence for the independent and knowledgeable political attitude that led to the creation of the United States Constitution by colonial statesmen. What the American Founders discovered was that natural law makes explicit our moral guides for equality, laws, freedom, virtue, and independence.

John Dickinson (1732-1808) from Philadelphia, Pennsylvania, and Wilmington, Delaware, was one of the nation's Founding Fathers, and was a successful attorney, a delegate from Pennsylvania to the First Continental Congress in 1775, and the Second Continental Congress in 1776. He wrote the "Olive Branch Petition" to attempt to negotiate peace with King George III. He was opposed to Independence from Britain, but he served in the Revolutionary War. Dickinson was a delegate from Delaware to the Federal Constitutional Convention, 1787, he signed the United States Constitution, and he worked for its adoption. In 1767 through 1768, he was nicknamed "Penman for the Revolution" for his *Letters From a Farmer in Pennsylvania*. These twelve pamphleteering letters were circulated throughout the colonies to unite the colonists against the Townsend Acts. Dickinson argued that Parliament's taxation against the colonies was done with the purpose of raising revenue, not regulating trade, therefore, the Acts were unconstitutional.

On March 5, 1770, British troops arrived in Boston and provoked an uprising called the Boston Massacre that led to the British troops killing three Americans, fatally wounding two, and injuring six. The Royal Governor of Massachusetts, Thomas Hutchinson, ordered the troops to withdraw to nearby islands. The British captain, Thomas Preston, and eight of his men were subsequently tried for murder; but convicted of lesser crimes.

More colonial opposition was generated when Parliament gave the nearly bankrupt British East India Company the right to ship large quantities of tea from India directly to the colonies without paying duties in England, therefore bypassing any middlemen, underselling American merchants, and gaining a monopoly on the tea trade. The Tea Act, 1773, reduced the tax on imported British tea giving an unfair advantage to British merchants who were selling their tea in America, and was unfair to American merchants who would lose business due to the cheaper tea. The colonists felt that this was arbitrary power by Parliament that was aimed at the colonial property. Following the famous dumping of the tea at Griffin's Wharf in Boston, Massachusetts on December 16, 1773 (The Boston Tea Party), Parliament passed the Boston Port Bill. The Boston Port Bill closed the Boston harbor and relocated the customhouse to

Salem, to let the Bostonians reflect on their sins until such time as reparations for the lost tea could be made.[204] Parliament also enacted measures to send British troops to the colonies. The colonists saw these acts as unrestrained power by Britain against the colonies. The colonists met in Councils of Safety and gathered arms to protect themselves against the British.

Britain passed the Coercive Acts, which the colonists called the Intolerable Acts of 1774. March 1774 was the first series of Coercive Acts, and a second series of Coercive Acts followed, which included the Massachusetts Regulating Act and the Government Act. These harsh legislative Acts known as the Intolerable Acts, were the Boston Port Act, the Massachusetts Government Act, the Administration of Justice Act, The Quartering Act, and The Quebec Act. The Quebec Act established a central British Crown government in Quebec and extended the southern boundary of Canada into territories that were claimed by Massachusetts, Connecticut, and Virginia. These acts ended any self-rule by the colonists. The Administration of Justice Act protected any royal officials in Massachusetts from being sued. In June 1774, Parliament passed a second Quartering Act which required the colonists to house and feed the British troops in their homes, taverns, and buildings. Parliament also ordered Governor Gage to seize the colonies weapons which were stored at Charlestown. The colonists were outraged by these Acts and knew that the Acts limited their freedoms and their rights, so when they met in the First Continental Congress in Carpenter's Hall in Philadelphia on September 5, 1774, they discussed whether to take action against the British. The First Continental Congress met from September 5 through October 26, with fifty-six delegates including Patrick Henry, George Washington, Sam Adams, and John Hancock.[205]

In 1774, there was a proliferation of pamphlets and political writings. The pamphleteers believed in natural law and wrote about the truth of men being born free and equal, and that no one has a power over anyone without his consent. James Wilson, a Philadelphia attorney, was one of the pamphleteers who drew from the theory of natural law to highlight their political views. James Wilson (1742-1798) was born in Scotland into a Presbyterian farming family. He moved to Philadelphia in 1765 and earned a living through teaching and tutoring. He passed the bar in 1767 and became one of the most prominent and successful lawyers of his time. Wilson was elected twice to the Continental Congress where he represented Pennsylvania.

In 1774, Wilson published *Considerations on the Nature and Extent of the Legislative Authority of the British Parliament*. (Wilson wrote this piece in 1770 but did not publish it until 1774). Wilson was critical of Britain, arguing that Parliament had no authority to pass laws over the colonies; and Parliament's taxation of the colonies was illegitimate because the colonies did not have any representation in Parliament. Wilson held the natural law view that all power derived from the people, and government was only legitimate through consent of the governed. Wilson was very familiar with British constitutional history, and his writing, along with John Adams, demonstrated a mastery of legal and constitutional arguments. However, at this time he stated that the colonists owed their allegiance to the British King — an opinion that he would soon change because he was one of the signers of the *Declaration of Independence*.

The colonists used many beliefs, approaches, theories, and ideas to advance their independence: natural law, natural rights, the theory that the origin of any government is through consent of the governed, and the colonial right of revolution if the government policy became tyrannical. Thomas Jefferson held a philosophy of natural rights and natural law, and he expressed this belief in his *A Summary View of the Rights of British America*. Written prior to the *Declaration of Independence* this pamphlet demonstrated Jefferson's intellectual skills as a gifted literary writer and established his reputation as a knowledgeable person on the principles of democratic government. *The Summary View* was written for presentation at the First Continental Congress and later printed in pamphlet form, and widely distributed in the colonies and in Great Britain. *The Summary View* was read and debated at the First Continental Congress (Jefferson was not present because he contracted dysentery en route to the Congress), but the language which expressed the colonial viewpoint was too strong for its adoption. Jefferson argued that the colonies had been independent of British rule since the colonies had formed, and that Parliament did not have the right to govern them. Jefferson further argued that the colonists owed allegiance solely to the British King, not to Parliament; and this allegiance is only to a king who acts justly for the interests of the colonists, not for a king who acts unjustly. Jefferson addressed the colonies grievances against the King and Parliament, and in spirited language he especially mentioned the Boston Tea Party. Jefferson refers to the "God who gave us life gave us liberty at the same time; the hand of force may destroy but cannot disjoin them." Jefferson believed in the universal truth that God bestowed liberty and rights upon everyone equally and independently. The natural rights that Americans possess included the rights of free trade, and the rights of human nature, which are wounded by the slave trade.[206]

Congress met on September 5, 1774, in Carpenter's Hall in Philadelphia. John Adams was a member of a committee that discussed the basis of American rights. Americans based their rights on the law of nature, the British constitution, and the American charters and grants. What authority does Parliament have over the colonies? The delegates agreed that Parliament can legitimately regulate external commerce, but that they do not have any authority to tax or raise revenue on the colonies without their consent.[207]

The Declaration and Resolves of the First Continental Congress was a statement given by the First Continental Congress on October 14, 1774, that outlined the colonial objections to the Intolerable Acts, provided a list of grievances against the mother country, and outlined a colonial bill of rights. *The Declaration and Resolves of the First Continental Congress* declares natural law as the source of the rights of the individual. The colonists had rights that they claimed due to the "immutable laws of nature", the principles of English constitutionalism, they are entitled to life, liberty, and property, and they do not dispose of any of these rights to a sovereign power without their consent. Congress proposed a boycott of trade with Great Britain until their grievances were addressed. The First Continental Congress denied that Parliament had the power or right to govern the colonies. This was a similar document to the *Declaration of Rights and Grievances* passed by the Continental Congress a decade earlier to protest the Stamp Act. On October 20, Congress formed the Continental Association to embargo exports and imports to Britain, and to discontinue the slave trade.

A provincial congress was held in Cambridge, Massachusetts, on February 1st, 1775, to begin preparations for a state of war against Great Britain. On February 9th, the English Parliament declared that Massachusetts was in a state of rebellion against the Crown.

The reaction to *the Declaration and Resolves of the First Continental Congress* by King George III was that he would not negotiate with the colonies. King George III said to his Prime Minister North, "The die is now cast, the colonies must either submit or triumph." British Minister, Lord North's "Conciliatory Proposal" was proposed on February 20, 1775 and passed by Parliament on February 27, 1775. (Lord North was Prime Minister in Great Britain from 1770-1782). The Conciliatory Proposal declared that any colony that would contribute to the common defense against any anti-Crown rebellion would be relieved of paying any taxes or duties, except for the regulation of commerce. The Conciliatory Proposal was sent to each of the individual colonies instead of the Continental Congress. Historians have concluded that the purpose of the Conciliatory Proposal was to divide the colonies and weaken their resolve and the will for revolution against the Mother Country.[208] Thomas Jefferson, who was becoming known for his articulate written expression of ideas, drafted the reply by the Virginians. Jefferson laid out a half a dozen reasons why the Colony of Virginia would not accept the proposal. The first reason articulated was that Parliament did not have any right to interfere with the support of the civil governments in the colonies.[209] Jefferson continued that the British Proposal only "changes the form of oppression, without lightening its burden." "The Virginia Resolution" declared unity with her sister colonies and left the decision for a final determination to the General Congress; while at the same time hoping that a wise direction may "reunite the colonies with the blessings of Liberty, Property, and Union with Great Britain."[210]

When Congress — as a Body — replied to Lord North's "Conciliatory Proposal" they chose Jefferson to draft it (July 25, 1775). Jefferson's Draft Resolutions stated, "That the colonies of America possess <an> the exclusive <right> privilege of giving and granting their own money;...". Congress rejected the "Conciliatory Proposal" in July 1775.[211] On March 23, Patrick Henry delivered his famous speech in Virginia, "Give me liberty or give me death."

Our Nation's development grew from colonies that were ruled by Great Britain to the colonists' call for independence from parliamentary misjudgments, restrictive laws, taxation, and unfair trade practices, to actual independence as a free republican democracy.[212] On March 30, 1775, Britain passed the New England Restraining Act to ban any trade between the New England colonies and any other country besides Great Britain, and later they extended this law to the other colonies. On April 1, 1775, Parliament ordered Governor Gage in Massachusetts to enforce the Coercive Acts and to use all necessary force to suppress the open rebellion by the colonies.

April 19, 1775 was the beginning of the Revolutionary War with the British troops stationed at Lexington and Concord. (Lexington and Concord were two farming towns that are located twenty miles north and west of Boston). Samuel Adams and John Hancock were warned about the arrival of the British by the fast-riding Paul Revere. (A Boston Silversmith and express rider).[213] The Second Continental Congress met on May 10, 1775, in Philadelphia: Congressional members passed resolutions for each colony to adopt a new government, a preamble on May 15th. (written by John Adams) declared that all authority under the Crown should be totally suppressed, and that the people of the colonies shall exert all the power of the colonies. Congressional members prayed for peace while preparing for war. Congress organized an army, and on June 15th. appointed George Washington as general and commander-in-chief of the army. Congress assumed military authority when they decided the pay rate for officers and men, secured the means for payment, secured the supplies for both rations and medical care, and drafted the rules for the army and what would later become the navy.[214] America's first battle against Britain was the Battle of Bunker Hill where Americans built an entrenchment north of Boston and inflicted heavy losses on the British forces.

On May 16, 1775, the Massachusetts Provincial Congress asked Congress for advice on how to proceed until civil government could be set up. Congress instructed Massachusetts to have a free representation of the people to set up a government that will "best produce the happiness of the people."[215]

On July 8, 1775, the colonies presented the Olive Branch Petition to Britain complaining of their unfair and severe treatment, while still pledging loyalty to the King.[216] In August, King George III issued a "Proclamation of Rebellion" and in the spring of 1776, the Continental Congress resolved to establish freedom of trade with the world with the exception of Great Britain.[217]

In December 1775, a bill was passed to cut off all trade with America: just one of Parliament's restrictive measures that lead to the Revolution, and then to the signing of the *Declaration of Independence* — the colonies eventually emerged as independent states unified under The Constitution of the United States. The foundation of our democratic Republic is built upon the knowledge of laws that are known to us through God's natural law. A written Constitution is the rational deduction of natural law thinking. Our written Constitution governs for the good of the people and is part of God's divine plan for us. Our written Constitution defines the parameters and boundaries of good government that is instituted for the good and happiness of all the citizens.

The Virginia Declaration of Rights, 1776, prepared the ideational path for the *Declaration of Independence* and for the Constitution of Virginia. George Mason, Thomas Jefferson, and James Madison attended the Virginia Convention of 1776, and contributed to its creation, but The Virginia Bill of Rights was primarily the workmanship of George Mason, (a planter from Fairfax County who replaced George Washington at the Virginia Convention, due to George Washington's appointment as commander in chief of the Continental Army that prevented Washington from attending The Virginia Convention). George Mason did not have formal legal training but did know his Locke and Montesquieu. The Constitution of Virginia, Bill of Rights, June 12, 1776, states, "That all men are by nature equally free and independent, and have certain inherent rights, of which when they enter a state of society, they cannot, by any compact, deprive or divest their posterity; namely, the enjoyment of life and liberty, with the means of acquiring and possessing property, and pursuing and obtaining happiness and safety."[218] The Virginia Constitution was adopted on June 29, 1776.

The Committee of five (John Adams, Benjamin Franklin, Thomas Jefferson, Robert R. Livingston, and Roger Sherman) were appointed by the Continental Congress to draft the Declaration of separation from Britain. The United States declared independence from Britain on July 2, 1776. Congress adopted the final text of the *Declaration of Independence* on July 4, 1776, and it was signed by the thirteen states on August 2, 1776. "We hold these truths to be self-evident, that all men are created equal, that they are endowed by their Creator with certain unalienable Rights, that among these are Life, Liberty, and the pursuit of Happiness."[219] This statement of rights which men hold in the state of nature is a statement of natural law. The wisdom of the self-evident truth of natural law is stated beautifully in the words of the *Declaration of Independence* where appeals are made to God our Creator and to natural law. It is a belief that was dominant and understood during the colonial era when the colonists were awakening to the moral and spiritual consciousness of independence from Britain. Natural law or the laws of nature are two terms that appear frequently in the founding documents. Historian Thomas G. West writes in *The Political Theory of the American Founding: Natural Rights, Public Policy, and the Moral Conditions of Freedom*, "that there are two predominant political uses of the term natural law: natural law as the ground of natural rights (without any explicit mention of duties), and natural law as defining the moral limits of the natural right to liberty."[220] West goes on to write that the laws of nature are recognized as the ground of natural rights, but how natural law leads to the rights of individuals is not clearly defined.

The Committee of five (John Adams, Benjamin Franklin, Thomas Jefferson, Robert R. Livingston, and Roger Sherman) worked together in drafting the document that would come to be known as the *Declaration of Independence*. All five Committeemen were superb leaders in the constitutional development of the new Nation, and three of the five would go on to meet at the Federal Convention in the summer of 1787 to found a national government when they drafted The Constitution of the United States. (John Adams and Thomas Jefferson did not attend the Federal Convention because they were both appointed as Ambassadors overseas: Adams to England (1778-1788), and Jefferson to France (1785-1789) where their influence and diplomacy overseas assisted the fledgling nation on her way to greatness).

There are excellent and extensive biographies of all three of these great-souled men (See the Bibliography online at socratesplace.com); however, this is a summary to place the reader within the time frame of colonial America. Thomas Jefferson, for example, was raised by his parents in the Anglican (Episcopal) Church. A young Jefferson attended the College of William and Mary in Williamsburg (1760-1762). Jefferson studied under William Small, a Scottish Enlightenment professor, who influenced Jefferson's religious and political thought. Jefferson studied law and was admitted into the Virginia bar in 1767. Jefferson was elected to the Virginia House of Burgesses in 1769 and served until 1774 when the British dissolved the House of Burgesses.

Lord Viscount Henry St. John Bolingbroke (1678-1751), whose belief in "Nature's God", and rejection of orthodox Christian doctrine, was another significant influence on Jefferson's religious and political beliefs. (In the 1760's Jefferson copied over 10,000 words from Bolingbroke's Philosophical Works, three volumes published in 1754. (John Adams claimed to have read Bolingbroke five times). Bolingbroke (along with Blackstone and Locke) viewed Parliament (where Bolingbroke served from 1701-1714) as being limited by natural law. American's presumptions about the nature of law in the mid-eighteenth century was that the laws of God, that is, natural law or the laws of our nature are the foundation and source of our rights and liberties; the idea of a written constitution and the codification of laws was the consequence of these presumptions about the nature of law.[221] Lord Viscount Bolingbroke's belief system was Deism where he believed in the existence of God that is the creative force of the universe — a universe whose laws were regular. God is unknowable and unseen, and His creation obeys the laws of nature, which are scientifically observable and verifiable. Bolingbroke questioned the truth of many important Christian doctrines, for example, the Biblical Creation story, the divinity of Jesus, original sin, atonement, the Biblical miracles, predestination, the doctrine of grace, revelation, and he believed in a God of deism whose orderly creation of the world obeyed the laws of nature, creating the universe and then leaving it alone — these natural laws are scientific and empirically verified by us.

Thomas Jefferson was influenced by Bolingbroke's ideas, and many historians write that Jefferson practiced Deism. There is a scholarly debate over Jefferson's religious beliefs; and the controversy includes questioning the faith and religious beliefs of George Washington, Benjamin Franklin, James Madison, Alexander Hamilton, and John Adams.[222] However, numerous historical records support the view that the religious foundations of these influential founding fathers was Christianity, and that they were influenced by Christian beliefs, ideas, and practices. Jefferson kept his own religious beliefs private, but we can discern from the records that he did embrace theism, because it is clear from his correspondence and the documented history, that he did believe in one God — "Nature's God" in the *Declaration of Independence* was a God that placed unalienable rights and the reason to discern the laws of nature in all men. Jefferson's "Nature's God" was a God who created the universe, and the laws of nature, and the innate ability to reason was given to all human beings. From the historical evidence, we can also conclude that Jefferson believed in natural law. The founders frequently referred to natural law, and the term "natural law" has a Christian connotation.

However, Jefferson disliked anything that was antithetical to reason — for example, supernatural and mystical doctrine — for Jefferson, our knowledge of God is through rational thought and an understanding and observation of His laws which govern the world and holds chaos in check. According to Jefferson, we do have an obligation to worship God. Jefferson did believe in an afterlife that would award and punish us accordingly for our deeds or misdeeds. Jefferson also believed in Jesus as an exemplary moral teacher who brought great wisdom into the world; in fact, he believed that Jesus was the first of human sages, and Jefferson held Jesus in devotion and admiration for His purity and the sublimity of His moral precepts. In 1803, Jefferson wrote to Benjamin Rush, "To the corruptions of Christianity, I am indeed opposed; but not to the genuine precepts of Jesus itself. I am a Christian, in the only sense in which he wished any one to be sincerely attached to his doctrines, in preference to all others; ascribing to himself even human excellence, & believing he never claimed any other."[223] However, Jefferson denied Jesus's divinity as the Son of God; Jefferson believed that it was Jesus's followers that imposed the idea that Jesus was divine after His death. Jefferson believed in the teachings of Jesus, for example, the principle of love which was the divine spark in our heart. Jefferson did not, however, believe in the virgin birth of Jesus, or in any of the numerous miracles in the Bible, original sin, grace, or the Resurrection of Jesus, or of personal revelations from God. Jefferson believed that God gave us the gift of reason so that we may individually find the truth. Freedom of speech and the free expression of our conscience, liberty and science were all important to Jefferson, and we use these in combination with our moral sense to create a political community that offers well-being for all its citizens. Jefferson did attend church throughout his life, and he also publicly prayed. In his second Inaugural Address, Jefferson asked his listeners to pray with him.

Some scholars write that historians who adhere to a strict dichotomy of beliefs for the Founding Fathers (where the Founders are depicted as either Christians or Deists) are not representing accurate views of the Founders' religious sentiments. Historian Gregg Fraser, for example, argues that theistic rationalism is a more accurate category for these early American thinkers like Thomas Jefferson, John Adams, George Washington, James Madison, Benjamin Franklin, and Gouverneur Morris. Fraser writes, "Theistic rationalism was a hybrid belief system mixing elements of natural religion, Protestant Christianity, and rationalism....Reason was the chief source and test of knowledge, and reason combined with their Christian upbringing convinced them that a creator God would not abandon his creation. Consequently, they rejected the absentee god of Deism and embraced a thesis of a God, to a significant extent, of their own construction."[224] Deists (generally speaking) deny that God intervenes in the material world, and that we receive any written revelation from God, as well as a denial of Christ as the Son of God. Thomas Jefferson, for example, believed that Christ was an exemplary moral prophet but not the divine Son of God. The major religious denominations at the time of eighteenth-century America shared beliefs in the divinity of Jesus, an omnipresent and omniscient God who intervened on behalf of mankind, the virgin birth of Jesus, revelation, the Bible as the Word of God, the resurrection of Jesus, and atonement for our sins.[225]

Jefferson believed in natural law and accepted the doctrine of the natural rights of man.[226] Jefferson believed that men had been born into a state of nature, (a Lockean philosophy that was in current practice during Jefferson's lifetime), and that men were free to govern their own persons and property; and that government was instituted by men through consent of the governed. Jefferson later summarized this philosophy of the consent of the governed in the *Declaration of Independence*. Historian Dumas Malone writes that Jefferson said little about the social contract (which according to Lockean philosophy preceded the formation of society and the consent of the governed); when Jefferson referred to contracts or compacts, he generally meant charters, constitutions, or a formal agreement of some sort. Jefferson believed in the exercise of freedom: freedom of opinion, intellectual freedom, religious freedom, and the separation of church and state. For Jefferson, freedom was the most important of all the rights, and the sanctity of the individual and the freedom of the mind were the inalienable rights.[227]

Jefferson's early studies centered on law; he was admitted into the bar of the General Court of Virginia in 1769, after two years of reading law with George Wythe. Jefferson practiced law on a circuit, and before the General Court in Williamsburg, specializing in land cases. Jefferson himself was widely read (he had one of the largest libraries at the time) — and fluently spoke and read French, Italian, Latin, and English, and in addition he could read Greek and Spanish. Historians often refer to his Commonplace Book where he copied out passages of various writers who struck him as memorial or of particular or practical use.[228] French political philosopher and judge Montesquieu's (1689-1755) *The Spirit of the Law* (1748) was read by Jefferson and passages were copied in his Commonplace Book with personal reflections and summaries.[229] Montesquieu's theory of the separation of powers influenced the Founder's thinking during the discussion and creation of the United States Constitution. Jefferson disagreed with Montesquieu's fondness for the British, and the believe that a republic could only be successful if formed over a small territory.[230]

Jefferson believed in and practiced intellectual freedom; believing that the only boundaries for intellectual freedom were in the moral sanction of everyone's heart, and in the laws of nature.[231] Jefferson argued against any religion that had absolute authority over the thinking of men and was also against any government that had supreme authority over its subjects. Thomas Jefferson believed in the universality of Christian ethics. In 1819, Jefferson commented in a correspondence that if he were to be the founder of a new sect, he would call them the Apiarians, after the example of the bee, who could extract the honey of every sect.[232] For those of us (like this author) who are honeybee keepers, this is a marvelous thought. Throughout his life, Jefferson was reticent to share his religious sentiments with others — keeping his own religious views private.

Jefferson's technical skill in drafting legislation was demonstrated in the document for the *Declaration of Independence*. Jefferson's commonplace book on government shows that he had researched many of the governments of other nations. Jefferson's interest in the best form of government, included an interest in the knowledge of formulating fundamental law. Jefferson's beliefs and correspondence show that he believed in the law of nature. While the Federal Convention was still in session debating the Constitution, Jefferson wrote to Edward Carrington, "It has been so often said, as to be generally believed, that Congress have no power by the confederation to enforce anything, e.g., contributions of money. It was not necessary to give that power expressly; they have it by the law of nature."[233]

The *Declaration of Independence* solidified America's continual movement toward independence from Britain. The *Declaration of Independence* is a document that was written utilizing a deductive argument, which is a reasoning tool for clarifying natural law concepts. Deductive reasoning begins with a universal concept (or a general concept), and argues with supporting particulars, to a conclusion. The universal principle 'that governments are established to secure our natural rights' was affirmed by this Founding document. The *Declaration of Independence* announced that the ties between Britain and the colonies were broken due to the misdeeds of England. Instead of addressing Parliament (whose legal authority over the colonies had always been debated), the colonial grievances were directed against George III, who had broken the law and the covenant to rule by disregarding the good of the people. The *Declaration of Independence* was a clearly stated philosophy of natural law, natural rights, equality and compact theory, the social contract, a clear statement that it is legitimate to resist despotic authority, and with a serious stated belief that government is derived from the consent of the governed — Lockean, Enlightenment, and Jeffersonian ideas that guided the American Revolution (1775-1783).

The *Declaration of Independence* states that the central philosophy of our government is for the protection of our rights, our safety, and ultimately our happiness. The eternal truths of the *Declaration of Independence* and natural law transcend space and time, and set the laws in place, where it is then the creation of the Constitution that provided the means to achieve the goals of liberty, equality, justice, and the pursuit of happiness. James Madison will later write in the *Federalist Papers* that in order to understand the Constitution, we must look to the words of the *Declaration of Independence*.

There are many theological, philosophical, and political influences on Thomas Jefferson's theology of equality as expressed in the *Declaration of Independence*. John Locke's (1632-1704) *Second Treatise of Government* had an enormous influence on Jefferson's thinking. "We hold these truths to be self-evident, that all Men are created equal, that they are endowed by their Creator with certain unalienable Rights, and that among these are Life, Liberty, and the Pursuit of Happiness."[234] We are familiar with the Lockean thesis that there are three natural rights: life, liberty, and property; and that no human being has a right to harm these rights in another person.[235] Jefferson divided rights into alienable and unalienable following the philosophy of Thomas Hutchinson.[236] The *Declaration of Independence* is a sound and logical justification for the American Revolution consonant with the laws of nature, and nature's God: a statement of universal truths, that is a statement about natural law, a clarification about the form and nature of government (government is formed to protect our natural rights), a list of the charges against the King and Parliament, and the justification for the American colonists to declare their independence and separate from the British empire.

Locke maintained that the end or purpose of government was for the public good.[237] Governments are created to secure our unalienable rights that are granted to us by God. When the government takes away our natural rights, then the people have a right to overthrow the government. Great Britain was guilty of taking away the colonist's God-given rights, therefore, they are justified in separating themselves away from the Mother Country. The specific abuses against the King of Great Britain in the Declaration begins with, "the king's refusal to Assent to Laws for the public good." The *Declaration* states that the American citizens may dissolve the government when the King refused to assent to laws which were "necessary for the public Good."

The second abuse alleged by the *Declaration* was that the King refused to allow the governors of the colonies to pass laws that were of immediate importance until the King's assent is given; this held the colonial legislatures in limbo until the king gave his assent (after long delays), and therefore the colonists were neglected while waiting for the king to assent. The King also did not allow the colonists to pass their own laws for the public good.

The third abuse was that the King would refuse to pass Laws for large Districts of People, unless those People would give up their right to representation in the legislature. Locke cautions that when an arbitrary will is set in place instead of the laws, then the Legislature is changed.[238]

The fourth abuse is that the King has called together the Legislative Bodies at unusual times, which are distant from the Depository of the public Records, and at unusual times and uncomfortable locations for the citizens to cause fatigue so that they will comply.[239]

The fifth abuse claims that the King has hindered the colonial legislative body by repeatedly dissolving their Representative Houses. The colonists believed in the right to govern themselves, and this legislative abuse by the king violated the right to self-governance.[240]

The list in the *Declaration of Independence* of abuses by the King against the colonists continues: the King has dissolved Representative Houses and refused for a long period of time to have other Representatives elected, prevented the Population of States, obstructed Justice by refusing to Assent to Laws for establishing Judiciary Powers, appointed Judges and erected new Offices and Officers that harass the People, kept standing Armies in times of peace without the consent of the Legislatures, established unfair trade laws, denied colonists a fair trial, and forced the colonists to go to Britain for a jury trial, waged war against the colonists and impressed the colonists into the British navy, and "He has combined with others to subject us to a jurisdiction foreign to our Constitution, and unacknowledged by our Law." This refers to the people of England, and to Parliament whose claim of legislative authority over the colonies is illegitimate since the colonial Americans had never authorized Parliament to make laws for them.

The philosophy of the *Declaration of Independence* establishes the unalienable rights of the colonists endowed by God, and the right to a government that will secure these rights. King George III, and

Parliament have violated the unalienable God-given rights of the colonists, therefore, the people have the right to overthrow a tyrannical government, and the people are absolved from all Allegiance to the British Crown and declare themselves as free and independent states. These free and independent states have the power to wage war, make peace, contract alliances, establish trade, and behave as independent states.

Jefferson's belief in a "Natural God" who Created the laws of nature is in harmony with God who also implants us with natural law: the moral compass for our moral reasoning. Most Christians will agree that natural law is the basis of both love and moral duties, moral obligations, and the moral law, and that we obey these duties because they are given to us by our Creator, whom we love. Our God-given natural law makes the foundation for our natural rights, that is, liberty-rights, freedom-rights, and equality-rights that are a part of God's play book for us to follow. A workable natural law morality lays the groundwork for our man-made laws and for justice. This natural law morality is also the foundation for a sound politics where each politician is bound to uphold his or her oath to protect and defend the Constitution of the United States, and the citizens that he or she represents.

Immutable archetypes of natural law emanate from God's Spirit and give us guidance for our thinking about natural law. The basis for constitutional thought was founded upon these immutable archetypes of natural law. Religious thought was bound to political thought in seventeenth century American minds: God was the Supreme ruler of the universe, and He embodies the laws, justice, equality, and covenant. The same spiritual energy that animates our worship of God, animated the language of constitutionalism in the early Republic.

Separation from the British Empire meant that the colonies were no longer subject to the British Empire and had to establish state governments to become self-governing commonwealths.[241] The different colonial states elected constitutional conventions to draw up constitutions to establish their own state governments. The duties and powers of the governments were to be written and specified, and these written principles were legally binding. Individual rights were deduced from the principles of equality and justice.

The Virginia Constitution in 1776 and the Massachusetts Constitution in 1780, are two prime examples of the patterns of natural law language that formed the archetypes that were utilized to form the *Declaration of Independence* and The Constitution of the United States. Scholar David G. Smith writes, "In some states — Virginia and Massachusetts most notably — local patriotism was strong, and pride in the institutions of self-government was a thriving spirit running counter to national attachments."[242] The moral attachment to the universal truth that all men are by nature equally free and independent was appealing to colonial Americans, and natural law language is evident in the early colonial State Constitutions.[243] This strong belief in natural law as a universal truth was a factor in breaking down the local patriotism and allowing the colonial states and individual citizens of the diverse states to slowly accept and then to embrace the Nation as national citizens united under The Constitution of the United States and the federal government.

The Massachusetts colony sent a letter to Congress on May 16, 1775, that asked for guidance and advice in setting up a civil government for representation of the people of Massachusetts.[244] After Massachusetts, additional states sought a general plan from Congress to govern its people. New Hampshire sent a similar resolution to Congress on October 18, 1775, South Carolina on November 4, 1775, and Virginia on December 4, 1775.[245] On May 10, 1776, Congress passed a resolution and a preamble on May 15, 1776, to declare that any authority under the Crown is suppressed, and that commonwealths should be established to govern a free and independent people by free and independent states.[246] The language of natural law is reflected in the State Constitutions.

The Massachusetts Constitution, October 25, 1780, Declaration of Rights, Article 1, states, "All men are born free and equal, and have certain natural, essential, and unalienable rights; among which may be reckoned the right of enjoying and defending their lives and liberties; that of acquiring, possessing, and protecting property; in fine, that of seeking and obtaining their safety and happiness."[247] The monarchical principles of the mother country with King, aristocracy, elites and governing classes within Parliament no longer worked for the American colonists whose vision created an extraordinary republicanism where self-governing citizens can live a life of freedom and happiness.

Chapter 9

Natural Law: Freedom, Justice, and Liberty

The Continental Congress wrote the Articles of Confederation for governing the nation. Congress approved The Articles of Confederation in 1777. They were ratified by the states in 1781. The national government under the Articles of Confederation was one legislative body with each state having a single vote. To pass a law, Congress required a two-thirds majority. Congress did not have any authority to enforce the laws that it passed. The Articles also lacked the power to regulate interstate commerce, trade, and the power of taxation. Under the Articles of Confederation, the states were not paying the money that they owed to the federal government, the states were ignoring treaties, they were attempting to regulate the trade of the other states, they were devaluing the currency, and the lack of a federal governmental power was leading to insurrection. For example, Shay's Rebellion (1786-1787) was a rebellion by veterans of the Revolutionary War who found that their farms were being foreclosed for nonpayment of taxes, so the farmers shut down the banks and courthouses in and around Springfield, Massachusetts. The revolutionary war veterans held scrip (promissory notes) for payment for their war services, and this script was being denied as payment for taxes.

The Articles of Confederation were laws for governing the new Nation passed by the Continental Congress' legislature. There were no checks on these laws. Contrast this with The Constitution of the United States which were laws for governing the new Nation that the representatives of the people had passed after the state delegates met in State Conventions where they discussed, questioned, argued, debated, and then voted for ratification of The

Constitution of the United States. There were checks built into the Constitution. This was after debates and arguments within each state on the strengths and weaknesses of the Constitution. These debates of the Federalists versus the Anti-federalists were arguments that Americans paid close attention to, and the alleged reasons given both for and against the Constitution. These debates and reasoned arguments are a sign of the ebb and flow of natural law dialectic. A turning point came in America when the Federalists and Anti-Federalists engaged in vigorous questioning and debate over the merits, strengths, and perceived weaknesses of the newly constructed Constitution. From the risk of the Union's dissolution under the Articles of Confederation, the Americans approved the Constitution which would empower the national government while at the same time ensuring that the state's retained their sovereignty in all areas that were not enumerated as a federal power in the Constitution.

The founders were well-versed in natural law philosophy. The Americans knew their Locke, and in 1787 they believed in Locke's theory of natural law, and frequently expounded upon his consent of the governed and natural law conception of the human being. The founders also followed the Swiss philosopher Jean Jacques Burlamaqui (1694-1748), whose book *The Principles of Natural and Political Law* (1747) was read by many of the eighteenth-century Americans who participated in the First Continental Congress. Like Locke, Burlamaqui philosophized about God who created and rules the universe and is omniscient and omnipotent. Burlamaqui argues that if we can come to understand our God-given essence as a created being, then we can also understand our duties, and the natural rights that are necessary for us to perform our duties.[248]

Underlying all the political, economic, and moral thinking of the founders was a moral commitment to natural law. Even today, we continue to understand — through natural law — the merits of the constitutional rights guaranteed by a government that was instituted by public constitutional consent. The moral foundation of natural law is a commitment to justice for each citizen.

A formative part of Constitutional history is discovered through a careful study of the delegates' debates during the Federal Convention. (The Convention was referred to as the Federal Convention, or the Grand Convention at Philadelphia, or the Philadelphia Convention in 1787. It was after the ratification of the Constitution of the United States that it was referred to as the Constitutional Convention). The delegates to the Federal Convention behaved in a reasonable manner during the rational debates and inquiries into what constitutes a sound republic. James Madison, for example, believed in strong moral principles: virtue, right-mindedness, individual rights, equality, honesty, and integrity. These beliefs are consonant with natural law thinking. For many of the Founders, the government must be impartial and promote lawfulness and due process. Natural law is woven into the fabric of our Constitution, for example, equality, rights, freedom of speech, freedom of the press, individual liberty, truth, respect for the law, religious freedom, the due process clause, the protection of property, and liberty of contract clauses.

The Constitution of the United States is an expression of natural law where the Founders used human reason to render the immutable laws of God into a remarkable document that serves to govern in a just manner. A first principle of natural law is that God is a just God. God is a Supreme Intelligence that has ordered all things in the wisest manner, and we are blessed that He has instilled natural law in us as part of our natural being. Recall from our earlier Chapter 4, "Natural Law and St. Thomas," St. Thomas taught us that the first principle of natural law is that we should seek the good and avoid evil. Along with this key principle is the maxim that we should seek God's truth. Our Founding Fathers were practicing natural law when they met together to discuss and deliberate a novel form of government that would honor God, honor the integrity of the citizens, and give the maximum dignity and autonomy to the citizens while holding the Union together with a workable form of government. A sound republic, individual freedom, individual rights, justice, democracy, and constitutionalism were conceived through the practical reasonableness of citizens practicing natural law. The delegates conceived of a constitutional republic that provides a measure of freedom and fulfillment within the rule of law that was unprecedented in history. Freedom flows from the understanding and use of natural law, and freedom is protected by the precepts and laws of The Constitution of the United States of America.

The practical reasonableness that is a key to natural law deliberations was active in the discussions and construction of the Constitution of the United States of America by setting the framework for citizens, future citizens, legislators, and judges to live within the legal form of the Constitution.

One of the keys to natural law thinking is practical reasonableness which was the type of reasoning power that the delegates used in their debates. One of the tools used for practical reasonableness is dialectic, i.e., the art of question and answer that was taught to us initially by Socrates, and later by Jesus.[249] Dialectic was part of the rational inquiry that the delegates used to formulate and clarify their ideas as they discussed the formation and structure of the Constitution.

Dialectic is more than the art of forming conceptions. It is a critical method that opened the intellectual horizons of the framers for a wider inquiry into the nature of governments. The founders searched for correct conceptions for creating a government, whereby everything (the particulars) will radiate from the general conception of what the most appropriate structure for a federal republic should be. Madison was instrumental in focusing the members' attention on the structure of the form of the government, and the practical operation of the novel constitution. The Convention members agreed to work toward the creation of a complex central government that would have authority over the states. With Madison's initial guidance, the members defined a common ground by using the Virginia Plan as a beginning outline for the debate on the creation of the Constitution.

Deductive reasoning is another tool for us to use in clarifying natural law concepts. Deductive reasoning argues from the general concepts to the particulars of that concept. The Founders used deductive reasoning during the Convention. They began with the fundamental and general concepts of a common defense, security of liberty, and the general welfare of the citizens, and argued deductively to the particulars of what constitutes a national government that will hold these three general concepts as fundamental.

Inductive reasoning is an additional tool for us to use in clarifying natural law concepts. Inductive reasoning moves from the particular cases to the general idea or concept; for example, goodness is a particular characteristic of an individual who upholds the precepts of natural law. Another example is virtue; virtue is a particular characteristic of an individual who adheres to natural law, and a virtuous person is one who practices natural law. The analytical framework for an individual who is practicing natural law is to recognize knowledge (wisdom), understand the knowledge (practical wisdom), correct usage of the knowledge (application), and the ability to draw distinctions (spiritual discernment).

These are the tools that we use to understand and utilize natural law, and they are the same tools that Socrates used in ancient Greece to teach philosophy. These analytical tools are the reasoning powers that are bequeathed to us by our Maker, and Jesus utilized these tools to teach us the Biblical truths that guide us in our knowledge and understanding of the Word of God.[250] The spiritual light of understanding of the Word of God is also revealed to us through natural law.

Historically, adherents to the principles of natural law are creative individuals whose thinking is creative, individualistic, imaginative, often visionary, and at times groundbreaking. We are created in God's image, and one of our unique characteristics as human beings is our creativity. The American Founder's, for example, demonstrated this God-given talent of creativity when they created the Constitution of the United States of America. We are created in

God's image; God gave form to the universe by speaking Holy words. God teaches us the power of words, and we learn to communicate our ideas into words. The Founders created the Constitution by taking the ideas of the past historical governmental structures and polities, the current state constitutions, and turning the confusion and lack of structure of the existing polity governed by the Articles of Confederation and shaping it into a coherent order that will function well under the rule of law as guided by the Constitution. The Constitution represents our ideas of justice, and we have the idea of justice as an innate and universal idea though natural law. The idea of justice is an archetype that transcends space and time; as human beings we are anchored in a temporal setting or space, but we utilize our ideas of natural law for a further understanding of those archetypes, for example, the idea of justice, which are critical for our development as members of a political community. We communicate with each other through this innate idea of justice, and it is through the words that correspond to our ideas of justice that we can take the abstract concept of justice and translate it into a concrete idea that relies on the rule of law to uphold its meaning and value. Unfortunately, today the utilization of the universal concept of justice is suffering due to a spiritual darkening that has been caused by those who have fraudulently misrepresented their natures in order to grasp power. For those of us who wait on the Lord, we know that God's power is superior to all powers and forces, and His light is more powerful than the darkness. "The light shines in the darkness, and the darkness has not overcome it." (John 1:5).

Natural law was always a key concept for colonial Americans. As we study our constitutional history, we appreciate the relevance of our growth as a republic within the concept of natural law. The dialogue of natural rights is a logical extension of natural law. Americans originally meant that natural rights were considered to be the same rights that Englishmen held until the American Revolution. The scholar John Phillip Reid examined American's original understandings of rights and concluded that there were numerous justifications for Americans' conception of rights: natural law, American rights as Englishmen, the colonial contracts used during emigration, the original contracts, equality with other British subjects, the use of the British constitution, and, finally, (after the Revolution) principles of the American Constitution.[251]

Natural law maximizes the greatest amount of good for a community since the individuals who follow natural law do so to bring about good both within their own lives and others. Natural law activity creates the good, and the good is pleasant and beautiful, pleasing to the eye, and a better proportion of said good thing is intricately patterned—the seeing of which delights. We are nourished through God's natural law and through the viscosity of God's nutritive good.

The delegates to the Federal Convention conducted themselves in a reasonable manner which is consonant with natural law practices. Although Madison rarely used the term 'natural law', his understanding of what constitutes a sound republic was based upon the principles of natural law. Madison believed the principles of the Constitution and the consent of the parties to the Constitution cannot conflict with the "law of nature and of nature's God" where all political institutions aim for the safety and happiness of society.[252] Natural law is woven into the fabric of our Constitution, for example, our freedoms protected by the Bill of Rights, the respect and belief in the rule of law, sovereignty of the individual, the due process clause, and liberty of contract. Madison's constitutional philosophy — a belief that the Constitution protects citizens' rights, a belief in moral principles, integrity, and the virtue of the Nation's citizens — is still our predominant view today. Constitutional scholar David G. Smith writes, "Madison's view is that a constitution protects the spirit of neutrality and probity upon which the will of the public is formed to protect common rights."[253] The Madisonian spirit of lawfulness, governmental impartiality, and due process are concepts that continue to animate good democratic government today.

The keys to the success of the delegates who attended the Federal Convention (Constitutional Convention of 1787) are found in the methods of natural law thinking where the delegates looked at the problems of the new nation and used reason, (practical reasonableness, deductive and inductive reasoning), debate, dialectic, communication, speeches, compromise, informed opinion, consent, and determination to examine the principles that would be the foundation for this new system of government. The delegates discussed the first principles of government: law or the laws of nature, and occasionally they used the term 'natural law,' the natural rights that govern human action, the virtuous actions of both the citizens and the government, political theory, equality, liberty, freedom, justice, equity, prudence, property, sovereignty, power, and abuse of power were all concepts that were discussed and debated by the delegates. James Madison gathered the meanings of democracy from the ancient and past governments, and it was his genius that discerned that the past meaning of democracy could be pressed into his logical millhouse for a conversion for use in American government. Madison rationally examined and interpreted every democratic variable to administer a clarity of vision for the current practice of government, and to successfully construct the Constitution of the United States of America.

The three fundamental axiological ideas that gave birth to the Constitution of the United States of America are freedom, justice, and liberty; and natural law crowns the apex of this triangular enumeration. Axios (worth or value) and logos (logic, theory, or meaning) are ancient Greek words that are fundamental in assisting us to develop a moral theory of value to live a full and spiritual existence. Axiological ideas help us to identify the moral values that influence our perceptions, decisions, actions, and deeds. Axiological ideas are the patterns for our thinking, and we utilize these ideas for subsequent connate notions. For example, there is a necessary connection between the idea of freedom and democratic rule. There is a necessary ideational connection between the idea of individual freedom and democratic rule. This is demonstrated from the Founder's discussion of axiological ideas and put into practice to form a government that would maximize freedoms while at the same time it could successfully govern the Nation through the rule of law. It is through natural law that axiological ideas will demonstrate to us that human justice is below divine justice, and human liberty is also below divine liberty, but both ideas touch the periphery of that which is Sovereign, Holy, and venerable, and in doing so the mind can participate in freedom. When the mind can access the axiological idea of freedom, then the human being follows with free activities and free acts. The most satisfying and successful historical form of government is democracy, and our experiment with a republican democracy is an active spiritual journey. Our Constitutional freedoms are unfolding as the wings of time across the spatial expanse of our natural law journey — this voyage unfolds as a discovery of individual freedom, and from our natural law perspective, religious freedom is the key to all our expansive freedoms.

Chapter 10

Natural Law and the American Founders

In 1787, the essential realities of creating a new nation, and the perspectives of a spiritual nation came together in the minds of the Founders who were energized with the task of creating a novel republican government. When the eager delegates met in Philadelphia in 1787 a majority of the states had expected the Convention to amend the Articles of Confederation to meet the needs of the Union. The delegates, however, did not recommend amendments to the Articles of Confederation, instead they drafted The Constitution of the United States of America. James Madison's concern, for example, was the defective structure of the Articles of Confederation.[254] Historian Lance Banning argues that Madison's chief concern over the Article of Confederation was its "irredeemably defective structure," i.e., at issue was the weaknesses of the framework of the Articles. Some historians have argued that the Convention delegates wanted a firmer union because of the oppressive behavior of the state legislatures.[255] James Madison did not advocate for a fundamentally radical and powerful national government. One of the primary concerns for Madison was the allocation of the amount of power between the national government and the states. In the final Constitutional document, all powers not enumerated as federal powers in the Constitution belong to the states. The powers reserved to the states concern the individual liberty and property of the citizens of the state, and the prosperity of the state. Madison clearly understood that the central government must be able to act without the intervention by the states, and that the states must have autonomous powers to act if the action does not infringe upon the federal government's powers as specified in the Constitution.[256]

James Madison's talent lay in his ability to challenge the workability of past governmental forms, to analyze the distinctions made within these past governmental forms, and to use these models to create a unique form of government that was appropriate for the new American Nation. The analytical framework that Madison prepared prior to the Federal Convention relied on deductive and inductive reasoning, with the utilization of the distinctions that are workable for governing a nation whose citizens would be the voice of the Nation through their votes. Madison's studies of past governments taught him that there had been numerous past federations and governments that ruled, and some were successful for democracy: for example, the ancient Greek city-states -- an example was the ancient Athenian system of government. Madison devised a unique federalism for America where the government exercised its constitutional governing powers but was at the same time responsible and answerable to the citizens. Madison's key idea was the insight that our government must be able to act directly on the body politic, and that the rule of law was the instrument through which the government acts. Madison's acute reasoning and analytical powers kept the Convention delegates focused, wherein the tools of dialogue, dialectic, reason, (both deductive and inductive reasoning skills), discussion, argumentation, and compromise shaped the delegate's ideas into The Constitution of the United States of America. Throughout history no nation's citizens had successfully created a document like the Constitution that established a government that has the power to govern a nation, and the citizens with the comparable generous size of the United States.

James Madison spoke over two-hundred times during the Federal Convention, and his practical and studied knowledge of past forms of government bequeathed to us the form of federalism, the three branches of government, i.e., the executive (a single executive, and the appointment, duration, and eligibility of the President), legislative (a bicameral legislature with the House and the Senate), and the appointment, duration and eligibility of Congress members, and the judicial branch of government, (the appointment, duration, and eligibility of the Supreme Court Justices, and judicial review), and the diffusion of the powers of each branch, the balance of power between the three branches of government, the balance of power between the federal government and state governments, the Constitutional rights of American citizens, the method of elections, the method of congressional representation, the terms of appointments, suffrage, slavery,[257] taxation, and to the future states' position on slavery upon joining the Union, power to raise armies, marine, and naval forces, common defense and general welfare, taxation, trade among states, infrastructure, international trade, and international relationships and treaties.

Seventy-four delegates from twelve states were appointed to the Federal Convention. (Rhode Island did not send any delegates to the Federal Convention). Nineteen of these delegates did not attend, leaving fifty-five delegates to attend; however, two came very late, five were absent for the majority of the proceedings, and seven left the Convention early. Forty-two delegates remained at the end of the Convention. There were thirty-nine signatures affixed to The Constitution of the United States of America after four months of dedicated debate and work by honorable men of good character.[258] The delegates were all men of exceptional abilities who had experience to some degree in fighting a Revolutionary War, drafting and signing the *Declaration of Independence*, drafting and implementation of their own respective state constitutions, experience in politics, and many had debated and approved the Articles of Confederation. The Convention delegates discussed and debated the strengths and weaknesses of the Articles of Confederation, the state constitutions, as well as the English constitution, and common law.

The delegates brought their political, legal, and professional experiences, along with their leadership, logic, reasoning, and oratorical skills, with them to the Grand Convention. The recorded debates of the Convention tell us that the delegates used their experience as a guide to the construction of the Constitution. The majority of the delegates had knowledge of historical events —

governments and politics of ancient Greece, ancient Rome, and they had read the historians, for example, Tacitus, and the philosophers, for example, John Locke, David Hume and Freiherr Samuel von Pufendorf. The delegates were influenced by the classical tradition of natural law, English constitutionalism, and common law. American documents, for example, the Massachusetts Constitution of 1780, state constitutions, and colonial documents were also a source of reference for the delegates. The delegates had personal experience in colonial politics, law, and the wisdom to know what type of government would work. The delegates, for example, had experience to some degree in the drawing and implementation of their own respective state constitutions, so the debates in 1787 appropriately examined the strengths and weaknesses of the state constitutions. Many of the delegates had experience in the American Revolution, knowledge of the British government, experience in politics, and had participated in the debates for the approval of the Articles of Confederation. The majority of the delegates were practicing attorneys. James Madison was not a trained attorney; however, he had a keen intellect and political perception that enabled him to understand the problems of governing under the Articles of Confederation, and the determination to remedy the structure of the government. The delegates were searching for a body politic that would form a strong union without destroying the states. They also had the wisdom to know what would not work, for example, a league of states, nor a confederation; and the delegates had the rational ability to compromise their own position for a workable Constitution.

The delegates' objectives were to create a Republic for the public good, to ensure liberty for all Americans, to protect property, and to end the disorder caused by a weak Articles of Confederation. The ability to utilize reason to compromise their own differences of opinions that were held between the large and small-state factions, and to achieve a workable Constitution is a notable achievement. The delegates used common-sense moral reasoning which was learned from the Scottish moral philosophers Francis Hutcheson (1694-17470), Thomas Reid (1710-1796), and Adam Smith

(1723-1790); philosophers who taught that ethics were grounded in human instincts that are universal in nature. The English philosopher, Francis Bacon, was also an influence with his scientific examination of consciousness as an object that gives us the data to use induction to reason from particulars to universals. For Bacon, laws about human nature can be discovered using induction arguing from a proposition that is self-evident. The moderate Enlightenment ideas of the philosopher John Locke, and the scientist, and mathematician, Isaac Newton, were also prime philosophical influences on American thought during this time.

The Founding Fathers came to the Convention with a belief in natural law — a universal belief that our individual rights are derived from the universal laws of God, and that government exists to protect our natural, inborn, and God-given rights. The most influential delegates (all Episcopalians) were James Madison from Virginia, Alexander Hamilton from New York, James Wilson from Pennsylvania (Some historians write that James Wilson was attracted to Deism in his later years.), and George Washington from Virginia. These delegates applied natural law as the source for the rule of law and government. Other delegates at the Philadelphia Convention also adhered to the concept of natural law: John Dickinson from Delaware (a Quaker, who became an Episcopalian in his later years), Daniel Carroll from Maryland (a Roman Catholic), and George Mason from Virginia (an Episcopalian). The majority of the delegates were practicing attorneys who were very familiar with William Blackstone's, *Commentarie on the Laws of England*, who believed in the law of nature which is dictated by God for us to discover through reason, and for us to obey. Lord Edward Coke, England's renowned jurist, also guided the delegates in understanding English Common Law as a practical application of natural law.

Delegate George Washington (1732-1799) was born in Westmoreland County, Virginia,[259] and was the most distinguished member (among many prominent members) of the Convention. He was a hero as a successful general and commander-in-chief of the victorious Continental Army (elected by the Continental Congress on June 15, 1775 and served through 1783) that defeated the British in the Revolutionary War. Washington's generalship led the colonies to victory over the British. Washington was a revered and respected presence in 1786 — tall, commanding, disciplined, dignified, reserved, moral, trustworthy, and visionary. During the French and Indian Wars, Washington served as a lieutenant colonel in the Virginia Regiment and as an aide-de-camp to General Edward Braddock (March 15, 1754). Washington was a leader as a soldier, a planter, an entrepreneur, and a politician (as America's first President serving two terms of office from 1789-1797). After Washington's Presidency, he served (in 1798) as Lieutenant General of the United States Army.

Washington was fifty-five years old at the time of the Convention. As a delegate from Virginia (the richest colony from the tobacco crop and was also the largest and most populous of the colonies) his participation gave a legitimate air to the success of the Convention. It had taken much persuasion, especially by James Madison, to get Washington to leave his beloved Mt. Vernon and lend his name, credibility, and prestige to the influential group of men gathering in Philadelphia. Washington's political sentiments lay with the nationalists, so his participation signaled hope for governmental reform, and calmed the citizen's fears over the fate of their fledgling nation. When Washington arrived in Philadelphia on Sunday, May 13th, he was met by saluting officers, dignitaries, an adoring crowd, a parade, and booming cannonballs.[260]

On Friday, May 25th a seven-state quorum allowed the delegates to officially begin their historical deliberations. Washington appeared in his old military uniform, and due to the prestige and visage of the hero of America's independence, he was unanimously voted as President of the Convention. He presided over the meetings with an aura of dignity while seated on a high-backed wooden chair carved on top with the sun, which visitors to the Pennsylvania State House (later known as Independence Hall) had remarked was reminiscent of a throne. We have the lasting impression of a powerful figure, and although he did not often speak during the debates, his presence indicated that the secret meetings were indeed conducted for the public good. Washington's role as President of the convention was to preside over the meetings so he did not enter the daily debates, but he was not a silent and inactive observer of the makings of the Constitution — he attended every meeting with a summary booklet of his own Convention notes that he had condensed, listened attentively, and carefully read all the information that set out the numerous debates.[261]

George Washington was a devout Christian, although he was not excessively verbal about his Christian believes which was the custom for the eighteenth-century man. During the American Revolution, General George Washington had knelt in prayer to seek God's guidance and protection for his soldiers and his country.[262] When George Washington took his oath of office as President of the United States, he established a tradition when he added the words "so help me, God," to the inaugural oath.[264] President George Washington (in his first year as President during his Thanksgiving Proclamation) acknowledged God's almighty providence and asked for His protection and favor over the United States. Washington believed that God's blessing gave us our good government, and that we should praise God, give Him thanks and be faithful to His calling. We are a spiritual nation, and Washington acknowledged this sacred calling for all American citizens, "every person may here worship God according to the dictates of his own heart."[264]

James Madison was a prodigious thinker and was energetically involved in the creation of the American Union. As purveyors of history, we are fortunate to have copious information and published material on which to draw our conclusions on Madison's life and works, especially his role in the formation of The Constitution of the United States. Madison left behind his meticulous notes on the proceedings, debates and speeches of the Constitutional Convention, extensive private letters, and correspondence, published and unpublished essays, his published papers, and state papers. James Madison (1751-1836) is often described as "the father of the Constitution," an apt epitaph for a man who came to Philadelphia on May 3rd, 1787, (Madison arrived eleven days before the scheduled convention meeting date of May 14th.) intellectually prepared with notes on the construction of past republics and anchoring his knowledge with the over two-hundred books that he brought with him.

James Madison was born in Port Conway, Virginia. He attended the College of New Jersey (1768). (Later called Princeton University). Madison's views of government, law, political philosophy, and religion were influenced by the Calvinism of the College's President, Reverend John Witherspoon (1723-1794). He received a baccalaureate degree in 1771. At the College of New Jersey, Madison learned the principles of the Scottish Enlightenment where there is a universal human nature, and the science of politics or the science of government can reveal to us knowledge of the natural laws. This knowledge of natural laws is important for an understanding of the natural rights of liberty. When James Madison returned home from college, he was a deeply moralistic young man, writing to a former college classmate that he was eager to enroll his name in the "Annals of Heaven."[265] As a youth, James Madison attended the Episcopalian Church, but he never received full communion or identified himself as an Episcopalian. Madison has been described by historians as a rational Christian. The eighteenth-century man was generally modest in their personal proclamations about religious affiliations. The measure of the Founders religious beliefs is noted through their words (verbal and written) and actions, and these salient features demonstrate a clarion call to a belief in God and natural law.

James Madison, thirty-six at the time of the Convention, was modest by nature, soft-spoken, slight in build, and always well-dressed with a preference for grey or black outfits. He was politically active in his home state of Virginia, and in Congress where he favored a revision of the Articles of Confederation. Madison had considered the ministry as a career. It may have been his soft voice or poor health that had kept him out of the ministry.[267] Madison had a long political career: he was the youngest legislative politician to the Continental Congress for the largest state of Virginia, and a signer of the *Declaration of Independence.* We can describe Madison as the most sophisticated constitutional scholar at the time of the Federal Convention. He was an effective politician in proposing both state and federal legislation, an ordered and deep thinker, a scholar, a republican, and he was modest in his analysis that the Federal Convention and the Constitution was the work of all the delegates, and that he had learned much as a delegate.[267]

Madison's long political career and accomplishments are consistent with the beliefs of a man who adhered to the philosophy of natural law. Madison was a staunch defender of republican freedoms, inherent equal rights, liberty, justice, and just laws, a just government, religious freedom, and freedom of religious consciousness, along with a belief in reason and logic. Madison believed that the Constitution cannot conflict with the "law of nature and of nature's God."[268] He believed in the inherent virtue of the citizens of the American polity. He advocated for private rights, property rights, and public liberty, all three are rights that are mutually beneficial for a natural law theorist. Madison's individual values were consistently moral, and his expectations for American freedom and self-governance were always optimistic. Madison's energy, intellect, and research lay the groundwork for the structure and formation of the Constitution of the United States. Madison's expert use of reason and logic overcame any arguments against the Constitution. Madison's prestige and writing ability in *The Federalist* helped Americans to overcome any questions, suspicions, or doubts that they had about the newly presented Constitution.

Throughout his career, Madison believed in religious freedom, and he believed that the liberty of conscience was sacred. Early in Madison's career, in 1773, he was involved in a protest to protect Baptist dissenters in Culpepper County, a neighboring County to

Madison's Orange County, Virginia. Madison also initiated a lead role in drafting the Virginia Constitution of 1776.

In 1776, Madison was elected to the Virginia state convention which framed a revolutionary constitution. George Mason's draft of a "Declaration of Rights" contained conventional language for the protection of religious dissenters, "that all men should enjoy the fullest toleration in the exercise of religion according to the dictates of conscience."[269] Madison amended Mason's language and Patrick Henry introduced it:

> *"All men are equally entitled to the full and free exercise of [their religion]*
>
> *According to the dictates of conscience; and therefore that no man or class*
>
> *of men ought, on account of religion to be invested with peculiar*
>
> *emoluments or privileges; nor subjected to any penalties or disabilities*
>
> *unless under color of religion, any man disturb the peace, the happiness,*
>
> *or safety of society."*[270]

The Virginia state convention delegates feared that this language could disestablish the Anglican Church, and the amendment failed. Madison then altered Mason's, "All men should enjoy the fullest toleration unpunished and unrestrained by the magistrate" to "All men are equally entitled to enjoy the free exercise of religion unless the preservation of equal liberty and the existence of the state are manifestly endangered."[271] Madison's perceptive nature realized that the word "toleration" evoked a special privilege that was only granted by the state. Madison replaced the word "privilege" with the concept that all men are equally entitled to the free exercise of religion. Madison's language is important because it writes into law equal treatment for different religious faiths, and distinctive spheres for church and the state.[272]

John Locke influenced Madison, and the Lockean separation of church and state, and religious freedom. Madison's colleagues, brothers George and Wilson Cary Nicholas, urged Madison to take a leadership role in Virginia to gain support in opposition to a proposed assessment bill. Madison wrote an anonymous appeal, "*Memorial and Remonstrance against Religious Assessments*," where he writes that religious liberty is unalienable: "It is the duty of every man to render to the Creator such homage and such only as he believes to be acceptable to Him." And further, "In matters of religion no man's right is abridged by the institution of civil society."[273] Written from a Christian point of view, the "*Memorial and Remonstrance against Religious Assessments*" argued that Christianity did not require state aid, and flourished best without it, individual and inherent rights are not surrendered when we enter society, and there are chartered bounds of government that cannot be transgressed.[274]

James Madison was more prepared than most Constitutional Convention of 1787 delegates with a knowledge and understanding of past and ancient forms of government. In 1787, while in New York waiting for a quorum for the Confederation Congress, he undertook a self-study of the history of all the confederations over the past thousand years in Europe. Madison's intensive study of the science of government included ancient Greece, Rome, the historian Tacitus, and the philosopher's Locke, Hume and Pufendorf.[275] Madison undertook his studies to make an independent judgment on what type of governmental structure and form would lead to a successful government for the flourishing of all Americans.[276]

Madison concluded that a confederation composed of independent states was weak, and thus the need for the sovereignty of a central government. The outline of a federal republic was something that Madison introduced, and he maintained that federalism was the proper structure for a practical, reasonable, and workable republic. Many of the participating convention delegates felt that the Articles of Confederation should be reconstructed to fit the needs of the Union. Madison shared his thoughts as to why lesser changes to the

Articles of Confederation would not work, and why an enlarged republic — with a sound structural form which placed limitations on the states — would be the correct structure to ensure private rights.

Madison was guided in the Convention by two goals: to preserve liberty and to create a stable and effective government. Madison introduced the outline of a federal republic as the proper structure for a practical, reasonable, limited, and workable republic. Madison believed that the national government should have authority over finance, commerce, foreign trade, and policy, and at the same time play an impartial role in neutralizing disagreements and the pursuit of interests on behalf of the state's actions which could be detrimental to the whole society. Madison's scholarly studies on the ancient forms of government, both past and present, equipped him with a knowledge and wisdom that was necessary to enable him to propose the unique structure of federalism for the United States. Madison's resolve to keep the Union from dissolving due to the current inadequate Articles of Confederation was of key importance, where he addressed the lack of governmental power, an ineffective central government, lack of ability to formulate laws and to enforce those laws which the government had formulated, lack of control over the states' actions and laws, lack of an independent source of revenue, no control over trade with other countries, and the lack of confidence that the citizens and other nations exhibited and felt toward the Union. Madison came to the Convention with workable ideas and thoughtful solutions that he felt would cure the numerous divisions and problems that were created by the weak central government under the Articles of Confederation.

Once the Convention began, Madison kept precise notes of the proceedings — the arguments of the various speakers, the motions, and the votes. These records were meant for historical posterity, and to share with his friend in Paris — Thomas Jefferson.[277] After the Federal Convention, Madison organized the ratification process, and in support of the Constitution, wrote *The Federalist* along with

Alexander Hamilton and John Jay. The authors were collectively known by the pseudonym of Publius. Madison then led the ratification debate at the Virginia Convention. Madison was elected (1789-1797) to the U. S. House of Representatives, where he was the sole drafter of the Bill of Rights. He was an advisor to President George Washington, he organized the Democratic-Republican Party, served as secretary of state under President Thomas Jefferson (1801-1809), supervised the Louisiana Purchase, which doubled the size of the nation, and he served two terms as the fourth President of the United States (1809-1817). After concluding a distinguished political career, Madison then served as rector of the University of Virginia (1826).

Madison was the first delegate to arrive in Philadelphia for the Federal Convention, where he met daily with the seven Virginia delegation members who arrived in Philadelphia by May 13th, and two Pennsylvania delegates, Gouverneur Morris, and James Wilson, while they waited for a quorum of seven states. The Federal Convention convened on May 25, 1787 and ended on September 17, 1787. After a process of discussion, investigation, analyses, explanation, arguments, dialogue, debate, and compromise, the fifteen-point Virginia Plan was formulated. Madison took a lead role in the daily caucuses that produced the Virginia Plan. The Virginia Plan served as a key outline for the historical deliberations that were about to take place.

During the Convention, Madison offered his opinion on the importance of forming a central government by demonstrating the weakness of the independent states. The important details of the overall constitution of a federal government were filled in by Madison: the three branches of government, the executive, judicial and congressional branches, separation of powers, checks and balances, candidate qualifications and selection of candidates, finance, commerce, foreign policy, justice, order, dignity, and script within a virtuous federal government were discussed and debated. Many Framers believed that the Revolution had unleashed vices, and that virtue was leaving the land with new faces (unvouched for and unprincipled men!) filling the numerous openings available once the Crown was gone. This was alarming for those who considered the social movements to be aligned with the political agendas.

Delegate Edmund Randolph (1753-1813) was the governor of Virginia and an important political figure. Randolph was born in Williamsburg, Virginia, and graduated from the College of William and Mary. He was thirty-four at the time of the Convention. His position as governor of Virginia gave him a prominent leadership role even though he did not speak very often during the Convention. On May 29th, Randolph introduced the fifteen resolutions of the Virginia Plan (also referred to as the Randolph Resolutions but thought to be primarily the work of James Madison), and these resolutions served as an excellent starting point for the deliberations. The Virginia Plan outlined a central republic at the head of a confederation of republics. (An example of the nationalist philosophy of union). The Convention delegates agreed that an effective central government was needed with an independent source of revenue, authority to regulate the nation's trade, and power to compel the states and citizens to obey legitimate rules and laws. The delegates with a national vision were James Madison, Alexander Hamilton, Charles Pinckney, and James Wilson.

George Mason (1725-1823) was the wealthy owner of Gunston Hall in Fairfax County, where he grew tobacco and wheat, and invested his money in land speculation west of the Appalachians. He was one of the main drafters of the Virginia Constitution of 1776, and the Declaration of Rights. He retired from politics for ten years, and in 1785 he attended a meeting at George Washington's home — his friend and neighbor — to discuss the navigation of the Potomac River. He preferred to stay in his familiar surroundings at Gunston Hall but was persuaded to attend the Federal Convention to lend his intellect to the politics and policy-making that would preserve the Union. George Mason as well as the entire Virginia delegation were Episcopalians, and included George Washington, James Madison,

Edmund Randolph, John Blair, Jr., James McClung, Edmund Jennings Randolph, and George Wythe.

The most loquacious delegate to the Convention was Gouverneur Morris (1752-1816) from Pennsylvania who was a brilliant lawyer, merchant, financier, and an eloquent and skilled speaker. (He was also an Episcopalian). Born in New York City, he graduated from King's College (later named Columbia University), and practiced law in New York City. He served in the New York Assembly from 1775-1777 where he, along with John Jay and Robert R. Livingston, drafted the New York Constitution. Morris settled in Philadelphia to practice law, and in 1787 he was chosen as a delegate to the Constitutional Convention. Morris aligned his thinking with Madison for a national government. Morris spoke on the floor of the Convention 173 times. He also served as head of the Committee on Style, showing how important the proper wording and phrasing of the Constitution was for the meaning and application of the rule of law. Governor Morris's political philosophy was formed around a biblical point of view which saw religion and morality as essential to a free society and the rule of law.

Benjamin Franklin (1706-1790) also from Pennsylvania and the oldest delegate at age eighty-one, was a Deist, however his call for prayer at the Convention stating that, "God governs in the affairs of men," is not consistent with the Deists' belief that God does not intervene in the affairs of men. He was born in Boston, Massachusetts, where he learned the printing trade at a young age, and held a worldwide reputation as a philosopher, political theorist, politician, statesman, diplomat, scientist, postmaster, humorist, printer, publisher, editor, polyglot, inventor, author, and colorful charmer. Franklin was raised in a Calvinist home, and although he questioned orthodoxy as an adult, his faith in God remained balanced by a belief in reason.

Franklin moved to Philadelphia in 1723, at the age of seventeen and soon after founded and published the *Pennsylvania Gazette* (at age 23), the *Pennsylvania Chronicle* (from 1767 to 1768), and published

Poor Richard's Almanack, under the pseudonym of Richard Saunders (1732). Later, he cataloged a list of virtues that he practiced taking each virtue singly on a weekly basis: temperance, silence, order, resolution, frugality, industry, sincerity, justice, moderation, cleanliness, tranquility, chastity and this author's favorite, humility, to imitate Jesus and Socrates.[278] Franklin served as a military commander, a delegate to the Continental Congress, a Minister to England (where he resided in London from the mid-1750s to the mid-1770s), Ambassador to France 1776-1785, Governor of Pennsylvania, and was a delegate to the Constitutional Convention. Franklin not only signed the *Declaration of Independence* (1776), but also the Treaty of Alliance with France (1778), the Treaty of Paris (1783), and The Constitution of the United States (1787).

James Madison met Benjamin Franklin for the first time at the Convention and held Franklin in high esteem and defended him from criticism when Franklin was in France acting as the representative from the United States. In Philadelphia, Franklin offered advice and stories while he entertained the delegates at his home on Market Street. The other delegate members praised him although his extreme democratic views were not always useful for the Convention. On the last day of the Convention, September 17th, 1787, before signing the Constitution, — in his role as peacemaker — Franklin wanted to present a speech to urge his fellow delegates to sign the Constitution. Franklin, however, was too weak to deliver his speech, so Pennsylvania delegate James Wilson delivered it for him.

Pennsylvania delegate James Wilson (1742-1798) was an able lawyer, land speculator, and politician. Raised in his native country Scotland by strict Calvinist parents, who were farmers, he attended the University of St. Andrews, Glasgow, and Edinburgh. Wilson intended a career in the ministry, but his plans were interrupted by the death of his father; and in 1765, he sailed to the New World where he became a tutor with the College of Philadelphia. He received an honorary M.A., and in 1767 was admitted to the bar, and in 1768 he set up a successful law practice in Reading, Pennsylvania.

Wilson was elected twice to the Continental Congress where he represented Pennsylvania. In 1774 he published, "*Considerations on the Nature and Extent of the Legislative Authority of the British Parliament*," where he was critical of Britain arguing that Parliament had no authority to pass laws over the colonies; and Parliament's taxation of the colonies was illegitimate because the colonies did not have any representation in Parliament. Wilson held the view that all power derived from the people, and that the colonists owed their allegiance to the British king. Wilson was one of six Patriots who signed both the *Declaration of Independence* and The Constitution of the United States, and he was forty-five at the time of the Philadelphia Convention in 1787. Wilson's understanding of past governments and political economics were valuable in the construction of the Constitution. Both James Wilson and James Madison are considered to be the most learned of the delegates at the Convention. Wilson helped to design the executive branch by proposing a chief executive that would be energetic, independent, and accountable to the American people. Popular sovereignty linked the interests of the people with the administration of the president, and dual sovereignty linked the nation and the states, and was an ongoing political problem that Wilson was competent to address. Wilson (along with Roger Sherman) proposed the Three-Fifths Compromise that counted slaves as three-fifths of a person to determine the allocation number of representatives in the House of Representatives. James Wilson also proposed the idea of the Electoral College. Wilson was a member of the Committee of Detail, and his contribution to the first draft of The Constitution of the United States (especially Article II), to the development of American jurisprudence, political theory, and the relationship between natural-law jurisprudence and Christianity is well-noted.[279]

After the Philadelphia Convention, James Wilson was a strong supporter for the ratification of the Constitution. His "speech in the statehouse yard" was delivered in the courtyard behind Independence Hall and was reprinted in newspapers to offer support for the document and voiced Wilson's strong commitment toward ratification. He focused on the fact that the people would hold the supreme power, and act by representation or collectively. Wilson had a clear, concise, and critical mind, and he was a nationalist in his thinking, along with Madison.

In 1789, President George Washington appointed James Wilson as one of the six original Justices of the United States Supreme Court, where Wilson served until his death in 1798. In 1789, the College of Philadelphia invited Wilson to give a series of law lectures where he would teach the foundations and science of American law. The first lecture was delivered on December 15, 1790, and they continued until 1792. Wilson hoped that his Lectures on Law would be an important American textbook for the law schools as an adjunct to William Blackstone's *Commentaries on the Laws of England*. The illustrious audience for these lectures on the principles of the American Constitution included President George Washington and his wife, Martha, John Adams, and both houses of Congress. Wilson addressed the moral, political, and legal philosophy of law. Wilson was critical of John Locke (1632-1704) and David Hume (1711-1776) because of their skepticism about the nature of the human being. Both philosophers, philosophized that human nature did not have the moral properties that are necessary to obtain a knowledge of justice. Wilson argued that their skeptical theories were not in harmony with a representative and democratic government that relies on a virtuous citizenry to sustain a democratic government.

Wilson believed in a common-sense 'moral sense' which is crucial to natural law, domestic law, international law, common law, and criminal law. Wilson argued that philosophical skepticism is an enemy to self-government. He taught that we do have the capacity for virtue because we have the innate capacity to know the natural law, and that the sovereignty and power of a nation resides in its people. (During the Constitutional Convention he argued for dual sovereignty). He further taught that moral properties are necessary for a knowledge of justice, with God being the source of justice, and the author of law. (Wilson was influenced by the Anglican theologian Richard Hooker whom he said was wiser than Locke. See Richard Hooker's *Of the Laws of Ecclesiastical Polity* written in approximately 1600). In Wilson's lectures and throughout his career, he appealed to the Christian natural law tradition and taught that all laws come from God. Wilson did not give a precise definition of law but did say that the origin of law is found in custom and received by the consent of the citizens of the society.

Wilson taught that the moral law is known by reason, and we can choose to obey or disobey the moral law. He divided God's laws into categories that are similar to the categories that Richard Hooker used in *Of the Laws of Ecclesiastical Polity*: the two-fold eternal law is further divided into the law of God for mankind, the laws of nature, and law celestial. The law of God for mankind is further divided into revealed law and natural law (natural law includes the law of nature and the law of nations). The revealed law and natural law both make up the human law. (Human law is made up of municipal law and the voluntary laws of nations which are part of the human law that we use to govern ourselves). The two-fold eternal law governs each of God's creatures according to the nature of the creature, i.e., natural law, law celestial, laws of nature, and human law. The eternal law is God's book of law that we are not able to access or open, while the celestial law is the law that rules the angels. The laws of nature are what governs and regulates all the phenomena of the material universe. Human law is made for the human beings in our present state. Human law flows from the taxonomy of revealed law and natural law. Wilson follows Richard Hooker's classification of law. See Richard Hooker's, *Of the Laws of Ecclesiastical Polity*. See also Saint Thomas Aquinas' *Summa Theologica* where St. Thomas also classifies law: the eternal law which is identical to divine reason and contains timeless truths, natural law, which is the goodness that we innately have, and our instincts that manifest our consciousness of God, divine law is the revealed Word of God in the Scripture, and human law is the human application of natural law.[280] Wilson believed that reason and revelation come from God — the incomprehensible Author and Creator of all things, and that they each flow in a different direction but are never separate nor in conflict with one another. Divine revelation is a friend to law. Wilson taught that Scripture supported and assisted reason, and that reason, revelation, and a moral sense all worked in harmony with one another.

Wilson taught that we possess our rights by nature. The Constitution of the United States did not create any new or novel rights; the goal of the Constitution was to preserve our rights and provide security for the recovery of rights that we already possessed. For Wilson, we all have a moral sense within our souls that enables us to know the moral forms. The moral principles that we rely on to form our government are due to our capacity for being a rational being. The first principles of natural law lie in our conscience. Wilson understood, and taught, that the first principles that underlie the positive law are the axioms of natural law. Blackstone taught that where the positive law was silent, then the natural law would come back into force.[281]

For James Wilson, natural law is the way that the human beings learn how to pursue their happiness, and how they achieve perfection. Wilson followed Blackstone's belief that God intended man to pursue his own true and substantial happiness. What separates us from the animal kingdom is that we have knowledge of the natural moral laws and are subject to these laws.[282]

One of the youngest members of the Convention at age thirty was New York delegate, Alexander Hamilton (1755-1804). Hamilton was born in Charlestown, the capital of the island of Nevis in the British West Indies.[283] He was self-assured and described by contemporaries as brilliant in his defense of a centralized government during the Convention. Later in his political career, his many accomplishments include his defense for a national bank. Hamilton believed in God-given natural law and natural rights, and as a Christian, he believed in original sin, which led him to a distrust of the "masses". In "The Farmer Refuted," (printed in 1775), Hamilton wrote, "the sacred rights of mankind are written in the whole of human nature by the hand of Divinity."[284] In 1777, General George Washington promoted Captain Hamilton to Lieutenant Colonel, where he served as a personal aide-de-camp to Washington during the Revolutionary War. During his wartime service to General Washington, Hamilton educated himself with reading philosophy, history, politics, economics, and geography. Historian Ron Chernow writes that Hamilton kept a prayer book that he filled with notes. Chernow observes that Hamilton "aspired to the eighteenth-century aristocratic ideal of the versatility of man conversant in vast areas of knowledge."[285] In 1782, Hamilton studied law, and was elected as a delegate to the Continental Congress (1782-83). In 1787, he served in the New York State Assembly, and then became a delegate to the Constitutional Convention. Jefferson did not play an active role in the Convention debates; his major speech at the Convention (on June 18th) was a lengthy six-hour speech that advocated a more centralized government. Hamilton's Federalist philosophy was overridden in the Convention by the other two New York delegates — Robert Yates and John Lansing, Jr. — who held Anti-Federalist positions. On September 8th Hamilton joined the Committee of Style and Arrangement with chair William Samuel Johnson, Rufus King, James Madison, and Gouverneur Morris. Gouverneur Morris was its chief draftsman, and within four days the Committee of Style and Arrangement condensed the articles from twenty-three to seven and wrote the historical preamble that is so familiar to all us, "We the People of the United States, to form a more perfect Union,..." Hamilton was the only New York delegate to sign the completed Constitution of the United States of America. After the Convention, Hamilton was instrumental in promoting and ratifying the Constitution when he wrote *The Federalist*, along with James Madison, and John Jay. Hamilton was again elected to the Continental Congress in 1787. Throughout his lifetime, Hamilton was a staunch abolitionist.

In 1789, Hamilton was appointed as secretary of the treasury under President Washington, where he served from 1789 to 1795. It was during this time that Hamilton strengthened the nation's finances with a budget system, funded the national debt, instituted a tax system, set up a customs service, created the Coast Guard, assisted in the creation of a powerful industrial nation which encouraged manufacturing, and formed the national bank and a national Mint.

In 1795, family commitments and financial burdens forced Hamilton to resign as secretary of the treasurer, thus he started the practice of law in New York City. He was appointed Inspector General of the Army from 1798-1800. On July 12, 1804, he died after suffering from a fatal wound that he received from a duel with Vice-President Aaron Burr.[286]

John Rutledge, an Episcopalian, and South Carolina delegate was born in Christ Church Parish, South Carolina, (1739-1800). He was a successful attorney who studied law in London and practiced in Charleston, South Carolina. Rutledge had been a Revolutionary leader prior to the Revolutionary War. (1739-1800). He was a colleague of Madison's in the First and Second Continental Congress until 1776 and served as attorney general and then governor of South Carolina (1779-1782). As Chairman of the Committee of Detail during the Constitutional Convention, his accomplished language ability gave the delegates a viable draft of the Constitution that was constructed from the original Virginia Plan, and modifications to the Virginia Plan after debates, arguments, disagreements, consensus, and agreements.

The New York delegates in attendance were John Lansing, Jr. (1754-1829), and Robert Yates (1738-1801). Robert Yates became a leader of the Anti-Federalist movement in opposition to the Constitution after the Convention.[287]

The Pennsylvania delegates in attendance were George Clymer (1739-1813), Thomas Fitzsimons (1741-1811), Jared Ingersoll (1749-1822), Thomas Mifflin (1744-1800), and Robert Morris (1798-1801). All the Pennsylvania delegates signed the Constitution.

On the first day, as well as the introduction of the Virginia Plan, Mr. Charles Pinckney's Plan was also introduced, but the details are obscure, and the plan was not debated or considered by the delegates in the debates.

The Founders discussed the law or the laws of nature, and

occasionally used the term 'natural law.' The legal protection of liberty and the rights and duties of a virtuous citizenry were part of their political theory. Equity and prudence were also moral guides.

John Adams and Thomas Jefferson were absent from the country during the Convention, with Adams in London, and Jefferson in France where both men were using their skills of diplomacy to convince Great Britain, France, Holland, and the power brokers in Europe that the United States could pay her debts and be trusted with commerce and treaties. Although absent from the convention, both men made their extensive and knowledgeable political views known through letters.

John Adams was born in Braintree, Massachusetts (1735-1826). He and his wife Abigail, both devout Christians, believed in natural law, and God's providence and guidance over the new nation. John Adams maintained that "rights are derived from the great legislator of the universe and are antecedent to governments."[288]

John Adams's book, *A Defence of the Constitutions of Government of the United States of America, Volume I* (London, 1787), was published in 1787, and read by Convention members. Convention members objected to the main argument in Adams's book that was favorable to a limited monarchy like the British constitution. James Madison, for example, wrote to Thomas Jefferson that men of learning will find nothing new in Adams's book. Madison complained in correspondence to Jefferson that Adams's book would "encourage the revival of the British Constitution in this country."[289] In his book, Adams examined the comparative governments of the democratic republics, the aristocratic republics, and the monarchical republics (both ancient and modern). The citations in his book included the use of Plato, Aristotle, Thucydides, Cicero, Swift, Franklin, Machiavelli, Montesquieu, Hume, Hobbes, and Joseph Priestley. Adams believed that Cicero was the greatest of all the philosophers and statesmen, and he followed Cicero's reasoning to recommend three branches of government. Like Socrates and Cicero, Adams was a dialectical thinker, and he believed that moral principles are self-evident, and are derived from rational intuition. Adams logical reasoning concluded that federalism, checks and balances in government with three parts to government — a strong executive, legislative, and judicial — and a bicameral legislature were the best forms of government for the new nation. The goal of law, for Adams, was public happiness, and this was achieved through justice and respect for rights. John Adams also felt that the social mobility that was created by the absence of the Crown was a positive thing for Americans, and he looked forward to the removal of the narrow constraints that had been imposed on the Nation by the British.

When John Adams read a copy of The Constitution of the United States of America signed at Philadelphia on September 17, 1787, and reaching London in the autumn, he viewed the document in a favorable light, but felt that the office of the presidency should have more power, and he was also concerned over the absence of a bill of rights.

Thomas Jefferson (1743-1826) was born in Shadwell in the Colony of Virginia. Jefferson was the author of the *Declaration of Independence*, a key Founding document stating our natural law heritage and affirming a belief in our Creator God, freedom, and individual liberty. He was a believer in individual rights, democracy, and republicanism, and was a gifted man of numerous talents including statesman, diplomat, lawyer, planter, politician, and architect. Jefferson served as the second Governor of Virginia, with two one-year-terms from 1779 to 1781, functioned as the United States Minister to France appointed in May 1785, served as the first secretary of state under President George Washington from 1790 to 1793, held the office of the nation's second vice-president from 1797 to 1801, and was the nation's third President from 1801 to 1809. Jefferson was an expert at surveying, horticulture, mathematics, mechanics, a philologist, and a prolific letter writer. However, the only book that he wrote was *Notes on the State of Virginia* (1785). His keen interest in philosophy and religion was noted throughout his life, and he founded the American Philosophical Society.

Jefferson was in France at the time of the Constitutional Convention, however, prior to the Convention he assisted Madison by sending him pertinent books on the history and philosophy of governing and the structure of the past governments of the world. The extensive correspondence between James Madison and Thomas Jefferson gives us an insight into two great minds who mutually benefitted from the ideas proposed to each other, and the letters show the perspicacious mind of Madison and Jefferson's capacity for theoretical speculation based upon reason and knowledge. Both men believed in natural law, the doctrine of the natural rights of man, freedom of the individual, religious freedom, political freedom, freedom of the mind, freedom of consciousness, the rule of reason, the rule of law, republican government, and government instituted for the enlightenment of the people with the goal of human happiness.

The Federal Convention convened on May 25, 1787, with the Virginia Plan being introduced to the convention on May 29, by Edmund Randolph, which would serve as an excellent starting point and outline for the deliberations that would ensue throughout the summer. The Virginia Plan was written by the Virginia state delegates after a process of discussion, investigation, analyses, explanation, dialogue, arguments, and compromise.

The delegates to the Federal convention met to revise the existing form of government under the Articles of Confederation. During the years before the Revolution popular leaders had relied on the concept of natural law to gain independence from Britain. Now that independence was won, the Convention delegates brought their belief in natural law with them to the Convention as a foundational concept. There was no need to define "natural law" — it was inherent in the beliefs of the delegates as demonstrated by Madison's notes of the convention. The "natural rights of the people", "public liberty", and "republican liberty" are phrases that are used by the delegates rather than "natural law".[290] Luther Marten used the theory of a state of nature when he argued in defense of state rights. The natural rights of individuals are protected by the state constitutions, and therefore, the state's rights must also be protected in the national constitution.[291] Hamilton argued that just like individuals give up shares of their liberty to enter society, the state's also give up a part of their sovereign power in order that a union of states may be formed.[292]

After independence, the Crown was no longer the sovereign power, so the colonists became the sovereign who created and constituted both state and national governments. The legal fiction of dual citizenship (See Article 1, Section 8, 9, and 10; Article IV, Section 2), where the citizens were citizens of both the state and national governments was an important concept. The concept of federalism was an entity that maintained its integrity and power while its constituent parts also maintained their freedom, power, and integrity.[293]

During the eighteenth-century including the ratifying debates for the Constitution, popular sovereignty was a widespread notion. The political system in the United States does not have a location for sovereign authority. Does sovereign authority reside in the federal government, in the state, in nature, in the cultural community, in The Constitution of the United States of America, in the laws, in reason, or in natural law? "See, the Sovereign Lord comes with power, and his arm rules for him." (Isaiah 40:10).

We examine James Madison for an understanding of the Constitution. The outline of a federal republic was something that James Madison introduced, and he maintained that this was a proper structure for a practical, reasonable, and workable republic. Madison stated that the two goals of the Constitution were to preserve liberty and create a stable and effective government. While many of the states felt that the Articles of Confederation should be reconstructed to fit the needs of the Union, Madison, however, shared his thoughts on why lesser changes to the Articles of

Confederation would not work, and why an enlarged republic with a sound structural form — with limitations placed on the states — would be the correct structure to ensure private rights.

Madison's political philosophy reflected the components of the dominant mid-eighteenth century thinking of the time that were influenced by the Cokean and Lockean philosophy. Coke's belief in natural law as a part of the laws of England, along with a jurisprudential approach to politics, and the Lockean philosophy that men are born into a "state of nature" and possess inalienable rights, but in a state of nature are without a government, and without the protection that a government guarantees. Some of these innate rights are deeded to the government when men join into the social contract to form a government bounded by laws. Both these philosophies were reflected in an egalitarian philosophy with the principles of a majoritarian democracy, where the members of the polity can discern and apply the laws of nature. Madison's political science reflects the practical outcome of this egalitarian philosophy. The Founders discussed the laws of nature, and occasionally they used the term 'natural law.' More common at the time was the usage of 'natural rights' language, that is, rights that govern human action, and these actions are virtuous. The legal protection of liberty and the rights and duties of a virtuous citizenry were part of this political theory. Equity and prudence were also moral guides to the creation of a government. While believing in natural law, Madison did not want to rely on natural law alone to preserve people's liberties. Madison understood that there needed to be limiting principles in place in the Constitution to prevent overreaching governmental power. He also knew that the enumeration of rights proposed in the Constitution were not a complete list, but that some enumeration was necessary to limit the scope of the federal government.

Republican theory prior to the Constitutional Convention claimed that the people had the authority to frame a constitution, and that the legal force of the constitution was taken from the authority of the people, who also restrict the abuse of power. The constitutional energy is generated from this authorizing power of the people, and it is an artificial authority because it is created by humans. The natural source of constitutional energy is given to us by nature and is an immutable and universal principle of our existence.[294] Robert J. Morgan equates the natural constitutional energy with the autonomy that a ruler has and the ruler's autonomous action; for example, the pursuit of fame or wealth, or even the power to wage war. In *Natural Law and The Constitution: The Law of All Laws*, this author equates the natural constitutional energy with the theory of natural law, which seeks the good of the individual and the nation. Both James Madison and Alexander Hamilton make references to constitutional energy and discuss the positive republican benefits that derive from a well-structured Constitution. James Madison writes in *The Federalist* No. 37, "Energy in government is essential to that security against external and internal danger and to that prompt and salutary execution of the laws which enter the very definition of good government."[295]

Hamilton and Madison also consider energy to be a necessary qualification for the federal government, but also for the executive office, i.e., the President of the United States.[296] Alexander Hamilton writes in defense of the Constitution in Federalist No. 15, "While they (those who oppose the Constitution) admit that the government of the United States is destitute of energy, they contend against conferring upon it those powers which are requisite to supply that energy."[297] Hamilton goes on in No. 70 to discuss the "necessity of an energetic executive....,"The ingredients which constitute energy in the executive are unity; duration; an adequate provision for its support; and competent powers."[298]

The natural law benefits of The Constitution of the United States are that the constitutional foundation sets a framework for the federal and state acts, with the interplay of the acts of the citizens, who are the beneficiaries of this sound constitutional structure — for the good of all the citizens. On a philosophical and religious level, natural law is an inspirational energy — a spiritual love for God;

wisdom for the past; understanding for the present; and happiness for the future.

In 1783, a pamphleteer called Tullius wrote *Three Letters Addressed to the Public*. Tullius distinguished between political sovereignty and juridical sovereignty, whereas political sovereignty belonged to Congress and juridical sovereignty belonged to the states. (3 Letters 12). Both Congress and the states exercised their spheres of sovereignty, where each sphere is independent, separate, and limited, (although Congress was invested with a more extensive authority), they both work toward the common goal of public safety and private happiness.

Madison was aware of the problems that had to be solved to bring together a consolidation of diverse states into a republic, while the states still retained some of their sovereignty. Madison searched for the Aristotelian middle ground that would generate a national authority that could generate enough power and energy to effectively govern the nation, while at the same time leaving the states with enough power to be useful for managing their own internal affairs.

The political models of Poland, and the Netherlands, as well as the Swiss cantons, were all loose confederations that were not adequate models for the governing of the American states. The ancient Greek republics, for example, the Achaean League and the Lycian Confederacy, were also examined by the delegates but could not be a guide for the American republic, because there were not enough details on the organization of these governments to be studied. The delegates decided that the separate states made up one unified political body. The philosophy of state sovereignty had to be reexamined to make way for the unified body of the republic.

While we study the intricacies of the Constitutional Convention, keep in mind the question of individual sovereignty? How do we, for example, progress from individual sovereignty to spiritual sovereignty? Ultimately, for the delegates involved with the formation of the Constitution, sovereignty was divided between the federal government and the states; then individual sovereignty (through State ratification committees) gave legitimacy to the Constitution and to the formation of the federal government, then spiritual sovereignty gives individual allegiance to God who governs through the natural law — while our Constitution gives us the formal construction for our behavior as members of the Nation. Politicians today are attempting to remove God's sovereignty from this equation, and to remove individual sovereignty from this equation, leaving the federal government alone as sovereign. We do not want this for our great Nation!

Two philosophies of union animated the delegates' discussion: a nationalist philosophy where the delegates argued for a powerful union, but to formulate this union the states must surrender some of their sovereignty; and a federalist philosophy where the delegates wanted the states to retain their sovereignty.[299]

The Convention delegates met daily in Philadelphia while they waited for a quorum. The Virginia Plan was Madison's agenda, and he had the goal of replacing the Articles of Confederation with a national government. With the establishment of a national government, the authority and power of the states would shift from the states to the federal level. After a process of discussion, investigation, analyses, explanation, arguments, dialogue and compromise, the Virginia Plan was formulated.

Chapter 11

Natural Law and the Federal Convention of 1787

On Friday, May 25th, the Convention delegates reached a quorum and entered the Independence Hall chamber to commence their business to form a federal government. Madison chose a seat front and center to take meticulous notes of the Convention and took it upon himself to preserve the historical record of the meetings to keep a clear and accurate record for future generations to use.

After the opening of the Federal Convention of 1787, the delegates unanimously elected George Washington as president of the Convention, then rules were set and agreed to on the 28th, followed by proposals agreed to on the 29th. One rule required that the delegates keep the contents of the meetings secret to avoid pressure from public opinion with the rule "that nothing spoken in the House be printed, or otherwise published, or communicated without leave."[300]

Delegate Edmund Randolph (Virginia) introduced fifteen resolutions of the Virginia Plan (also referred to as the Randolph Resolutions) on May 29th, and these resolutions served as an outline for a starting point for the deliberations. The Virginia Plan noted the need for correcting and enlarging the Articles of Confederation. The Virginia Plan conceived of a central republic at the head of a confederation of republics. (An example of the nationalist philosophy of the union). The Virginia Plan also provided for a national legislature with two branches (houses), the method of election for representatives for the two branches was by population and outlined some legislative powers, and a national executive and the method of election. A Council of Revision that had the power to veto Executive and

Judiciary Acts was recommended. A National Judiciary was to be set up with legal jurisdiction over admiralty, citizenship disputes, national revenue cases, impeachment cases, and legal issues involving national peace. There was provision for admitting new states to the union, with a guarantee of state territory and state governments. The Legislative, Executive, and Judiciary officers in each state were bound by an oath to support the articles of Union.[301] Delegate Randolph completed his presentation with a prompting to the other delegates, "not to suffer the present opportunity of establishing general peace, harmony, happiness and liberty in the U. S. to pass away unimproved."[302]

When Randolph finished his presentation of the Virginia Plan, it was submitted to a committee of the whole. Charles Pinckney, the statesman from South Carolina, also presented a plan known as the Pinckney Plan. Historically, we do not have a copy of the original Pinckney Plan but can deduce from supporting original sources that it was similar in its provisions to the Virginia Plan and called for the establishment of a central government with power and authority.[303] State representation in Congress was a contentious issue — whether the states would have an equal vote in the national legislature, or should representation be based upon population? After the debate, the delegates voted that representatives in the lower house should be elected by the people. The delegates wisely decided to act initially on matters of general agreement before they addressed the more provocative issues. (May 31 and June 1).

The delegates discussed, argued, and debated the numerous topics and agreed to discard the Articles of Confederation. Within a two-week period, the delegates had agreed to a legislature consisting of two houses that were proportioned to population, a national veto for state laws, a national judiciary to enforce federal laws, and outlined how to proceed for ratification.[304]

Luther Martin, Elbridge Gerry, William Paterson, and several other delegates were concerned that the proposed principles had gone beyond the Articles of Confederation, and that these principles were untried. On June 14, 1787, the Convention adjourned until the next morning so that the delegates might digest the details that had been proposed for the government system under consideration.[305] On June 15th, the delegates reconvened with the submission of the New Jersey Plan by William Paterson, the delegate from New Jersey. The New Jersey Plan was also known as the "Federal" Plan (Also referred to as the Patterson Resolutions, it reflected the federalist philosophy of the delegates), it did not alter the Articles of Confederation, but did provide for some amendments that established a supreme tribunal and taxation; however, the powers of the central government rested with the states.[306] The New Jersey Plan provided for a Congress with one house, for a plural Executive, a supreme tribunal, provisions for the admission of new states, and the states were to be bound by the laws of the United States. A Compromise Committee was appointed on June 30th after the delegates debated the Virginia and New Jersey Plans. Two weeks of debate ensued over the New Jersey Plan, also referred to as the "revolt of the small states."

The delegates who had lived during the American Revolution relied on the conception of the law of nature as the basis of their reasoning to resolve the difficult problems of the Convention. The rights and powers of the states and how the states should be represented in the legislature was a contentious political problem that nearly dissolved the Convention.

Luther Martin of Maryland, for example, had been sent to the Convention to protect states' rights, and he later attempted to prevent the ratification of the Constitution. Luther Martin spoke frequently during the Convention to argue for states' rights. On June 27th, Martin read passages from Locke, Vattel, and Lord Summers-Priestly to prove that individuals in a State of Nature are equally free and independent. He argued that "the States like individuals were in a State of Nature equally sovereign & free. That the States being equal cannot treat or confederate so as to give up an equality of votes without giving up their liberty."[307] New York delegate Robert Yates agreed with Martin and responded that, "the first principle of government is founded on the natural rights of individuals, and in perfect equality."[308] Massachusetts delegate Rufus King further questioned, "As the fundamental rights of individuals are secured by express provisions in the State Constitutions; why may not a like security be provided for the Rights of States in the National Constitution."[309]

The delegates that held a nationalist philosophy (George Washington, James Madison, Alexander Hamilton, Charles Pinckney, Benjamin Franklin, James Wilson, and Gouverneur Morris) and the delegates that held a federalist philosophy (Elbridge Gerry, George Mason, Oliver Ellsworth, and John Dickinson) understood that a compromise was needed to work toward the unity that would form the government. On June 30th, Benjamin Franklin stated that the delegates must compromise as a body "to make a joint."[310]

From June 15th through June 30th, the delegates debated the Virginia and New Jersey Plans. The debates revealed to both sides — the nationalists and the federalists — what their philosophy of government and governance was, and both sides clearly saw that they needed a compromise. On June 3rd the Compromise Committee was adopted and their findings were reported to the Convention on July 5th and debated from July 5th through July 16th. The outcome of the debates was the Connecticut Compromise which recommended a lower house (the House of Representatives) based upon proportional representation (the population of the state), and all money bills would originate in the lower House; and the Senate, where each state would have equal representation with two Senators.

The recommendations of the Connecticut Compromise were adopted on July 16th by a vote of 5 to 4 (Connecticut, New York, New Jersey, Delaware, and Maryland voted for the Compromise; Virginia, Pennsylvania, South Carolina, and Georgia voted against the proposal). Madison was disappointed and suffered a further setback to his agenda when the legislative veto was rejected by seven states. A further Convention measure made the legislative acts of the United States the supreme law of the land, known as the supremacy clause, a clause which would be strengthened during the remainder of the Convention.

Following the Connecticut Compromise, the delegates debated the "three-fifths clause" where three-fifths of the slaves would be counted for representation and taxation, the federal judiciary, Congress, the Presidency, the electoral college to elect the President, the provision for admitting new states, foreign commerce, and domestic commerce. On July 26th the delegates agreed upon a single executive — a President who would be elected for a term of seven years and ineligible for reelection. On August 6th a Committee of Detail gave Congress the power over the military establishment, taxation, and commerce.[311]

The draft of the Constitution provided for key protections of liberty. Scholar John P. Kaminsky writes in *The Constitution Without a Bill of Rights*, "that a number of individual rights were incorporated into the draft of the Constitution that were protective of individual liberty: the prohibition of the suspension of the writ of habeas corpus except in case of rebellion or invasion, the prohibition of bills of attainder and ex post facto laws, the provision for impeachment of all civil officers, the guarantee of jury trials in criminal cases, the narrow definition of treason, the ban on religious qualifications for office holding, and other clauses protected the rights to private property."[312] On September 12th, late in the Convention, George Mason (the author of the Virginia Declaration of Rights) introduced the idea of a Bill of Rights to preface the Constitution. Elbridge Gerry of Massachusetts agreed and proposed the motion that a committee be set up to draft a Bill of Rights. The delegates defeated the motion; they were focused on strengthening the federal government, not in limiting the governments powers. The omission of a Bill of Rights became the one important issue that (until it was resolved, and the rights of individuals were guaranteed with an inclusion of a Bill of Rights) would prevent the ratification of the Constitution of the United States. The Convention delegates agreed that an effective central government was needed with an independent source of revenue, authority to regulate the nation's trade, and power to compel the states and citizens to obey legitimate rules and laws.

Madison

Chapter 12

Natural Law: The Ratification of the Constitution

The Constitution of the United States was published on September 19, 1787, in a special issue of the Pennsylvania Packet. Congress read the Constitution on September 20th, and scheduled September 26th for its consideration. Congress resolved to transmit the Constitution to the state legislatures for their submittal to state conventions for deliberation and a vote on the ratification of the Constitution (September 28th, 1787). A vote for ratification was a vote for approval of the Constitution as it is, and any amendments, including a Bill of Rights, would be added later. If a state voted against ratification that state would not be a member of the new government. The Constitution was at first received with a favorable impression, but it quickly became evident that a successful adoption had to first overcome a strong opposition by the key states of Massachusetts, New York, and Virginia. The pamphlets and debates for and against the Constitution demonstrate the concerns and fears of the people on both sides: the Federalists favored ratification, and the Anti-federalists argued against ratification — both sides offered cogent arguments and asked thoughtful questions. Both sides believed in natural law and natural rights as the foundation for our government and individual actions.

The Federalist versus the Anti-Federalist debates were important historical dialogues that demonstrated our Constitutional foundation in natural law. The interchange of a dialectic between the Federalists and the Anti-Federalists is a sign of natural law. Dialectic, debate, rational arguments, a questioning nature — are all indications that the intrinsic nature of natural law is present. Natural law is a gift from God, and when functioning, it sets boundaries for our thoughts and actions. The Federalist versus Anti-Federalist debates clarified the political philosophy and science of the Constitution. The ongoing debates generated The Federalist, an important documentation of the political science of the Constitution, and the outcome of the debates led to the ratification of the Constitution, and the subsequent adoption of a Bill of Rights — key Constitutional Amendments for our freedoms.

The Anti-Federalists argued that there was no legal basis for the Constitution because the Philadelphia Convention had violated its purpose that was to revise the Articles of Confederation, and instead the Convention members created a whole new government. The Anti-Federalists also objected to the ratification of the Constitution through state conventions instead of Congress or state legislators, and the requirement for nine states for ratification instead of thirteen states, both provisions were also requirements for amendments to the Articles of Confederation.

The Anti-Federalists feared the new government and that the ensuing powers would rob them of their liberties — both individual liberty and state sovereignty. These threats posed a danger to the stability of established politics and law, to the inherent principles of the *Declaration of Independence*, and to the principles of federalism. They feared that the centralization of the government would create an all-powerful government that would take away the citizen's and state's rights. They also argued that all three branches of the proposed government were capable of tyranny, and the debaters were especially suspicious of the powers of the judiciary. There was also concern that the state laws would become subservient to the federal laws. The power of the Presidency was seen to lend itself to a monarchy or a potential tyranny. The congressional power to raise an army and navy cast doubt on the citizens to put their trust in this new government, along with the government's power to levy taxes, to regulate elections, and to make treaties. They also argued that the Constitution's elaborate theme of separation of powers and checks and balances did not protect the people from minority faction. The Anti-Federalist questioned how the Constitution would be responsive to the people? They continued to argue that by strengthening the federal authority through consolidation of the federal government, then the federal principles would be violated.

The opponents to ratification argued that there should be a Bill of Rights to protect the rights of the people. Hamilton argued that a Bill of Rights for the proposed Constitution was unnecessary because the Constitution itself is a bill of rights.[313] Madison agreed with this position, but later changed his mind in order to gain the confidence of the people that the people's rights cannot be encroached upon by the Government. On June 8, 1789, Madison proposed a Bill of Rights to Congress that was modeled on the ones that were submitted by Virginia. The proposed amendments were submitted to the states on September 25, 1789. The first ten amendments to the Constitution were ratified by the states by December 1791. The natural rights of the citizen may not be deprived by the government; and the powers not delegated to the United States are reserved to the States.

Alexander Hamilton, James Madison, and John Jay met the challenges to the opponents to the Constitution as they penned *The Federalist* that was published as a series of newspaper articles in New York under the pseudonym of Publius. (*The Federalist* first appeared in New York newspapers on October 27, 1787. The pen name "Publius" was chosen by Hamilton, named after Publius Valerius Publicola, the Roman counsel in 509, 508, 507 and 504 B.C., and one of the founders of the Roman Republic). *The Federalist* was an argument of support on behalf of the proposed Constitution and remains today a classic work of political theory and history that assists us in understanding the Constitution of the United States.

There were many prominent Anti-Federalists, including the Governor of New York, George Clinton, (who wrote as "Cato"), Mercy Otis Warren (who wrote as "A Columbian Patriot"), Richard Henry Lee, George Mason (Virginia delegate to the Constitutional Convention, who did not sign the document because it did not contain a Bill of Rights), Samuel Bryan of Pennsylvania (he or his father were thought to pen their opposition as "Centinel"), and Robert Yates, a delegate from New York, who left the Convention early in protest over the aims of the other delegates to disregard the Articles of Confederation and start fresh with a new document. The anonymous Anti-Federalist writer "Brutus" was thought to have been Robert Yates.

For many philosophers and political scientists, the truths of political science are tested by our experience. David Hume, for example, regarded political truths as defended through experimental or empirical reasoning.[314] Publius believed in the human essence that was created by the omnipotent Creator whose wisdom and love has blessed us with the law of nature. James Madison reflected in *The Federalist* that it was the almighty finger of God that guided the Philadelphia Convention to its successful agreements on the Constitution.

It was the skillful logic and clear explanations of Publius (Alexander Hamilton, James Madison, and John Jay) that defended the Constitution against the opponents' complaints — who were afraid of this new government. Publius' skillful arguments, analysis, practical reasoning, and concise writing skills are abilities that we learn from the wisdom of natural law. Natural law, natural rights and the laws of nature are at the root of the Founder's political theory. The laws of nature and natural rights govern our actions, and the practical experience of politics is successful to the degree that this experience maintains itself within the spirit of natural law. When we reflect on all the good that comes from practicing natural law, we envision the protections that are afforded to us by our Constitution: the goal of the Constitution is justice and happiness which entails natural rights, liberty, freedom, equality, and preservation of life, liberty, justice, peace, happiness, and prosperity.

For Publius natural law was an undeniable axiom in a demonstrative science (See John Locke and his attempt to develop morality as a demonstrative science). Although Publius presented the ideas of the Constitution in a practical manner which could be understood by the citizens, the truth of the politics of the construction and implementation of the Constitution would be understood through the actual experience of governing. James Madison believed in natural law, but he did not want to rely on natural law alone to preserve people's liberties. Madison understood that there needed to be limiting principles in place in the Constitution to prevent overreaching governmental power. He also knew that the enumeration of rights proposed in the Constitution was not a complete list, but that some enumeration was necessary to limit the scope of the federal government. Madison's political philosophy was demonstrated through his participation in the delegates' debates during the Constitutional Convention of 1787, and again in his writing in *The Federalist* to defend the Constitution.

Today, animating our experiential political system are the fair and equitable laws of our Nation that are governed by the laws of the Constitution of the United States of America. As citizens, we have a duty to obey the laws of our Nation — the statutes, and subsequent judicial review of our laws are intricate and constitutional guides for a Nation founded upon law. These constitutional laws were implemented through the wisdom of the Founders who had an understanding and obedience to natural law. As citizens of the United States of America, we owe our allegiance to the Constitution, and our ultimate sublime duty is to obey natural law for our spiritual allegiance is to God.

The Federalist discusses the fundamental principles of the Constitution: federalism, checks and balances, separation of powers (the legislative, the executive, and the judiciary. Montesquieu was the most cited philosopher in *The Federalist*; his discussion on the separation of powers from the legislative and executive powers is an archetype for the Madisonian separation of powers.), pluralism, and representation. James Madison writes in *The Federalist* No. 39 that the character of the novel republican government is a system of government which derives its powers directly or indirectly from the body of the people. The writers of *The Federalist* maintained that the citizens did not have to choose between confederation and consolidation. In *The Federalist* No. 39 Publius (James Madison) argued that the Constitution was a new form of government, partly national and partly federal. The Anti-Federalists argued that the Constitution placed sovereignty in the federal government and in the states, and dual sovereignty was not possible. The Constitutional argument for federalism was a fundamental concern for the Anti-Federalists.

James Madison wrote in *The Federalist* No. 43, "The transcendent law of nature and nature's God...declares that the safety and happiness of society are the objects at which all political institutions aim and to which all such institutions must be sacrificed."[315] Justice and happiness are both the ends of government.[316] We recall from our discussions about Plato, Socrates, and Aristotle that these wise philosophers taught the same idea — that justice and happiness are the ends of government.

The premise of *The Federalist* No. 55 (James Madison) is that there is sufficient virtue among us for self-government. But Madison states that government is not in the business of cultivating virtue and caring for the soul. So, the majority of us have a little virtue, a few of us have exceptional virtue, and we all insist on liberty that is found in every person by nature. It was John Locke who wrote about the necessity to replace the idea of choice, and hence virtue was replaced with interest. *The Federalist* talks about self-interest. We reflect on self-interest and think about Socrates who taught us how to develop our souls and virtue, where this is in our best interest. The Constitution is our American framework for a just legal system that provides the national stability and security so that we are free to develop our souls. The government may not be in the business of cultivating virtue, but the representatives of our government should, by the understanding of natural law, exhibit virtuous actions and honesty. Our leaders should also take the interests of the citizens to heart and provide the maximum amount of national stability and safety for the citizens to be able to exercise their freedoms — life, liberty, and the pursuit of happiness — unhindered and in peace.

The Anti-Federalists believed that there was a natural connection between the states and individual liberty and that the Constitution would abolish the constitutions of the states and, therefore, abolish individual liberty. They claimed that the governments that were created to secure individual rights in the *Declaration of Independence* were state governments and held that the government of the Union was to be subordinate to them. The Anti-Federalists also argued that the size of republican government should remain small to maintain a homogeneous population with similar cultures, interests, and habits, and in doing so, it would be able to maintain its responsibility to the people, and thus they would voluntarily and with confidence obey the laws.

The Federalists and Anti-Federalists agreed that the republican Government should rest directly upon the people so that they would have confidence and respect for the laws. The Federalists and Anti-Federalists disagreed on what form the government should take with the Federalists forming one republican government for the United States, and the Anti-Federalists preference was for a confederation of states. The Anti-Federalist believed that the representatives of the people should hold similar views, have compatible circumstances, be homogeneous in their thinking, and be sympathetic to their problems. This was an adequate description of the characteristics of state legislators, but this congruity and sameness in personal characteristics would be impossible on a federal level where the proportion of the representation would be too large and unwieldy. The Anti-Federalists then proposed that the yeomanry (the men who owned and cultivated estates and land) of the country would promote the public good because they are temperate and control their passions and appetites.

The Anti-Federalists argued that the proposed Constitution would undermine the trial by jury and stipulated that commerce would threaten the republican virtue as citizens would desire more wealth and luxury. They were concerned with civic education and feared that the Constitution showed an indifference to religion. The opponents to the ratification of the Constitution used the theory of natural rights to argue that the proposed Constitution was perverting the liberties and rights of the individuals and the states. As we have seen from the discussions by the delegates at the Federal Convention, the proponents of the Constitution were conversant with the theory of natural law and employed it for their benefit to urge the passing of the Constitutional document in order to create the new republican government.

The debates, arguments, and disagreements over the ratification of the Constitution brought out the strengths of the Constitution and the similarities of the philosophy and the beliefs of the Federalists and the Anti-Federalist. For all their differences, there was a common belief in natural law and fundamental natural rights that were inalienable. Each citizen participated in the contract, and therefore each citizen was a watcher and protector for our Constitutional rights.

Living in a Constitutional Republic defined by the Constitution, we have the freedom to choose our leaders. Socrates taught us that choice is an activity of the soul. Hamilton wrote in *The Federalist* No. 1 that our republican government depends on the people of this country to establish good government from "reflection and choice," not "accident and force." So, to protect our republican nation is the bedrock for the protections for our individual souls. The Framers used the scientific concept of interest to describe the difficult notion of the soul; instead of looking into our souls, we consult our self-interest. John Locke wrote about necessity to replace choice, and hence virtue was replaced with interest. The Federalists talk about self-interest, and we reflect on Socrates' words. The Constitution is our framework that provides the national stability, so we are safe and free to develop our souls.

As mentioned earlier, *The Federalist* No. 55's premise states that there is sufficient virtue among us for self-government. The government may not be in the business of cultivating virtue, but the representatives of our government should, by the understanding of natural law, exhibit virtuous actions and honesty. Our leaders should also take the citizens interests to heart and provide the maximum amount of national stability and safety for the citizens to be able to exercise their freedoms — life, liberty, and the pursuit of happiness — unhindered and in peace.

The dialogue and differences between the Federalists and Anti-Federalists strengthened the arguments of *The Federalist* which has enriched us with a better understanding of the Constitution of the United States. The differences between the Federalists and the Anti-Federalists does not overshadow their similarities, i.e., they were united in the belief in natural law and the purpose of the government was to protect individual rights, and that this was best achieved through some form of republican government.

Natural law is the body of innate principles that guide us as we govern ourselves. Our lawmakers, representatives, and judges respect natural law, and their laws and rulings are in harmony with natural law. Natural law is not a substitute for positive law, but it is the reasoning framework that guides our intellectual understanding of the rule of law. We inhabit natural law; natural law lives within us and operates as our guiding moral principles.

During the Convention of 1787, the delegates did not incorporate the specific guarantees of rights into the Constitution, with rare exception. Madison specifically felt the need to protect freedom of the press and the rights of conscience — however, both were not specified in the body of the Constitution. Historians agree that this omission was due to the task of the Convention — to enlarge the powers of the federal government not to restrict those powers. When George Mason voiced his concerns and expressed a desire for a Bill of Rights, all the state delegates unanimously rejected his proposal. Later, James Madison promised his constituents that he would support a Bill of Rights in the House of Representatives if they would elect him, and he kept his promise by focusing on the Virginia convention, and George Mason's "Virginia Declaration of Rights of 1776."

The Constitution presupposes natural law doctrine, and the content of this natural law is the common good that we all seek as human beings. We have learned from St. Thomas, for example, that the content of our morality is good and is to be done and pursued, and evil is to be avoided.[317] This is the first principle of practical reason for St. Thomas. Our seeking a good is directed to action because we all seek that which is good. St. Thomas also taught us that the goods of human beings are to preserve our life, sexual intercourse, the education of our children, living in society, living according to reason, and to know the truth about God.[318] The natural law is our common moral knowledge that we obey because of our natural inclination to do that which is good and avoid that which is evil.

The Founders and the nation's citizens knew that absolute limitless power belonged only to God. When the Founders wrote the Constitution, they enumerated powers granted by the Constitution; however, they did not specify all the powers to be granted to the various governmental institutions. Instead, they vested power only in those institutions enumerated in the Constitution: to the President of the United States of America (the executive Power, Article II), the legislative Powers (vested in a Congress which consists of the House of Representatives and the Senate, Article I), and the judicial Power (vested in the Supreme Court and inferior courts that are established by Congress, Article III). All these institutions and the individual citizens that are voted into these offices or appointed by Congress are bound by the text of the Constitution of the United States.

The Federal government performs only the governmental tasks which cannot be performed by state and or local government. If the federal power is not enumerated in the Constitution, then it belongs to the States. The principle of subsidiarity was defined in the Tenth Amendment, adopted in 1791: "The powers not delegated to the United States by the Constitution, nor prohibited by it to the States, are reserved to the States respectively or to the people." Therefore, powers are reserved to the States if not delegated to the United

States, and there are some powers that do not belong to the government and are reserved to the people."

The original document of the Constitution did not contain a charter of rights, because the delegates feared that an enumeration of rights would guarantee more rights to the national government than it possessed. During the ratification process it was agreed that a Bill of Rights would be added to guarantee traditional rights. In the first session of Congress twelve amendments were initially proposed with only ten being ratified. Our freedom and rights existed before the Constitution, so the Bill of Rights does not create them but merely serves to make certain that the national government does not invalidate them. These rights are derived from the Common Law tradition, and therefore from Natural Law.

James Madison famously wrote in *The Federalist* that we are not angels, nor are we depraved.[319] The states and federal government are natural institutions. The Constitution does not exist to perfect mankind (which it cannot do) or to repress him (which it should not do). The Constitution does not attempt to control every virtue or vice. The Founders did not explicitly state that they were applying natural law principles to the Constitution, but the goal of the Constitution was to promote the common good by acting or not acting according to the circumstances as prescribed in the Constitution, and the nature of man. We have learned that one of the goals of natural law is to promote the common good of all human beings. For the writers of *The Federalist*, the goal of good government was to establish justice and promote the welfare or happiness of the people (citizens) as a whole.

One of the most widely read *The Federalist* No. 10, defends the republican form of government — a republic is where representation takes place — that is proposed by the Constitution. Madison discusses his theory of factions, and writes, "By factions, I understand a number of citizens, whether amounting to a majority or a minority of the whole, who are united and actuated by some common impulse of passion, or of interest, adverse to the rights of other citizens, or to the permanent and aggregate interests of the community."[320] Madison explains that the latent causes of faction are sown in our nature and take many forms: different religious opinions, different views about government and our leaders, ambition, power, jealousy, oppression, conflicts, and the most common cause of faction is an unequal distribution of property.[321] The causes of faction cannot be removed but relief can be sought by controlling its effects.[322] He then states, "To secure the public good and private rights against the danger of such a faction, and at the same time to preserve the spirit and the form of popular government, is then the great object to which our inquiries are directed."[323] Madison continues, "Men of factious tempers, of local prejudices, or of sinister designs, may, by intrigue, by corruption, or by the means, first obtain the suffrages, and then betray the interest of the people."[324] He concluded that a strong united Republic can effectively control factions, and the multiplicity of a diversity of interests and opinions found in a larger Republic can effectively control factions.

In *The Federalist* No. 43, he defended the legitimacy of the Constitution, "the transcendent law of nature and of nature's God...declares that the safety and happiness of society are the objects at which all political institutions aim and to which all such institutions must be sacrificed."[325]

Madison's *The Federalist* No. 51 is an examination of the checks and balances of the branches of government created by the Constitution. We maintain constitutional boundaries by "exterior provisions." When exterior provisions fail, then we rely on auxiliary precautions, "By so contriving the interior structure of the government as that its several constituent parts may, by their mutual relations, be the means of keeping each other in their proper places."[326] The end of government is justice. Power is separated but it must also be checked. The Constitution provides for the important parameters of the three branches of government with separation of powers (with separate functions but shared power), checks and balances, and bicameralism. There are many crucial governmental checks written into the Constitution: the president can veto legislation, (the executive has the power of the veto (the negative) — Madison thought that the executive was the weaker branch, but it too could exceed its constitutional boundaries. "The interest of the man must be connected with the constitutional rights of the place.",[327] the legislature can override the President's veto with a two-thirds majority vote, treaties made by the President must be approved by the Senate, the Senate must approve presidential appointments, Congress can make lower courts, or dismantle lower courts, Congress can determine the size of the Supreme Court, Congress can determine the appellate jurisdiction, Congress can set the salary for the executive and the judiciary, and Congress can impeach members of the executive and judicial branches."

The Federalist Nos. 78 through 83 written by Alexander Hamilton, discusses the judiciary: the manner of constituting the judiciary, the mode of appointing judges, the independence of the courts of justice, the powers of the judiciary, the authority of the judiciary, and the distribution of the judicial authority between the supreme court and the inferior courts of the Union. Our Justices are bound by the Constitution, the text of the Constitution, precedent, and *stare decisis*. The Judiciary Act of 1789 completed a part of the political system left out in the Constitution, as did Chief Justice Marshall's Supreme Court ruling in Marbury v. Madison (1803).

The ineffectiveness of The Articles of Confederation was solved with the construction of the Constitution of the United States which created a republic with the direct involvement of the citizens who elected Congressional members who then passed laws that affect those citizens who elected them. All the authors of *The Federalist* (the Publius triad of James Madison, Alexander Hamilton, and John Jay) believed in natural law and an egalitarian government. Natural law is reflected in the Constitution of the United States of America through the establishment of a limited government, the establishment of subsidiary, and the guarantee of traditional rights. The writers of *The Federalist* were not philosophers, and they did not define natural rights, or natural law, nor justice. However, they did write that the goal of good government is both justice and the happiness of its citizens. The Founders have given us the form of good government in the Constitution of the United States of America. For the Founders of our Nation, justice and happiness were married to natural law, and we are the fortunate progeny of that belief. We leave this chapter with a question for the reader to think about within the religious dimension: what role will America take in the millennial apocalyptic context of grace where Christ's reign over the saints will usher in an American utopia with the perfection of our human capacities to understand natural law?

Chapter 13

Natural Law: No Higher Law

"The law of the Lord is perfect, reviving the soul. The statutes of the Lord are trustworthy." (Psalm 19:7).

Our blessing as a nation is that we already possess a workable form of a republican government in the Constitution, but we must remind ourselves that the guardianship of government is the responsibility of each citizen so that our protections under the Constitution for individual rights does not degenerate into an autocratic regime. The Founders' vision of a good government was based upon fundamental rights and these principles were based upon natural law.

The principles of freedom are alive in the minds of each individual prior to its extension in a societal class. Everyone has a unique function, as does the community, but where they are similar is the end toward which they seek, varying in degree but not in kind. This end is freedom. Freedom is the natural heritage of humankind. Freedom is our natural heritage from God. For the individual living within a free community, freedom is superadded to existence even when the individual is passive in relationship to furthering the ends of freedom for the community. However, freedom is contiguous with existence when the individual is actively seeking the ideals, ideas, and practice of freedom. The most expeditious way to restore our republican faith — and our trust in the Constitution — is for the rise of innovative ideas, and a vigorous growth of freedom. Freedom as an idea will necessarily lead to free activity. Freedom evolves as we participate in freedom as citizens; a work of freedom entails a work toward freedom, and the idea of freedom leads to the practice of acts by citizens living within a free society; a society that is freedom loving.

If we become passive in relationship to our freedoms, we can pick up the Bill of Rights — written laws that establish the principles of natural law — and we then remember the safeguards of freedom and liberty that are written in the positive laws of the United States. The First Amendment, for example, protects our civil liberties: freedom of religion, freedom of speech, freedom of the press, freedom of assembly, and freedom to petition the government.

In the eighteenth century, the individual was the center of society and rights were considered as an absence of power, and power was circumscribed by the law. Liberty was exercised when there is the absence of power to restrict its exercise. The Bill of Rights limited the power of the government by enumerating the powers of the government, and by delineating how the citizens can express their will through the government. With the development of the Constitution, rights can be considered to trump power.[328] Today, expanded government control and extensive regulations over the polity, with more interference and supervision over the affairs and activities of individuals, have led to a dark philosophy that believes that rights can be limited through government interference. Government control over our lives, along with censorship on social media, and false news broadcasts have led to American citizens today who are skeptical about our future, and unhappy over the censorship of the truth. We need to work harder to find the sources that will reveal the truth. Be a truth-seeker, and support those who stand in the light of truth.

We are studying natural law because we seek truth; and God has given us the anchor of natural law to understand truth. The moral ground of the law is based upon natural law. We have lost sight of this eternal truth which has been camouflaged by the sociologist, progressive, and atheistic practices of those in power who deliberately want a confused and divided community. The understanding of natural law provides the template necessary for us to understand the eternal truths of God's presence in our lives.

Our prayer is that God heals our Nation that is currently divided: we have those who believe in the truths of the Constitution of the United States of America, the freedoms of the American citizens under the Constitution, the inalienable rights of American citizens, that we are a Nation under law, that we are a Nation under God, and that as human beings, we have an innate Natural Law instilled in us by our Creator God. We have discovered that natural law theory is universal, and that our purpose as humans is to seek the good, and this good is discovered through reason. Moral principles are universal and objective and discovered through reason that is bequeathed to us by God through natural law. If we follow natural law, then we strive to be a good person, and we also do our best to be good citizens of our community. The concept of natural law is fundamental for our intellectual development, and this development fulfills a basic need within us for justice.

Natural law are laws that are applicable to all human beings and are universal in nature, immutable, and inalienable. When we obey natural law, we are cooperating with God's divine plan for us. Natural law lays down our foundation for an understanding of our rights and duties. Individual rights are rooted in natural law. Our individual rights are those that we are entitled to due to our God-given nature. Any infringement upon our individual rights is an act that is not in harmony with God's laws for us. We act in accordance with natural law to fulfill the ends of the human being according to God's plan for us. God bestows upon us our freedom to act in accordance with natural law, and we develop a self-conscious knowledge of ourselves acting in spiritual fulfillment with natural law. Our self-conscious acts develop into a social consciousness where we develop a social nature which leads to friendships within the community. Religion and the pursuit of the truth as it relates to our life as one of God's creatures gives our life meaning and depth. This knowledge is the development of the soul and our spiritual relationship to God. He gives us experiences in which we may exercise our natural law, and these experiences lead to spiritual wisdom. Aesthetic experiences in life reinforce the beauty of God's kingdom and His earthly creation, and God has given us, as well, the capacity to reason and think in depth and ask the abstract and difficult questions about God and our relationship to God; and, He has also given us the joy of love and play and rest.

And we have those in our nation who currently condemn the Constitution and want to discard it to redefine our government to justify a Marxist government without limits. The leading progressives of the past are the philosophers Georg Wilhelm Hegel (1770-1831), Karl Marx (1881-1883) and Friedrich Engels (1820-1895), (See the Communist Manifesto), Herbert Croly (1869-1930), and John Dewey (1859-1952). The Progressive political movement believes that we should adapt our government for the social changes that are occurring. The progressives want to change the government, politics, and human nature through social engineering, and they believe in a process ideology that replaces God with the consciousness of a whole community. This community is accepted as valid only if it meets the criteria of constructivism, scientism, social experimentation, societal progress and process, and the administrative state of a centralized government. The progressives want to take the knowledge away from the individual and place it into the hands of the committee which has the "learned expertise" to solve our problems. For the radical progressives, the history of the past is not relevant to our current circumstances because each historical period is incomplete, and therefore, is not relevant to our current circumstances. The individuals' freedom, free will, and independence is absorbed by the state for the good of the whole. Everything is relative to the moment; there is no universal moral order. There are no universal or external truths. There are no inalienable rights. There is no natural law. There is no God — the progressives disparage constitutional republicanism, democracy, and capitalism. For those of us who worship God Almighty, we know that God gives us the means to create and express our talents, and there is nothing more humanly creative than the free individual, who still has the power to exert positive change within an historical period.

For the radical progressives, our modern law has become positivistic with a detachment from truth, true beliefs, our ties to family, our cultural heritage, and social organizations. Law is used to govern our behavior, and more laws are then applied to existing laws. Our national moral values have become disconnected from our polity. With a loss of a shared national vision and a loss of believe in natural law, we are witnessing abhorrent human behavior. It is hard to imagine how a human being can shoot masses of other human beings for no reason at all, it is abhorrent that a human being will murder another human being because his or her beliefs are different, and it is heart-breaking that a human being will kill a child for no reason at all. But that is sadly what we are witnessing today! From the words of wisdom of American Gospel preacher, Reverend Bill Owens, "these indiscriminate murders are not going to be fixed by the politician but is a tragedy of a spiritual disconnect from God," and all the effects of this disconnect are seen in the dysfunctional family unit, disharmonious social structures, and cities that are broken and unsafe.[329]

The modern cynical and hateful views of some of our leaders who hate our Nation, our Constitution, and our Founders are given a voice and a platform by the bitter and savage press, who are complicit in trying to tear down our government, our duly elected President, our democracy, our capitalism, our free-market economy, and our freedoms. The self-defeating liberals who avow a hatred for the United States want the Constitution "out of the way" so that they may promulgate progressive ideas that are Marxist in origin. For the Marxist there are no individual rights, just rights that are artificially bequeathed to us by the general collective will. For the Marxist, there is no God, and no higher spiritual realm, no human universal nature, and no human soul. This deliberate disintegration (through violence and bloodshed) of our nation's laws, our Constitution, our Bill of Rights, our President, our police force, our culture, our heritage, our statutes, our history, our government, our politics, our leaders, our personal views, our beliefs, and religion is taking place as, horrified, American's watch in silence because they are threatened, intimated, and bullied by the left.[330]

A polity relies on the reasoned exchange of ideas by its citizens to have a healthy republic. Political discourse and dialectic are critical to enrich the citizen body and should not be used to divide and diminish the political body. Our republican government relies on public debate of ideas that is full, open, and unhindered. Civil discourse is valued to enliven our polity and the quality of the debate raises the consciousness of the listeners. Reasonableness and candor are qualities that our extraordinary Founders used, and they are also modern qualities that should help us to maintain and value our freedoms and secure American constitutionalism.

The hate-mongers and pessimists have tried to frighten the God believers into silence by verbal and physical assaults; but we will not be silent! We believe in God! We believe and obey God's natural law! We follow the precepts of our Lord. We worship God. We believe in our Nation and our Constitution. We respect and obey our Constitution and our Bill of Rights. And most importantly we pray; and our prayers are for God to Bless the United States, for God to heal our Nation, for God to bless our Constitution and our Bill of Rights, and for God not to remove His divine protection from the United States of America. We believe in individual spiritual sovereignty that is bestowed upon us by God's natural law.

For those who walk and pray in the light of the Lord, our belief in the universal truths of natural law continues to ground our moral values. Historian Grant Gilmore reminds us that a perfect society needs no law. "In heaven there will be no law, and the lion will lie down with the lamb. In hell, there will be nothing but law."[331] The Holy Bible reminds us in Isaiah, "The wolf and the lamb will feed together, and the lion will eat straw like the ox, but dust will be the serpent's food.

They will neither harm nor destroy on all my holy mountain, says the Lord" (Isaiah 65:25). "The wolf will live with the lamb, the leopard will lie down with the goat, the calf and the lion and the yearling together; and a little child will lead them." (Isaiah 11: 6). The Holy Bible continues, "For the earth will be full of the knowledge of the Lord as the waters cover the sea." (Isaiah 11:9)

The Constitution is a visible written form of law and a reminder that God has bequeathed to us a Nation indivisible under God. Our cultural ethos flows from the true proposition that God is the ruler of our Nation. How blessed we are to experience His beneficence, and to live under Constitutional guidance that gives us a visible form for the rule of law. Our love for God is under attack by the believers in the Progressive and socialist agendas where they are trying to break down our Christian and religious traditions to have unlimited power for the government and themselves. We will not allow them to succeed. And we will not stray from our path toward God, and our worship for His Holiness. Do not be afraid, we are under God's protective wing!

We are gathered within the Body of Christ, and proclaim our love, worship, and devotion to God. We are battling the collective vision of progressives, and Marxist ideology that wants to remove the individual uniqueness of the American citizen. Progressive liberalism (and its sister Marxism) places an emphasis on atheism and agnosticism and puts their belief in the large administrative state. Progressives demand that all men and women be made equal even though it be made at a heavier cost to others, so that it is not true equality. The liberals call it "equity." Progressives remove God from the individual belief, from the state, the government, and from the nation. Progressives manipulate the polity to conform to their politics of remaking our human nature as divorced from God. The Progressives teach that human beings are malleable and can be remade in a Utopian Marxist vision where the individual is "perfected" through the government institutions, the culture, economic structure, legal and political institutions. The individuality and uniqueness of the human being created in the image of God is recast by the liberals to project a malleable being whose rights are not inalienable but dispersed by a government which dispenses every privilege to its citizens (if the citizen is adhering to the government's propaganda) to achieve an equality of outcome, i.e., equity! Progressives dislike pragmatic philosophy: conservatives, however, see a problem and want to fix the problem with reasoning, common sense, and constructive dialogue. Progressives want to shut the conversation down by calling the opponent a racist, bigot, or shaming the opposition into silence.

We will not be silenced! The United States was founded by individuals who freely inquired into the nature of good government, and their role within that government, and their role within the community. Americans are intelligent and inquisitive individuals who will not be bullied into silence by elite charlatans who do not have the best interests of the United States of America and her citizenry at heart. We carry the Christian spirit within us; a spirit of natural law which requires that we freely choose the best moral leaders for the interests of our Nation and its citizens. The natural law spirit requires that we ask questions, that we dialogue with each other, and that we freely debate the issues that affect all of us. This is our heritage; a heritage paid for with the blood of our ancestors who fought to keep the American freedoms and Constitutional government alive.

Chapter 14

The Constitution and the Law of Laws

The United States was founded as a natural rights republic. There were many influencing ideas on the founders of our Republic, but natural law and natural rights were the foundational ideas. The role of classical Greece and ancient Rome are considered to be strong influences on the thoughts of the founders. English common law and Whiggish thought also had an influence on republican ideas. John Locke and the Enlightenment philosophers also had an influence on our Nation. We have taken all these ideas into consideration and maintain that the key for our republic was the idea of natural law and what the founders most often referred to as natural rights.

Democracy is an outgrowth of our understanding of natural law. Freedom, equality before the law, justice, liberty, freedom to choose our state and federal representatives, freedom to choose our President, religious freedom, autonomy, individual rights, property rights, economic rights, and human rights are all the outgrowth of God's natural law. The concepts of natural law are the criteria for judging all these areas, and our spiritual inspection can lead to an enlightened age of human freedom. We can flourish as a nation under God's guidance with natural law, as it is revealed to us as the will of God and thought in His Holy Word. Our ultimate purpose is to love God with our whole heart. We are also commanded to love our families, neighbors, and others. Our ultimate goal is human happiness, and loving God and others brings us happiness. We have the most fertile ground for the exercise of natural law within the United States where the Constitution is our guide for the rule of law, and the rule of law is where we find God's natural law and His Will to preserve our nation.

Natural law keeps us mentally and spiritually situated in a holy perspective in relationship to God and to each other. Our religious ideas transform into our philosophical ideas, and these ideas influence our political ideas. Constitutional scholar Edward S. Corwin writes, "In the American written Constitution, higher law at last attained a form which made possible the attribution of it of an entirely new sort of validity, the validity of a statute emanating from the sovereign people."[332] Corwin goes on to teach us that this statutory form has been backed up by judicial review.[333] What has happened today in our current political climate to our individual sovereignty as citizens of a nation that has now regulated the creation of our laws to bureaucrats who are not elected by the citizens? There is a shadow penumbra of doubt about whether our current President was legitimately elected by the citizens, and this uncertainty is carried over into the question of "Who is running the Presidency?" — When the President does not make any public appearances and appears to be confused, does not take any questions from reporters, and has not scheduled a State of the Union address. Add this to the fact that he is "ruling" by Executive Order, and none of the Executive Orders will benefit American citizens, neither are they neutral Executive Orders — their impact will have a negative impact on American's livelihood, economy, jobs, quality of life, diminishing the rule of law, and damaging our domestic and national security. Biden's Executive Orders are designed to carry out the progressive agenda: open borders, the Green New Deal, reliance on solar and wind power to the detriment of the United States being gas and oil energy independent, and not to mention the immediate job losses from the energy sector, overturning all the Trump initiatives that have proven to be positive for the health, wealth, and security of American citizens, and giving preferred precedence to illegals coming into the United States, many who have tested positive for COVID. The Republican Governor of Texas, Greg Abbott, recognizes the health, job, and security threat to Texan citizens, and he has ordered the National Guard, the State

Troopers, air, ground, marine and tactical border security assets in "Operation Lone Star" to the Border to counteract Biden's Executive Order's allowing illegals to cross the Border and be released into the American communities. Governor Abbott recognizes that the Biden Administration's immigration policies have instituted a "Border crises," a humanitarian crisis, and is an act that endangers the lives of Texans. The Biden Administration plans to process immigrants and release them into the United States sovereign territory within seventy-two hours. This overturns the Trump Administration's policies which forced asylum seekers to remain in Mexico until their cases were heard in the United States. The Trump administration's policies curtailed the actions of the Mexican Cartels and smugglers who are now actively moving drugs and people into Texas and the United States. Biden's actions do not have the welfare of American citizens in mind; their policies are not in conformity to the United States Constitution; Biden's policies violate federalism by ignoring state laws and interests, and even suing (through the politicized Department of Justice) state laws that they disagree with; Biden's policies violate the separation of powers by making the executive branch of government the superior branch by attempting to pass laws without congressional debate and approval.

The safety and security of American citizens is a sacrosanct responsibility of any American president. Our armed forces also expect competent military leadership when they are deployed on a mission. The failure of the Biden Administration to protect our American citizens and American troops with their hasty and incompetent withdrawal from Afghanistan is a monumental failure and demonstrates the Biden Administration's inability to govern. We lost thirteen United States service members on August 26, 2021, when a suicide bomber detonated a bomb outside the Kabul airport. As well as the loss of the lives of our military, and Americans abandoned in Afghanistan, the military left behind an estimated 85,000,000,000 dollars in abandoned weaponry, and abandoned Bagram Air Base -- a strategic air base. As American citizens we question why the Biden Administration would allow the Taliban (a brutal regime) to gain control of Afghanistan? This botched handling of the military withdrawal of Afghanistan does not leave American citizens more secure or safe.

The progressives have always had the goal of a more powerful executive branch of government. The administrative state is another progressive goal, which they claim is based on scientific principles; but it is a goal for a power grab, where any rational dissenter is labeled a "racist" or worse. For example, Marine Lt. Colonel Stuart Scheller, Jr. was recently imprisoned without any charges for demanding accountability for the botched Afghanistan withdrawal. We see how the progressive scientific methodology works, for example, when the current administration frequently changes the COVID narrative to fit their political narrative. The progressives work toward their end goal of consolidated power, it does not matter to them how many American citizens are put out of work or have lost their freedoms and liberties. For Americans watching this debacle, the evidence shows that the progressives are tearing down our Nation, our United States Government, and our United States Constitution! Supporters of Donald J. Trump, and conservative republicans have been demonized by the press, by the current administration, and have been silenced by Big Tech! For those of us who believe in our Constitution, believe in our Republican democracy, believe in the rule of law, believe in God's natural law, and believe in God, we have turned to prayer. Christian believers are being demonized by the demon! Let us remember that God is an all-powerful God! We pray that God does not withdraw His protection from the United States of America and American citizens.

Natural law provides the foundation for the Constitution, and this foundation entails the natural rights and popular sovereignty of the people. Constitutional dialogues and reason are the instruments that keep the Constitution at the forefront of our focus to maintain our rule of law and our liberties. Judicial review is a key element of our natural law, where the power of judicial review binds us as citizens to the Constitution. Citizens today are questioning why the Supreme Court — the Highest Court of authority in our land — did not hear any of the cases that gave the evidence for voter fraud, unconstitutional mail-in ballots, questionable voting machines, illegal interference by other nations, questionable tabulation of votes, ballot harvesting, unconstitutional denial of republican observers at the polling places, voter irregularities, and unconstitutional behavior by state courts and officials. Some political writers and commentators have speculated that the Supreme Court did not want to examine any of the cases that would nullify the 2020 election results because they were afraid that it would ignite riots: there is evidence that this was a coup against our legitimately re-elected President Trump, and this cannot stand unchallenged, election fraud must be exposed to protect the integrity of our election system and to protect our United States Constitution and our Republic. The truth must be revealed so that our legitimate Constitutional right to choose our elected officials will be recognized and not be nullified, and so that our Republic is not overthrown. If the claims by President Trump and his allies that the election result were illegitimate are false claims as the democrats maintain, then let us examine the evidence to determine what is the truth. An unwarranted fear of violence is nothing compared to what American citizens must endure if our Nation is compromised and overthrown!

Aristotle wrote about four forms of government: monarchy, aristocracy, democracy, and mixed government. The form of the United States government is none of these — its uniqueness and workability are unparalleled in history. The genius of Madison's thinking was to create a republican government with the working idea of federalism — an idea that had no prior historical prototype to follow in his analysis. The Madisonian Constitution — with the distribution of the powers of the three branches of government, i.e., the executive, legislative and judicial, creating checks and balances to keep the necessary tension to keep the Constitutional document alive — is the symbol of our polity.

Nineteenth-century Christian writer, preacher and activist, Orestes Augustus Brownson (1803-1876) defended the United States Constitution when he wrote that the American system of government is better than any other system of government, "because it accords more nearly with the principle of things, the real order of the universe."[334] There are many factors for good constitutional decisions: judgement, discretion, precedent, policy, original intent, common law, cultural factors, and custom. And, we must add courage to this list, as it appears that this human quality was lacking in our recent Supreme Court refusals to hear or take up the numerous documented disputes related to the 2020 election. For the citizens, judgments on our laws also take these factors into consideration, and individuals also bring their own creativity into problem-solving. Human creativity is a sign that the human being is indeed utilizing natural law. Along with human creativity is imagination, and the ability to exercise the creative imagination for a better Nation. As creatures of God and as His children who are endowed with natural law, we utilize our creative spirit to propose positive changes (and challenges) to our government that will enrich the future for the well-being and happiness of all Americans. And we pray for the courage to be able to achieve a better Nation; God gives us courage and we take our courage from the strength that we gain in the Lord!

How we think about the Constitution matters as we approach the constitutional cases, documents, and judicial review from our natural law understanding, and as lay persons without legal or judicial training. We do not have to be a constitutional scholar to read and understand our Constitution, we must make the effort to understand our Constitution — because freedoms that are not guarded by the individual are freedoms that are at risk of being taken away by those who seek power for themselves! We understand that our allegiance is first to God, and we live within the framework that He has blessed us with — He (along with the Founders) has created a space within our Constitutional Republic for our autonomous freedoms to flourish. Human flourishing is vital to God's Commandments and plans for us. And our creative thinking about our freedoms enlivens the dialogue that enriches our Republic. The current censorship of conservative thinking, surveillance, and labeling Christians, conservatives, and those citizens who hold political views that are opposite from the democratic party as "domestic terrorists" is a very dangerous practice and must be strongly denounced by our leaders. We can make an argument that the lack of original and creative thinking led to the downfall of ancient civilizations, for example, ancient Greece, and ancient Rome.[335] Today, American news bias and Big Tech censorship cannot be healthy for the lives of our citizens, for the advancement of our knowledge, for our spiritual growth, and for progress and advancement of our Nation.

In examining the story of how the Constitution was created, and the originality of the Founders' ideas that developed into the structure and form of our Constitution, we are learning to understand the Constitution, and what it means for us today. Our belief in natural law strengthens the current meaning of the Constitution in that the entelechy of the Constitution, or the soul of the Constitution, remains constant, and we bring our virtue as human beings, and our Constitutional knowledge to bear, as we exercise our natural rights guaranteed to us by natural law and protected under the Constitution of the United States of America.

The Bill of Rights (ratified in 1791) are laws written by humans, but these laws are in harmony with Natural Law. All the rights that were subsequently written in the National Bill of Rights were first written in the original States' Bill of Rights. Although the state legislatures enacted the States' Bill of Rights (and not by a vote by the people), the rights were drawn from inalienable and inherent natural rights.

The draft of the Constitution provided for key protections of liberty. Scholar John P Kaminsky writes in *The Constitution Without a Bill of Rights*, "that a number of individual rights were incorporated into the draft of the constitution that were protective of individual liberty: the prohibition of the suspension of the writ of habeas corpus except in case of rebellion or invasion, the prohibition of bills of attainder and ex post facto laws, the provision for impeachment of all civil officers, the guarantee of jury trials in criminal cases, the narrow definition of treason, the ban on religious qualifications for office holding, and other clauses protected the rights to private property."[336] Late in the Convention on September 12th, George Mason (author of the Virginia Declaration of Rights) introduced the idea of a Bill of Rights to preface the Constitution. Elbridge Gerry of Massachusetts agreed and proposed the motion that a committee be set up to draft a Bill of Rights. The delegates defeated the motion with a vote of ten states to none. The delegates were focused on strengthening the federal government, not in limiting the government's powers; however, the omission became the one important issue that (until it was resolved, and the rights of individuals were guaranteed with its inclusion) would prevent the ratification of the United States Constitution.

The Ninth Amendment, for example, states, "The enumeration in the Constitution, of certain rights, shall not be construed to deny or disparage others retained by the people."[337] We know which rights that we retain as referenced in the Ninth Amendment through our wisdom in understanding natural law. Sovereignty is inherently individual sovereignty, and we surrender a portion of our natural rights to form a social compact under the Constitution. There is a portion of our rights and liberties, however, which are natural to us as human beings, and this portion cannot be relegated to another or to a governmental institution, because they are our God-given rights under Natural Law. One precept is our growth as human beings as we utilize our natural will to follow God's eternal law. A second precept is the growth of our spiritual body as we follow Christ's teachings and develop as Christians. A third precept is the strengthening of our moral nature because God teaches us that we follow in God's light as moral creatures. Another Natural Law precept is that we extend love to God, love to family, love to one another, and love to our fellow creatures. Love is a maxim of Natural Law. This natural endowment is our human essence and the stimulus for us to improve our souls. The unenumerated individual rights that are protected under the Ninth Amendment are the indicators of our God-given natural law. The Ninth Amendment and the Privileges or Immunities Clause of the Fourteenth Amendment establish the existence of fundamental, unenumerated rights.

God is interested in our spiritual development, i.e., "nearer my God to thee," and the Ninth Amendment is the most significant clause in the Constitution to recognize that the spiritual nature of mankind is the essence of the goal of our democracy. The Ninth Amendment recognizes that the sovereignty of the individual remains intact even after we have surrendered a small portion of our inherent rights to our Government to form a more perfect union; however, the sovereignty that remains intact with the individual is the essence of what makes us successful as moral agents of the natural law.

The Framers designed a constitutional republican government based upon the principles of natural law. These principles are the shields for the protection of our individual liberty and rights that keep safe our freedoms of speech, freedom of expression, freedom of discussion, freedom for investigation, religious freedom, freedom of conscience, sovereignty, dignity, progress in consciousness, creative freedom, freedom of consciousness (temporal freedom), right to consciousness of the self, social rights, working rights, spiritual freedom, moral freedom, freedom of the will, virtue, freedom of personhood, individualism, right of association, creativity, freedom of movement (spatial freedom), the right of habeas corpus, our life, our property, our intellect, our reasoning power, equality under our laws, equality of race, gender, religion and creed, and our protections under the rule of law, right to a jury trial, our pursuit for happiness, and freedom to seek the truth and speak the truth. Our natural rights that are protected by the Constitution are the protections of our moral space where all these enumerated rights may thrive. Our God-given natural law is the essence of this moral space where we exercise our spiritual nature that is bequeathed to us by our Maker, yet this is not a comprehensive list of the blessings bestowed upon us by God, and the protection of our rights under our Constitution. Our Constitution safeguards our ability to worship our Creator, to freely seek God's truth and guidance, to live our lives within that truth, and to develop our soul within the light of God.

An important part of our natural law is the development of

ourselves as moral individuals. Our Constitution provides the legal framework in which to do this. Our inalienable rights are established by God, and our Constitution allows us to develop our spiritual rights without governmental interference. As moral individuals, we are a part of God's divine plan, and as a Nation under God, our Nation is also a part of God's divine plan. Fitting in with His divine plan, we exhibit the divine characteristics of love, faith, kindness, compassion, patience, virtue, toleration, helpfulness, humanity, goodness, morality, truthfulness, and happiness. The citizens of the United States of America are united in their exhibition of these Godly qualities. Love carries forth our national heritage, our commitment to liberty, and our freedom — all are symbolic to our reciprocal love for our Nation.

Natural law circumscribes natural rights; there is no natural right that is not bounded by natural law. When we experience these, we are also under the guarantee of natural law that demonstrates to us that we are moral creatures and we obey God's natural law — the precepts are given to us for our advantage that we may develop ourselves, our bodies, and our souls. Moral principles should always determine our positive laws; and these have their common root in natural law and are self-evident principles.

Magna Carta taught Americans about due process, and the two due process clauses of the Constitution are found in the Fifth Amendment, i.e., "no person shall be deprived of life, liberty, or property, without due process of law.", and the Fourteenth Amendment which imposes the same limitations on state governments. In the same way that the Constitution protects claims that are part of the implicit concept of liberty, the Constitution also protects claims that are implicit in the concept of natural law. Our liberty protections under the Constitution are not all specific enumerations, some protections are abstract, deemed and brought to light through the wisdom of the courts. The Constitution provides the citizens with the means to promote their own individual liberty and maintain their own spiritual status while recognizing and returning to the first principles of natural law.

The modern American philosophy of politics includes the philosophy of natural law. Our relationship to God is part of our political science since good governance includes the theory of natural law. God has ordained us with natural law and has blessed our Nation with a remarkable Constitution that allows the maximum amount of freedoms for each individual citizen. People must have freedom to practice their religious beliefs. A governmental structure that allows legal reasoning to be in harmony with moral reasoning is a proper structure for spiritual growth. God has given us power and authority in our community, and we exercise this responsibility by transferring some of this power to those leaders who have accepted public and governmental leadership positions. Natural law judgments are implicit in the act of sound judgments for those who are in positions that require legislation and laws for the community and nation to follow.

The United States Constitution is committed to fundamental rights, and these rights are known through our belief in natural law. We frame our reason in service of God's universal truth of natural law. God has given us the wisdom to order our relationship to Him, while at the same time we live in our Republic. Our lives are whole in God and this wellness includes our human relationships of love, fellowship, worship, and sound stewardship of our natural resources; our resources include our tools for sound economic practices. Past historians have criticized the Founding Fathers for bringing their economic interests and property interests to bear in the framing of the United States Constitution.[338] Our moral interests are inextricably bound to our economic interests. God has provided us with the tools to achieve economic prosperity, and as stewards of His earth, it is our responsibility to use His resources in a wise manner. Current politicians disparage Americans using natural resources, and these same politicians have a platform that views economic success as a negative quality. The spiritual citizens of the United States of America hold that individual success is a positive quality: the natural law philosophers hold that economic success is a positive quality, and we thank our Creator for the Blessings that He has bestowed upon our Nation.

We are the children of Light and are Blessed with God's natural law. Our soul is bound to God by His love for us; and we strengthen this attachment by returning our human love to Him, to others, and to all God's creatures. We are learning natural law to strengthen this spiritual bound of love, and to be properly fitted for our battle armor to fight against the dark forces of Satan whose legions have gained a foothold in the government of the United States of America. "I can do everything through him who gives me strength." (Philippians 4:13). America is a Nation under God; a Nation of freedom under God; She is a nation of liberty under God. Satan will be vanquished by the loyal soldiers of God's army — follow God's banner, God's flag is the flag of unity in Christ and freedom. "If God is for us, who can be against us?" (Romans 8:31). We loyally follow God's Saints into the battle against Satan and his dominions; we have our armor perfectly prepared and fitted for us; God's mighty and powerful shield will protect us; Almighty and Holy God gives us strength and victory over the enemy for the Glory of God and His son, Jesus Christ.

We pray that God will continue to bless The United States of America. We pray that God will continue to bless us — His children. We pray that God will continue to bless The Constitution of the United States of America. We pray that God will continue to bless us with Natural Law — the Law of all Laws!

And Jesus taught the Apostle Thomas, "I am the way and the truth and the life. No one comes to the Father except through me. If you really knew me, you would know my Father as well. From now on, you do know him and have seen him." (John 14:6).

Chapter 1 Endnotes

...Mark R. Levin's *American Marxism.*
See also, Charles R. Kesler, *Crisis of the Two Constitutions: The Rise, Decline, and Recovery of American Greatness* (New York, London: Encounter Books, 2021), Ben Shapiro, *How to Destroy America in Three Easy Steps* (New York: Broadside Books, 2020), and Sean Hannity, *Live Free or Die: America (and the World) on the Brink* (New York: Threshold Editions, 2020). Page 2

...within the truths of natural law.
I use the term "founders" in the same sense that historian Thomas G. West uses the term: to refer to colonial thinkers, leading government officials, and politicians during the period from 1760 through 1800. In this sense "founders" would also refer to Thomas Jefferson and John Adams, although both men were absent from the Convention of 1787 — Jefferson was serving as diplomat to France, and Adams was serving as diplomat to England. Thomas G. West, *The Political Theory of the American Founding: Natural Rights, Public Policy, and the Moral Conditions of Freedom* (New York: Cambridge University Press, 2017), p.1. I use the term "Founding Fathers" to refer to the fifty-five delegates who attended the Constitutional Convention sessions in 1787. Of the fifty-five delegates who attended, only thirty-nine delegates signed the United States Constitution. Page 6

...influence on the American Founders.
I do not examine (in depth) the complex subject of Roman law and jurisprudence in *Natural Law and the Constitution: The Law of All Laws*. (Hereafter referred to as *Natural Law and the Constitution*). The subject of Roman law and its relationship to natural law, and to American law requires a separate book that concentrates on that topic alone. Pages 7

...from his book, Summa Theologica.
St. Thomas Aquinas, *The Summa Theologica of St. Thomas,* Second and Revised Edition, 1920, trans. by Fathers of the English Dominican Province, 2d rev. ed. Vol. I, II, III, IV, and V. (New York, NY: Benzinger Bros., 1948). I do not approach the subject of natural law from a Catholic doctrinal perspective; however, St. Thomas is included in *Natural Law and the Constitution* because of his unique and enlightening perspective on natural law. Page 7

...we consult our "self-interest."
James Madison, *The Federalist Papers,* Clinton Rossiter, ed. (New York: Signet Classics, 1961), No. 10, pp. 71-79. Page 9

...the suffrages, and then betray the interests of the people."
Ibid., p. 77. Page 9

...and to act in unison with each other."
Ibid., p. 78. Page 10

...government will set boundaries to check this behavior.
Ibid., p. 79. Page 10

...the local and particular to the State legislatures."
Ibid., pp.77-78. Page 10

...and the weak and strong nuclear forces,
Michio Kaku, *Physics of the Impossible: A Scientific Exploration into the World of Phasers, Force Fields, Teleportation, and Time Travel* (New York: First Anchor Books Edition, 2009), pp. 6-8. Page 10

...in harmony with God's natural law.
Politicians today use the term "scientific" to try to give legitimacy to their platform when they generally are referring to an agnostic belief system. Natural law believers are not against science; they in fact believe that scientific principles are always in harmony with natural law. Page 11

...the goal of colonial Americans was individual liberty.
Paul A. Rahe, *Republics Ancient and Modern: Classical Republicanism and the American Revolution* (Chapel Hill: University of North Carolina Press, 1992). Page 11

...and the Constitution of 1787 is without dispute.
Jerome Huylar, *Locke in America: The Moral Philosophy of the Founding Era* (Lawrence, Kansas: University Press of Kansas, 1995). Page 11

...and an expert on English constitutionalism.
Andrew C. McLaughlin, *A Constitutional History of the United States* (Safety Harbor, FL: Simon Publications, 2001) Vol I, p. 93. Page 11

...among these are Life, Liberty, and the pursuit of Happiness."
Larry P. Arnn, *The Founder's Key: The Divine and Natural Connection Between the Declaration and the Constitution and What We Risk by Losing It* (Nashville, TN: Thomas Nelson, 2012), pp. 127-132. https://archives.gov./America'sFoundingDocuments/DeclarationofIndependence. Transcript. National Archives and Records Administration, July 24, 2020, September 28, 2020. Page 12

...used by the delegates to express "natural law."
Max Farrand (ed.), *Records of the Federal Convention* (1911), I, 48, p. 124; 135, and II, 56. Page 14 & 15

...state's rights must also be protected in the national constitution.
Ibid., I, p. 437; 440; and 493. Page 15

...in order that a union of states may be formed.
Ibid., II, 666. Page 15

...the validity of a statute emanating from the sovereign."
Edward S. Corwin, *The "Higher Law" Background of American Constitutional Law* (Indianapolis, Indiana: Liberty Fund, 2008), p. 84. Originally published: Cambridge, Mass.: Harvard Law Review XLII, 1928. Page 17

...these documents have prescribed to us our freedoms.
Joan Arnsteen, (Neumann), *Socrates, Jesus and Freedom: A Philosophical Reflection* (Alger, MI: Proud Daughter Publishing, 2016), p. 235. Page 19

...created political life through Noah.
Richard Tuck, *Natural Rights Theories: Their Origin and Development* (Cambridge: Cambridge University Press, 1979), p. 43. Dr. Tuck explains how there was a synthesis between humanism and religious arguments by the seventeenth century Calvinists. Dr. Tuck also argues that the theory of natural rights was developed in Europe in the seventeenth century. Page 20

...whereas written laws often do change.
Aristotle and Richard McKeon, ed., *The Basic Works of Aristotle*, (New York: Random House, 1941), *Rhetoric* 1375a31-36, p. 1374. Page 20

...as "the first grace of God."
Francis Russell Hittinger, *The First Grace: Rediscovering the Natural Law in a Post-Christian World* (Wilmington, DE: ISI Books, 2007), p. 7. Page 21

...*lex humana* (the human law), and *lex vetus* (the old law).
Ibid, p. 7. Page 21

...through legal statute and confirmed through judicial review.
Edward S. Corwin, *The "Higher Law" Background of American Constitutional Law* (Indianapolis, Indiana: Liberty Fund, 2008), pp. 84-85. Page 22

...documents also reflect natural law language.
Thomas G. West, *The Political Theory of the American Founding* (New York: Cambridge University Press, 2017), pp. 25-28. Page 23

...life, liberty and the pursuit of happiness."
Declaration of Independence. A transcription can be found online at the National Archives, https://www.archives.gov/founding-docs/declaration. A transcription of The Constitution of the United States can be found online at https://www.archives.gov/founding-docs/constitution-transcript.
The Bill of Rights can also be found online at https://www.archives.gov/founding-docs/bill-of-rights. Page 23

Chapter 2 Endnotes

...The Greeks destroy Troy, and ...
Homer, *The Iliad*, trans. Robert Fagles (New York: Penguin Books, 1990). Page 30

...to win back his kingdom in Ithaca.
Homer, *The Odyssey*, trans. Robert Fagles (New York: Penguin Books, 1996). Page 30

...and he rescued my armor as well,"
Plato, *Plato: Complete Works*, edited by John M. Cooper (Indianapolis: Hackett Publishing Company, 1997), Symposium 220e 1-2. Page 32

...because of birth status to the rule of wealth.
Mogens Herman Hansen, *The Athenian Democracy in the Age of Demosthenes: Structure, Principles, and Ideology*, Trans. J.A. Crook (Norman: University of Oklahoma Press, 1999), p. 30. Page 35

...tyranny that continued from 561 until 510 BC.
Ibid., pp. 31-32. Page 36

...community a shared sense of purpose and cohesion.
Thucydides, *History of the Peloponnesian War*, trans. R. Warner (London: Penguin Books, 1972), 2.34-2.46. Page 39

...divine laws which led to that of natural laws."
John Wild, *Plato's Modern Enemies and the Theory of Natural Law* (Chicago: University of Chicago Press, 1953), p. 135. Page 40

...a point which needs to be stressed."
Ibid., p. 136 Page 40

...by the philosopher John Wild.
Ibid., p. 64. Page 41

...had wisdom that surpassed what we have.
Plato, *Plato: Complete Works*, John M. Cooper, ed. (Indianapolis, Cambridge: Hackett Publishing Co., 1997), *Apology* 23a. Page 43

...more important than tending the body.
Ibid., 30a Page 43

...be harmed either in life or in death,..."
Ibid., 41d. Page 43

...Virtue depends on knowledge.
Ibid., 26a. Page 43

...good versus what is good by convention.
Ibid., *Republic* 538d3-4; *Statesman* 296e8-9. Page 43

..."The unexamined life is not worth living."
Ibid., *Apology* 38a5-6. Page 46

...Socrates hears a "divine voice."
Ibid., *Apology* 31d1. Page 46

...course of action that he should not take.
Ibid., *Apology* 31d1-4; 40a2-c1 Page 46

...divine being of intelligence and power.
Ibid., *Apology* 33c4-7. Page 46

...excellence is moral or ethical virtue.
Ibid., *Laws* 643b-647c; *Republic* 430c, and Aristotle, *The Basic Works of Aristotle,* Richard McKeon, ed., (New York: Random House, 1941), *Nicomachean Ethics*, Book III, Chapter 8. Page 46

...Socrates thought courage was knowledge."
Aristotle, *The Basic Works of Aristotle,* Richard McKeon, ed., (New York: Random House, 1941), *Nicomachaen Ethics,* III.8.116b3-5. Page 46

...that law is intelligence without desire.
Ibid., *Politics,* III.16.1287a32. Page 47

..."the law of nature" infrequently...
Plato, *Gorgias* 484; *Timaeus* 83e. Page 47

...motion of the stars, and the laws of change in nature.
Ibid., *Republic* 515b5; *Phaedo* 103; *Protagoras* 315c5. Page 47

...holds the norms of justice within this nature.
Ibid., Laws, 715e7. Page 48

...his words were later transcribed onto possibly papyrus.
Diogenes Laertius, *Lives and Opinions of Eminent Philosophers, 3.37;* Quintillian, *Institutes,* 8 6.64. Page 49

...applicable to all men everywhere, required by human nature.
John Wild, *Plato's Modern Enemies and the Theory of Natural Law* (Chicago: The University of Chicago Press, 1953), p. 64. Page 50

...whose existence is legislated by arbitrary human interests.
Ibid., p. 62. Page 50

...and in this case it was Athens.
Mogens Herman Hansen, *The Athenian Democracy in the Age of Demosthenes,* J.A. Crook, trans., (Norman: University of Oklahoma Press, 1999), pp. 55-64. Page 50

...true Forms of knowledge, truth and beauty will emanate from.
Plato, *Republic,* VI, See "Analogy of the Divided Line." Page 51

...we can learn to comprehend the Form of justice itself.
Ibid., *Republic,* VI. Page 51 & 52

...evils of the soul are worse than evils of the body;
Ibid., *Apology*, 29b; 39a. Page 52

...integral to our moral development than the body,
Ibid., 30a; 41e. Page 52

...and that virtue depends upon knowledge.
Ibid., 26a; John Wild, p. 11 Page 52

...people who've been unjust here must pay the penalty there..."
Ibid., *Republic*, I.330d4-7. Page 55

...defined as giving back what is owed."
Ibid., *Republic*, I.331b-d. Page 55

..."the art which gives goods to friends and evil to enemies."
Ibid., *Republic*, I.334e-335e. Page 55

...then will he be equally clever at stealing it?
Ibid., *Republic*, I.334e Page 56

...the function of his opposite, an unjust person?"
Ibid., *Republic* I.335d11-12. Page 56

...hurled himself at us as if to tear us to pieces."
Ibid., *Republic*, I.336b3-5. Page 57

...for I won't accept such nonsense from you."
Ibid. Page 57

...Thrasymachus defines justice as the advantage of the stronger.
Ibid., *Republic.*, I.339a-340b. Page 57

...confesses ignorance on the definition of justice.
Ibid., *Republic*, I. Page 57

...where an unjust person is ignorant and bad.
Ibid., *Republic*, I.350c3-4. Page57

...and this leads to a happier person.
Ibid., *Republic*, I.353a-e; I.354c. Page 57

...vice is the disordered or corrupted nature of the soul.
Ibid., *Gorgias, 478; 503.* Page 58

...will find harmony within the whole state.
Ibid., *Republic*, IV.443d-e Page 58

...refer to the social or economic spheres of the polis.
Mogens Herman Hansen, p. 81. Page 59

...city recognizes, but some other new religion."
Plato, *Apology, 2b. Page 59*

...better lot is known to no one except the god."
Ibid., *42a3-4. Page 59*

..."The unexamined life is not worth living for men."
Ibid., 38a. Page 60

Chapter 3 Endnotes

...human beings is the realization of human nature.
John Wild, *Plato's Modern Enemies and the Theory of Natural Law,* p. 157. Page 61

...ultimate good for man is a realization of human nature.
Ibid., p. 157. Page 63

...activities are ordered together to serve a common end.
Aristotle, *The Basic Works of Aristotle,* Richard McKeon, ed. (New York: Random House, 1941), *Metaphysics,* 1075a18. Page 64

...will always obey and are bound by moral law.
Ibid., *Metaphysics,* 1075a19. Page 64

...and what is generated has a certain form.
Ibid., *Rhetoric,* 1360a5. Page 64

...their acts and are bound by the moral law.
Ibid., *Metaphysics,* 1075a18-19. Page 65

...any changing entity, and this matter is called *nature*.
John Wild, *Plato's Modern Enemies and the Theory of Natural Law*, pp. 159-160. Page 65

...Greek god(s) had no interest in the universe or mankind.
Aristotle, *Physics,* II.3; *Metaphysics,* V.2. Page 65

...change for something is its essence or form.
Ibid., *Metaphysics*, IV.1015a17. Page 65 66

...example of the essence or structure of the human body
Aristotle, *De Anima (On the Soul)*, 415b11. Page 66

...soul is also the source of movement and tendency
Ibid., 415b12. Page 66

...of locomotion
Ibid., 415b21. Page 66

...of growth
Ibid., 415b23. Page 66

...of nutrition and reproduction,
Ibid., 416a19. Page 66

...and the source of all the vital powers.
Ibid., 413b11. And, John Wild, *Plato's Modern Enemies and the Theory of Natural Law*, p. 161. Page 66

...made possible as well as the correct prediction of future events.
Plato, *Laws*, 792b1; 875d4. And, John Wild, *Plato's Modern Enemies and the Theory of Natural Law*, p. 161. Page 66

...and makes it perform its function well.
Aristotle, *Nicomachaen Ethics,* 1106a15. Page 67

...eudaemonia, which means "doing well and living well."
Ibid., 1095a15-22. Page 67

..."that for the sake of which a thing is done.
Aristotle, *Metaphysics,* V.2.1013a33. Page 67

...conventional justice, (nomikon dikaion.)
Aristotle, *Nicomachaen Ethics*, 1134b18-1135a5. Page 67

...can be called natural law (or natural justice) principles.
Ibid., II.6.1107a9-14. Page 68

...these principles as secondary precepts of natural law.
St. Thomas Aquinas, *Summa Theologica*, Translated by Fathers of the English Dominican Province in Five Volumes (Notre Dame, Indiana: Christian Classics, 1981), I-II, Q. 94, Art. 4. Page 68

...concept of justice by relating it to the notion of equity.
Aristotle, *Nicomachaen Ethics*, V.9. Page 68

...'specific determination' of certain generalities.
St. Thomas, *Summa Theologica*, I-II, Question 95, Article 2. Page 68

...the principles of legal or conventional justice.
Tony Burns, *Aristotle and Natural Law* (United Kingdom: A & C Black, 2011). Page 69

...his spiritual teaching of Christ in legal language.
Holy Bible, I Corinthians 6:1-9. Page 69

...was by nature a political animal (zoon politikon)".
Aristotle, *The Politics,* 1253a1-3. Page 69

...somehow escape conventional punishments."
Cicero *On The Republic* (London: Cambridge, MA.: Loeb Classical Libraries), 3.22.33. Page 71

...natural law may be changed in certain situations.
Aristotle, *Nicomachean Ethics, V. 7. Page 71*

Chapter 4 Endnotes

...to the divine governance of the world by a Holy God.
The terms "mankind", "man", "humankind" or "human being" are used to refer to human beings in general. Page 74

...a theology that would achieve the status of a science.
A catalogue of St. Thomas' extensive works can be found in Etienne Gilson's *The Christian Philosophy of Saint Thomas* (New York: Random House, 1956). Page 76

...everything that he had written seem to be straw by comparison.
J. Budziszewski, *Commentary on Thomas Aquinas's Treatise on Law* (New York: Cambridge University Press, 2014). This author acknowledges Dr. Budziszewski's *Commentary* as an indispensable book for a beginning understanding of St. Thomas. The events of St. Thomas's childhood and early years are retold by many authors, and I am especially thankful to C.K. Chesterton who told the story of St. Thomas so vividly in C.K. Chesterton, *The Dumb Ox (*Nashville, Tennessee: Sam Torde Book Arts, 2010) Page 77

...through which it is discovered (the human intellect)."
Russell Hittinger, *The First Grace: Rediscovering the Natural Law in a Post-Christian World* (Wilmington, Delaware: ISI Books, 2003), p. 9. Page 78

...the human mind or first in nature in St. Thomas"
Ibid., p. 9. Page 78

...who has care of the community, and promulgated."
St. Thomas Aquinas, *The Summa Theologica of St. Thomas Aquinas* (*ST*) Trans. Fathers of the English Dominican Province (Notre Dame, Indiana: Christian Classics, 1948), I-II, Question 90, Article 1. Page 78

...rational creature is called the natural law."
Ibid., *ST,* I-II, Question 91, Article 2. Page 79

...be pursued and done, and evil is to be avoided.
Ibid., *ST,* I-II, Question 94, Article 2. Page 79

...divine intelligence, and the divine Designer.
Ibid., *ST*, Vol. 1, a, Question 2, Article 3. Page 80

...fulfilling the desire to preserve our own existence.
Ibid, ST, I-II, Question 94, Article 2. For a helpful discussion of St. Thomas's ethics see: Edward Fesner, *St. Thomas: A Beginner's Guide* (Oxford, England: Oneworld Publications, 2009), p. 180-183. Page 80

...knowledge of God constitutes man's happiness.
Ibid., *ST*, I-II, Question 2, Article 8. Page 81

...precepts of the natural law are based upon this."
Ibid., *ST,* I-II, Question 94, Article 2. Page 81

...and avoid that which we take to be evil.
Ibid., *ST,* I-II, Question 2, Article 1; Question 90, Article 1. Page 81

...all the particular attributes to the general conclusion.
See Joan Arnsteen (Neumann), *Socrates, Jesus and Freedom: A Philosophical Reflection* (Alger, MI: Proud Daughter Publishing, 2016). See this book for a discussion on both Socrates' and Jesus' use of dialectics as a teaching tool. Page 83

...the intellect and the will when performing a moral act.
Vernon J. Bourke, PhD., *St. Thomas and the Greek Moralists* (Milwaukee, Wis.: Marquette University Press, 1947), pp. 14-16. Page 84

...comparison of the act with the nature of things).
Ibid., pp. 22-24. Page 84

...good is to be done and evil is to be avoided.
St. Thomas, *ST*, I-II, Question 94, Article 2. Page 84

...it is proper for us to act according to reason.
Ibid., *ST,* I-II, Question 94, Article 4. Page 85

...effort to perfect our knowledge of natural law.
ST, I-II, Question 94, Article 4. Page 85& 86

...we avoid offense, and shun ignorance.
Ibid., *ST,* Question 94, Article 2. Page 86

...is to have perfect union and contemplation of God.
Ibid., *ST,* I-II, Question 2, Article 8. Page 86

...of the community, and this rule is promulgated"
Ibid., *ST,* I-II, Question 90, Article 4. Page 87

...God utilizes to create and govern the world.
Ibid., *ST.*, I-II, Question 91, Article 1. See, Treatise on Law, I-II, Questions 90-97. Page 87

...by following our natural inclinations.
Ibid., *ST*, Questions 91, Article 6. Page 88

...creature's participation of the eternal law."
Ibid., *ST,* Questions 91, Article 2. Page 88

...have a reflection or participation of the eternal law.
Ibid., *ST*, Question 94, Article 2. Page 88

...defines prudence as right reason about how to act.
Daniel Mark Nelson, *The Priority of Prudence: Virtue and Natural Law in St. Thomas and the Implications for Modern Ethics* (University Park, Pennsylvania: A State University Press, 1992), pp. 106-107. Page 88

...that are contained within natural law precepts.
St. Thomas, *Summa Theologica*, I-II, Question 91, Article 2. Page 88

...following our natural inclinations (inclinations naturales).
Ibid., *ST,* I-II, Question 91, Article 6. Page 89

...understand the precepts of the natural law.
Ibid., *ST, I-II,* Question 91, Article 2. Page 89

...St. Jerome, Bonaventure, and St. Albert the Great.
For an excellent discussion of St. Thomas's concept of *synderesis* see Michael Bertram Crowe, *The Changing Profile of the Natural Law* (The Hague, Netherlands: Martinus Nijhoff, 1977), Chapter VI, pp. 136-165. Page 89

...knowledge of the first principles of thinking.
St. Thomas, *ST,* I, Question 79. Page 89

...part of learning to live in harmony with natural law.
Ibid., *ST,* I-II, Question 94, Article 2c. Page 90

...general way by starting from the things themselves.
St. Thomas, *Summa contra gentiles,* III, Question 81, Article 1. Page 90

...eternal law in the rational creature."
St. Thomas, *Summa Theologica,* I-II, Question 91, Article 2. Page 90

...proceeding from a sort of practical wisdom and reason."
Aristotle, *Nicomachean Ethics*, Book X, 9, 1180 a 21. Page 91

...to be done and evil is to be avoided.
ST, I-II, Question 94, Article 1a and 2ae. Page 91

...the day that you eat from it you will surely die.'"
Genesis 2: 16-17. Page 92

...rational creature's participation of the eternal law."
ST, I-II, Question 91, Article 2. Page 92

..."good is that which all things seek after."
Ibid., I-II, Question 94, Article 2. Page 92

...be done and pursued, and evil is to be avoided."
Ibid. Page 92

...into man's mind so as to be known by him natural."
Ibid., *ST,* I-II, Question 90, Art. 1., ad. 1. Page 93

...the Ethics, advanced the concept of natural justice.
Aristotle, *Nicomachean Ethics,* V 7, 1-2. Page 94

...is replaced with the language of natural rights.
John Finnis, *Natural Law and Natural Rights*, 2nd., ed., (Oxford University Press, 2011). Page 95

Chapter 5 Endnotes

...and corrupt social influences may all lead us astray.
Ibid., *ST,* I-II, Question 91, Article 6. Page 98

...accords with the order of natural inclinations."
Ibid., *ST,* I-II, Question 94, Article 2c. Page 98

...these wise thinkers will be discussed in this book.
See the Bibliography published in socratesplace.com for the titles of the books written by the key thinkers who influenced the writing of the Constitution of the United States of America. Page 107

...destiny in following God's covenant plan to the new land.
Bernard Bailyn, *Ideological Origins of the American Revolution* (Cambridge, MA: Harvard University Press, 1967), pp. 32-33. Page 107

...James Harrington, Adam Smith, and William Small.
All of the major works of these profound thinkers are listed in the Bibliography. Page 108

...and Locke's *Letters on Toleration* (1689).
Historians do not generally agree on the beginning date of the Enlightenment, or "Age of Reason" where reason, science and progress were developed and discussed; however, an approximate range of dates for the Enlightenment can be given as 1685 through 1815. Page 108

...Thomas Made, Robert Brady, and William Petyt.
Ibid., p. 31. Page 109

...but also on the Nation's belief in God.
See: *Torcaso v. Watkins,* 367 U.S. 488 (1961): *Engle v. Vitale,* 370 U.S. 421 (1962). Page 111

Chapter 6 Endnotes

...English Constitution was useful for their debate.
Forrest McDonald. *Novus Ordo Seclorum: The Intellectual Origins of the Constitution* (Kansas: University Press of Kansas, 1985), p.120 Page 115

...dissenting Protestant colonists understood so well."
Donald S. Lutz, *The Origins of American Constitutionalism* (Louisiana: Louisiana State University, 1989), p.153 Page 115

...of a document that was so historically unique.
Ibid., pp. 10-11 Page 116

...Whig idea that did not apply to the Americans.
Ibid., p. 151. Page 117

...authors of this era including Blackstone and Hume.
Ibid., pp. 142-143. Page 117

...political literature between 1760 and 1805.
Ibid., pp. 140-141. Page 117

...achieve a stolen victory for Vice-President Joe Biden.
See "Defending the Republic.org" where all of the data, sworn testimony, evidence, statistical analysis, mathematical analysis, sworn witnesses, mathematical anomalies that demonstrate that votes where "shaved" with an algorithm, that is, votes were weighed 1.26 points for Biden and .74 for Trump, votes were flipped in the six key states, voting centers were closed down and votes were flipped, video evidence of suitcases of filled out ballots brought out from under a table to be counted in the early morning after the observers were told that they were stopping the count for the evening, and foreign government interference took place in the 2020 Presidential election. In Dinesh D' Souza's podcast "Sidney Powell Discusses What's Actually Happening in America," Sidney Powell stated that "Facts do not lie; President Trump won the election." Attorney Powell stated that this was an organized, powerful, and fully funded coup of our government, and the failure of the United States government to have an investigation is a "complete institutional failure of every arm of the government to enforce the rule of law." (Podcast accessed on April 6, 2021). See also Sidneypowell.com. Page 120

...does not degenerate into an autocratic regime."
Joan Arnsteen (Neumann), *Socrates, Jesus and Freedom: A Philosophical Reflection* (Alger, MI: Proud Daughter Publishing: Alger, MI 2016), p. 141. Page 121

...current American understanding of our republic?
Alexander Hamilton. *The Federalist Papers*, No. 68. Hamilton discusses the electoral college and how it is designed to prevent fraud and corruption. See *The Constitution of the United States,* Article 2, Section 1.2. Page 122

Chapter 7 Endnotes

...(in his speeches) often invoked "God Bless America."
See, for example, socialist House of Representatives member Alexandria Ocasio Cortez who tweeted, "Is anyone archiving these Trump sycophants for when they try to downplay their complicity in the future." Twitter, November 6, 2020. This tweet was followed by a link to the "Trump Accountability Project," that lists journalists, editors, commentators, and others who are targeted for retribution if America succumbs to a socialist regime. Page 125

...believed that natural law can be independent of God.
Hugo Grotius, *De Jure Belli ac Pacis Libris Tres* (1625). Classics of International Law, James Brown Scott, general ed., 2 vols. Volume 1, Latin text, facsimile of 1646 ed.; Vol 2, English text, *On the Law of War and Peace,* translated by Francis W. Kelsey et. al. (Washington D.C., 1913, vol. 1; Oxford, 1925, vol. 2). Page 125

...natural law in his famous *Two Treatises of Government*.
John Locke, *Two Treatises of Government,* Peter Laslett, ed. (Cambridge: Cambridge University Press, 1960) Page 126

...by that very fact commanding or prohibiting."
John Locke, *Essays on the Nature of Law,* Edited by W. Von Leyden (Oxford: Oxford University Press, 1954), Folio 12. Also see, John Locke, *Questions Concerning the Law of Nature,* Edited by Robert Horwitz, Jenny Strauss Clay, and Diskin Clay (Ithaca, N.Y., 1990). Page 126

In Locke's *Essays Concerning Human Understanding* (1689),...
John Locke, *An Essay Concerning Human Understanding,* Volume I and Volume II, Annotated by Alexander Campbell Fraser (New York: Dover Publications, Inc., 1959). Page 126

...and therefore, there is no innate knowledge.
John Locke, *Essays on the Law of Nature,* W. von Leyden, ed., (Oxford: Clarendon Press, 1954), Folio 12. *The Reasonableness of Christianity* and *a Discourse of Miracles,* and part of *A Third Letter Concerning Toleration* were published in 1695. *Essays on the Law of Nature* was published after Locke's death in 1704. Page 127

...John Trenchard and Thomas Gordon around 1720.
John Trenchard and Thomas Gordon. *Essays on Liberty, Civil and Religious, and Other Subjects,* Ronald Hamowy, edited and annotated, *2 vols.* (Indianapolis: Liberty Fund, 1995). Page 127

...placed liberties beyond the legal reach of Parliament.
Calvin R. Massey, *Silent Rights: The Ninth Amendment and the Constitution's Unenumerated Rights* (Philadelphia: Temple University Press,1995), p. 28. Page 127

...therefore we should all be equal to one another.
John Locke, *Two Treatises of Government, Second Treatise*, chap. 2, sec. 6. Page 128

...therefore, we may not harm each other.
Ibid., chap. 2, sec. 4. Page 128

...from design" as a sound argument for God's existence.
Ibid. Page 128

...of the Messiah, witnesses to Jesus, and Jesus's miracles.
John Locke, *An Essay Concerning Human Understanding*, in Two Volumes. Collated and Annotated by Alexander Campbell Fraser (New York: Dover Publications, Inc., 1959). Page 129

...and for this reason commanding or prohibiting.
John Locke, *Essays on the Law of Nature* (1663-1664). In M. Goldie, ed., *Locke Political Essays* (Cambridge Texts in the History of Political Thought, pp. 79-133, Cambridge: Cambridge University Press,1997. doi:10.1017/CBO9780511810251.008)., III.
See also: John Locke, *Essays on the Law of Nature,* W. Von Leyden, ed., (Oxford: Oxford University Press, 1954), Folio 12, and John Locke, *Questions Concerning the Law of Nature,* Robert Horwitz, Jenny Strauss Clay, and Diskin Clay, eds., (Ithaca, New York: Cornell University Press,1990). Page 129

...passions are not impressions of truth on the understanding.
John Locke, *An Essay Concerning Human Understanding,* II, pp. 21, 35, 41, and 44. Page 129

...and within the bounds of the Law of Nature.
John Locke, *Two Treatises of Government* (New York: Mentor Books, 1965), 2nd. tr., par. 4. Page 130

...public that ought to control and regulate the government."
James Madison, *The Federalist Papers,* No. 49, p. 314. Page 131

..."that which either commands or forbids some action."
John Locke, *Essays on the Nature of Law*, Edited by W. Von Leyden (Oxford: Oxford University Press, 1954), Folio 11. Page 132

...through the natural inclinations of mankind.
Ibid., Folio 61. Page 133

...known to a few through rational proof.
Ibid., Folio 33, 38, 41-42, 64-66, 68-72. Page 133

...bring us comfort, peace, joy, and happiness
Saint Thomas Aquinas, *Summa Theologica.* See: J. Budziszewski, *The Line through the Heart: Natural Law as Fact, Theory, and Sign of Contradiction* (Wilmington, DE: ISI Books, 2009). Page 135

...be evil even if no evil consequences ensued."
Ibid., p. 200. Page 135

Chapter 8 Endnotes

...original contract between the king and the people."
Andrew C. McLaughlin, *A Constitutional History of the United States* (Safety Harbor, Fl.: Simon Publications, 2001), Vol. I, p. 91. Page 139

...but also by the sermons of the preachers.
Ibid., Vol. I, pp. 91-92. See also: Alice Mary Baldwin, *The New England Clergy and the American Revolution* (New York: F. Ungar Publishing Company, 1958), and Henry Martyn Dexter, *The Congregationalism of the Last Hundred Years as Seen in the Literature: With Special References to Certain Recondite, Neglected, or Disputed Passages* (New York: Harper & Brothers, 1880), Vol. I. Page 140

...and an expert on English constitutionalism.
Andrew McLaughlin, *A Constitutional History of the United States* (Safety Harbor, Fl.: Simon Publications, 2001), Vol. I, p. 93. Page 140

...called upon to help write the new state constitutions.
Thomas Paine, *"Common Sense"*, in *Writings of Paine,* ed. Foner. Page 142

...and confirmed by the Glorious Revolution of 1688.
Ibid., p. 76. Page 142

...interests through the defense of her colonies.
Ibid., pp.8-9 Page 143

...and founding and organizing new settlements.
Ibid., p. 13. Page 143

...no probable cause, and for no given reason.
Ibid., p. 25. Page 143

...dwelling and personal property of the colonists.
Ibid., p. 26. Page 143

...long-established in English constitutionalism.
Ibid., p. 28. Page 144

...natural rights by linking natural rights to representation.
https://oll.libertyfund.org/titles/collected-political-writings#1f1644 label 235; Online Library of Liberty, Liberty Fund, Inc., 2019, accessed December 29, 2019. Page 145

...Britain would respect the rights of colonial legislation.
https://oll.libertyfund.org/tites/2703#1f1644 label 097; Online Library of Liberty, Liberty Fund, Inc., 2019, accessed December 29, 2019. Page 146

...nature freeborn, as indeed all men are, white or black."
James Otis quoted in "Subjecthood and Citizenship: The Context of James Otis's Radical Critique of John Locke," author T.H. Been printed in *The New England Quarterly* Vol. 71, No. 3 (Sep. 1998), pp. 378-403. Published by: The New England Quarterly, Inc., in JSTOR. Page 146

...the universe and are antecedent to governments."
John Adams, *"A Dissertation on the Canon and Feudal Law,"* August 12, 1775. http://founders.archives.gov/documents/Adams/06-01-02-0052-0004. Accessed on July 11, 2019. Page 147

...New York, 1765, to protest the Stamp Act.
Ibid., pp. 35-36. Page 147

...reparations for the lost tea could be made.
Ibid., p. 72. Page 149

...George Washington, Sam Adams, and John Hancock.
Ibid., pp. 75-80. Page 149

...human nature, which are wounded by the slave trade.
Ibid., pp. 80-82.
Thomas Jefferson, "A Summary View of the Rights of British America. Set Forth in Some Resolutions Intended for the Inspection of the Present Delegates of the People of Virginia Now in Convention." Printed at Williamsburg, reprinted in Philadelphia and in London. See Thomas Jefferson, *Works* (federal ed.), II, pp. 47-89. Also see: Thomas Jefferson, *The Papers of Thomas Jefferson*, ed. Julian P. Boyd, and others. (Princeton, N.J.: Princeton University, 1950-), Vol. I: 1760 to 1776, p. 124. Also printed at https://avalon.law.yale.edu/18thcentury/jeffsumm.asp. Accessed on March 28, 2020. Page 151

...to tax or raise revenue on the colonies without their consent.
Andrew C. McLaughlin, *A Constitutional History of the United States* (Safety Harbor, Fl.: Simon Publications, 2001), Vol. I, pp. 84-85. Page 151

...the will for revolution against the Mother Country.
Pauline Maier, *From Resistance to Revolution: Colonial Radicals and the Development of American Opposition to Britain, 1765-1776* (New York: W.W. Norton, 1974), pp. 241-242. Page 152

...with the support of the civil governments in the colonies.
Dumas Malone, *Jefferson and His Time: Jefferson The Virginian,* Vol. 1 (Boston: Little Brown and Company, 1948), Vol. 1, p. 200. Page 153

...of Liberty, Property, and Union with Great Britain."
Thomas Jefferson, *The Papers of Thomas Jefferson,* Vol. 1, 1760-1776, ed. Julian P. Boyd (Princeton: Princeton University Press, 1950), pp. 170-174. Also see: "Virginia Resolutions on Lord North's Conciliatory Proposal 10 June 1775," *Founders Online,* National Archives, accessed May 8, 2020, https://founders.archives.gov/documents/Jefferson/01-01-02-0106. Page 153

...rejected the "Conciliatory Proposal" in July 1775.
Ibid., pp. 225-230. Page 153

...actual independence as a free republican democracy.
Andrew C. McLaughlin, *A Constitutional History of the United States* (Safety Harbor, Fl.: Simon Publications, 2001), Vol. 1, p. 89, note 17. Page 153

...(A Boston Silversmith and express rider).
Pauline Maier, *American Scripture: Making the Declaration of Independence* (New York: Alfred A. Knopf, 1997), p. 3. Professor Maier's book is a lively history of the events preceding the Declaration of Independence, and the complex drafting of the document. Page 153

...what would later become the navy.
Ibid., p. 11. Page 154

..."best produce the happiness of the people."
Ibid., p. 13. Page 154

...while still pledging loyalty to the King.
Olive Branch Petition, C. Ford Worthington, et. al. ed., *Journal of the Continental Congress, 1774-1789* (Washington, D.C.: 1904-1937), 2:158-162). See also, Larry P. Arnn, *The Founders' Key* (Nashville, Tennessee: Thomas Nelson, Inc., 2013), p. 45. Page 154

...the world with the exception of Great Britain.
Andrew C. McLaughlin, *A Constitutional History of the United States* (Safety Harbor, Fl.: Simon Publications, 2001), Vol. I, p. 90. Page 154

...pursuing and obtaining happiness and safety."
Quoted in Hillsdale College Lecture "Constitution, Lecture 2." Accessed December 26, 2019. Reprinted in Richard P. Perry, *Sources of Our Liberties* (New York: New York University Press, 11th. in the Series, 1952, 1959). Page 155

...Life, Liberty, and the pursuit of Happiness."
The text of the Declaration of Independence is reprinted in many sources. See Larry P. Arnn, *The Founders' Key* (Nashville, Tennessee: Thomas Nelson, Inc., 2013), pp. 127-132. See *The Declaration of Independence and the United States Constitution*, Booklet, Compliments of Hillsdale College (Hillsdale, Michigan: Hillsdale College). Also see: *Founders Online,* National Archives. Page 155

...moral limits of the natural right to liberty."
Thomas G. West, *The Political Theory of the American Founding: Natural Rights, Public Policy, and the Moral Conditions of Freedom,* (Cambridge: Cambridge University Press, 2017), p. 37. Page 156

...these presumptions about the nature of law.
Gordon S. Wood, *The Creation of the American Republic*, 1776-1787 (Chapel Hill: The University of North Carolina Press, 1998), pp. 292-294. Page 157

...James Madison, Alexander Hamilton, and John Adams.
Two authors that claim that these six founding fathers did not practice a Christian belief, but that their thinking and beliefs were deistic, and secular are: Gary Kowalski, *Revolutionary Spirits: The Enlightened Faith of America's Founding Fathers* (New York: Blue Ridge, 2008), and Brooke Allen, *Moral Minority: Our Skeptical Founding Fathers* (Chicago: Ivan R. Dee, 2006). Page 157

...human excellence, & believing he never claimed any other."
"From Thomas Jefferson to Benjamin Rush, 21 April 1803," *Founders Online,* National Archives, https://founders.archives.gov/documents/jefferson101-40-02-0178-001 (Original source: *The Papers of Thomas Jefferson, vol.* 40, 4 March-10 July 1803, ed. Barbara B. Oberg. (Princeton: Princeton University Press, 2013), pp. 251-253). Accessed on May 8, 2020, and October 18, 2020. Page 158

...to a significant extent, of their own construction."
Greg Fraser, "Gouverneur Morris and Theistic Rationalism in the Founding Era," in *Faith and the Founders of the American Republic,* eds., Daniel L. Dreisbach and Mark David Hall (New York: Oxford University Press, 2014), p. 208. Page 159

...the resurrection of Jesus, and atonement for our sins.
Ibid., p. 209. Page 159

...accepted the doctrine of the natural rights of man.
Dumas Malone, *Jefferson The Virginian,* Vol. 1 (Boston: Little Brown and Company, 1948), Vol.1, p. 179. Page 159

...freedom of the mind were the inalienable rights.
Dumas Malone, *Jefferson and The Rights of Man,* Vol. 2 (Boston: Little Brown and Company, 1951), Vol. 2, p. 154. Page 160

...as memorial or of particular or practical use.
Thomas Jefferson, *The Commonplace Book of Thomas Jefferson. A Repertory of His Ideas on Government.* With an introduction and notes by Gilbert Chinard (Baltimore: John Hopkins Press, 1926). Page 160

...Commonplace Book with personal reflections and summaries.
Ibid., arts. 777-778, and pp. 31-38. Pge 160

...only be successful if formed over a small territory.
Dumas Malone, *Jefferson The Virginian,* Vol. 1, (Boston: Little Brown and Company, 1948), Vol. 1., p. 176. Page 160

...sanction of each individual's heart, and in the laws of nature.
Ibid., p. 175. Page 161

...who could extract the honey of every sect.
Thomas Jefferson to Thomas B. Parker, 15 May 1819, *Jefferson Papers,* 38400. S1 R150, reprinted in Jayne Allen, *Jefferson's Declaration of Independence: Origins, Philosophy & Theology* (Lexington, Kentucky: The University of Kentucky Press, 1998), p. 39. Page 161

...they have it by the law of nature."
Thomas Jefferson to Edward Carrington, August 4, 1787, *The Writings of Thomas Jefferson,* Paul Leicester Ford, ed., (New York: G.P. Putnam's Sons, 1892-1899) Vol. IV, p. 424, reprinted in Dumas Malone, *Jefferson and the Rights of Man,* Vol 2 (Boston: Little, Brown, and Company, 1951), p. 161. Page 161

...Life, Liberty, and the Pursuit of Happiness."
The Declaration of Independence and the Constitution of the United States of America (Hillsdale, Michigan: Hillsdale College) Compliments of Hillsdale College. Page 162

...has a right to harm these rights in another person.
John Locke, *Two Treatises of Government*, 1690. Peter Laslett, ed. (New York: Mentor, 1965). Page 162

...following the philosophy of Thomas Hutchinson.
Garry Wills, *Inventing America: Jefferson's Declaration of Independence* (New York: Vintage Books, 1979), p. 213. Page 162

...purpose of government was for the public good.
John Locke, *Two Treatises of Government, 1690*. Peter Laslett, ed. (New York: Mentor, 1965), pp. 355-356; 363. Page 163

...place instead of the laws, then the Legislature is changed.
Ibid., p. 408. Page 163

...the citizens to cause fatigue so that they will comply.
Ibid., p. 409. Page 163

...the king violated the right to self-governance.
Larry P. Arnn, *The Founders' Key: The Divine and Natural Connection Between the Declaration and the Constitution and What We Risk by Losing It* (Nashville, Tennessee: Nelson Books, 2013), pp. 20-37; and, Jayne Allen, Jefferson's *Declaration of Independence: Origins, Philosophy & Theology* (Lexington, Kentucky: The University of Kentucky Press, 1998), pp. 48-51. Page 164

...state governments to become self-governing commonwealths
Andrew C. McLaughlin, *A Constitutional History of the United States* (Safety Harbor, Fl.: Simon Publications, 2001), Vol. 1, p. 106. Page 165

...thriving spirit running counter to national attachments."
David G. Smith, *The Convention and the Constitution: The Political Ideas of the Founding Fathers* (New York, University Press of America, 1987), p. 3. Page 166

...in the early colonial State Constitutions.
Andrew C. McLaughlin, *A Constitutional History of the United States*, Vol. I (Safety Harbor, Fl.: Simon Publications, 2001), Vol. I, See Chapter XI for a detailed and engaging history of the early colonial state constitutions. Page 166

...for representation of the people of Massachusetts.
Ibid., pp. 106-107. Page 166

...November 4, 1775, and Virginia on December 4, 1775.
Ibid., p. 107. Page 166

...independent people by free and independent states.
Ibid., pp. 107-108. Page 166

...seeking and obtaining their safety and happiness."
Quoted in Hillsdale College Lecture *Constitution 101*, Lecture 2, accessed December 26, 2019. Reprinted in *Sources of Our Liberties*, Richard L. Perry, ed. (New York: New York University Press, 1952, 1959), 10th In the Series, p. 25. Page 167

Chapter 9 Endnotes

...that are necessary for us to have to perform our duties.
Jerome Huyler, *Locke in America: The Moral Philosophy of the Founding Era* (Lawrence, Kansas: University Press of Kansas, 1995) p. 247. Page 170

...was taught to us initially by Socrates, and later by Jesus.
See this author, Joan Arnsteen (Neumann), *Socrates, Jesus and Freedom: A Philosophical Reflection* (Alger, MI: Proud Daughter Publishing, 2016). Page 172

...knowledge and understanding of the Word of God.
Ibid. Page 173

...(after the Revolution) principles of the American Constitution.
John Phillip Reid, *Constitutional History of the American Revolution: The Authority of Rights* (Madison, Wisconsin: The University of Wisconsin Press, 1986) p. 66. Page 175

...institutions aim for the safety and happiness of society.
James Madison, *The Federalist Papers*, Clinton Rossiter, ed., (New York: Signet Classics, 2003), No. 43, pp. 275-276, hereafter *Federalist. Page 175*

...the public is formed to protect common rights."
David G. Smith, *The Convention and the Constitution: The Political Ideas of the Founding Fathers* (New York: University Press of America, 1987), p. 80. Page 175

Chapter 10 Endnotes

...defective structure of the Articles of Confederation.
Lance Banning, *The Sacred Fire of Liberty: James Madison and the Founding of the Federal Republic,* (Ithaca: Cornell University Press, 1995), p. 116. Page 179

...the oppressive behavior of the state legislatures.
See, for example: Gordon S. Wood, *The Creation of the American Republic, 1776-1778* (Chapel Hill, N.C.: University of North Carolina Press, 1998). Page 179

...federal government's powers as specified in the Constitution.
Federal vs. State governmental powers have been in the focus recently during the Corona virus epidemic, where some states have kept the businesses within the states closed for extended periods of time; whereas the federal government has encouraged reopening of the businesses to stimulate the Nation's economy which has been damaged due to the pandemic. The issue has become politically volatile where all the states that have remained closed have Democratic governors and Democratic mayors who want to damage the Republican President's (President Trump) reelection image. The same political problems have persisted with the recent violent protestors, rioting, looting, burning of cities, and murders taking place in cities that have Democratic governors and Democratic mayors. Federal vs. State governmental powers have been in the focus recently when President Trump has responded to the continued violence, arson, looting, destruction of property, injury, and violence (and even death) directed at police officers, law-abiding citizens, businesses, and public and private property —(Homicides in New York City, Chicago, Portland, and Seattle have risen during this time of unlawful riots— where all these cities are run by democratic governors and democratic mayors) by issuing a memorandum on September 2, 2020, entitled "Memorandum on Reviewing Funding to State and Local Government Recipients That Are Permitting Anarchy, Violence and Destruction in American Cities." In response to President Trump's memorandum, on September 21, 2020, the Department of Defense identified cities that have refused to take reasonable actions to prevent and counteract criminal activities. The "Department of Justice Identifies New York City, Portland, and Seattle as Jurisdictions Permitting Violence and Destruction of Property," and listed the criteria for evaluating whether a city has performed its basic function of government to protect their own citizens. See: https://www.justice.gov/opa/pr/department-justice-identifies-new-york-city-portland-and-seattle-jurisdictions-permitting.

The decades long "progressive indoctrination campaign" in America's schools and universities, has led to the undermining of American patriotism in our Nation's youth. *The New York Times* "1619 Project", for example, makes the false claim that our democracy's founding was based upon false ideals. *Natural Law and the Constitution: The Law of All Laws* was written to dispel the anti-American ideas, and to restore our Nation's truths through natural law, and a respect for American citizens, The Declaration of Independence, The Constitution of the United States, and the Bill of Rights. It is the responsibility of each citizen to again read and reread these documents, and the Founder's stories to let the truth shine through the anti-American dogma. The reader will soon discover that one of the greatest joys is to read *The Records of the Federal Convention of 1787,* and *The Federalist Papers.* Page 179

...the terms of appointments, suffrage, slavery, ...
The Founders' beliefs about slavery (which varied) and the founding of The Constitution of the United States, and the question of slavery addressed at the Federal Convention is a very deep subject which is beyond the scope of this book. Constitutional historians address the subject of slavery, refer to the Bibliography for suggested authors. The words" slave" and "slavery" were not mentioned in the Constitution, but were implied in Article I, Section 2, Article I, Section 9, and Article IV, Section 2 (The fugitive slave laws were repealed by the ratification of the Thirteenth Amendment in 1865, which abolished slavery). The northern states did not want the slaves counted at all for representation in the House of Representatives, and the southern states wanted the slaves counted to increase their number of representatives in the House of Representatives. The original language of the Constitution compromised on the question of slavery with the "Three-Fifths Clause," Article I, Section 2 states, "Representatives and direct Taxes shall be apportioned among the several States which may be included within this Union, according to their respective Numbers, which shall be determined by adding to the whole Number of free Persons, including those bound to Service for a Term of Years, and excluding Indians not taxed, and three fifths of all other Persons." James Madison expressed his belief in *The Federalist Papers, Number 54,* by defending the compromise of the Three-Fifth Rule, by writing that the slaves had mixed characteristics of property and person. This of course was changed by Section 2 of the Fourteenth Amendment, ratified on July 9, 1868. The Founding Fathers believed that slavery would eventually die out, and their purpose in constructing the Constitution was to uphold the Union and protect the rights and liberties of the American citizens. An argument can be made that the Constitution neither authorized nor prohibited slavery. An expedient political solution should never be the answer to a moral question, and the subsequent Civil War demonstrated that. Believers in God's natural law are opposed to slavery in any form. Page 181

...debate and work by honorable men of good character.
Andrew C. McLaughlin, *A Constitutional History of the United States,* Vol. I (Safety Harbor, Fl.: Simon Publications, 2001), Vol. I, p. 148. A list of the seventy-four delegates that were appointed from twelve states, with a brief biography of each can be found in the Index in: David G. Smith, *The Convention and the Constitution: The Political Idea of the Founding Fathers* (New York: University Press of America, 1987), pp. 93-97. A copy of The Constitution of the United States and the Amendments are also found in Smith's book, pp.99-112. Page 181

...was born in Westmoreland County, Virginia, ...
The following brief biographical sketches on the Founders are meant to stimulate the reader to read the excellent biographies that have been written about the Founders. See the Bibliography at socratesplace.com for examples of some of these important books. Page 183

...adoring crowd, a parade, and booming cannonballs.
Ron Chernow, *Washington: A Life* (New York: Penguin Books, 2010), p. 526. Ibid., p. 530. Page 184

...read all of the information that set out the numerous debates.
Ibid., p. 530. Page 185

...and protection for his soldiers and his country.
William J. Johnson, *George Washington the Christian* (Milford, Michigan: Mott Media, 1919), pp. 102-107. For a biography that presents Washington as a committed Christian, see Mason Locke Weems, *The Life of George Washington; with Curious Anecdotes, Equally Honourable to Himself, and Exemplary to His Young Countrymen* (Cambridge, Massachusetts: Belknap Press of Harvard University, 1809 edition, reprinted in 1962). See also: John A. Eidsmoe, *Christianity and the Constitution: The Faith of Our Founding Fathers* (Grand Rapids, Michigan: Baker Books, 1987) Page 185

...added the words "so help me, God," to the inaugural oath.
George Washington, "First Inaugural Address, April 30, 1789; quoted in William J. Johnson, *George Washington the Christian* (Milford, Michigan: Mott Media, 1919), pp. 161-162. Page 185

...worship God according to the dictates of his own heart."
George Washington, Quoted in Paul F. Boller, *George Washington and Religion* (Dallas, Texas: Southern Methodist University Press, 1963), p 116. Page 185

...eager to enroll his name in the "Annals of Heaven."
James Madison to William Bradford, November 9, 1772, 1:75, William T. Hutchinson, William M.E. Rachal, Robert Rutland, et al., eds., *The Papers of James Madison* (Chicago and Charlottsville, 1962-1991) 17 vols. (covering 1751-1801). James Madison corresponded with other former classmates, for example, Hugh Henry Brackenridge and Philip Freeneau, but there is not a lot of surviving written material from Madison's youthful days, see *PJM* 1:71-72. See also: Lance Banning, *The Sacred Fires of Liberty: James Madison and the Founding of the Federal Republic* (Ithaca and London: Cornell University Press, 1995), Chapter 3, Footnote #9. Page 186

...soft voice or poor health that had kept him out of the ministry.
Irving Brant, *James Madison: The Virginia Revolutionist, 1751-1780* (Indianapolis: Bobbs-Merrill Company, 1941), Vol. 1, p. 100. Page 186

...and that he had learned much as a delegate.
James Madison, *The Federalist Papers* (New York: Signet Classics, 1961). Page 187

...with the "law of nature and of nature's God."
Ibid., No. 43, p. 276 Page 187

...exercise of religion according to the dictates of conscience."
Lance Banning, *The Sacred Fires of Liberty: James Madison and the Founding of the Federal Republic* (Ithaca and London: Cornell University Press, 1995) p. 85. Page 188

...any man disturb the peace, the happiness, or safety of society."
PJM I:173-175. Page 188

...and the existence of the state are manifestly endangered."
Lance Banning, *The Sacred Fires of Liberty: James Madison and the Founding of the Federal Republic* (Ithaca and London: Cornell University Press, 1995), p. 86. Page 188

...distinctive spheres for church and the state.
Ibid., p. 86. Page 188

...is abridged by the institution of civil society."
James Madison *Records of the Federal Convention,* Vol. I, p. 135. Page 189

...chartered bounds of government that cannot be transgressed.
PJM, 8:298-306. Page 189

...the philosopher's Locke, Hume and Pufendorf.
See *The Federalist Papers*, Numbers 18, 19 and 20. Page 189

...successful government for the flourishing of all Americans.
Ibid., James Madison Nos. 37 and 47, and Alexander Hamilton, No. 9; See James Madison "Notes on Ancient and Modern Confederations," in William T. Hutchinson et al., eds, *The Papers of James Madison,* 17 vols. (Chicago and Charlottesville, VA., 1962-91) 9:3-24, and James Madison "Vices of the Political System of the United States," Ibid., 9:315-358. Page 189

...to share with his friend in Paris — Thomas Jefferson.
Catherine Drinker Bowen, *Miracle at Philadelphia: The Story of the Constitutional Convention, May to September 1787* (Boston: An Atlantic Monthly Press Book, 1966), pp. 29-30. The official Convention secretary was Major Jackson of South Carolina; however, other delegate members also took notes: Alexander Hamilton, Robert Yates and John Lansing, from New York, James McHenry of Maryland, William Paterson of New Jersey, Rufus King of Massachusetts, William Pierce of Georgia, and George Mason delegate from Virginia. The most comprehensive notes were taken by James Madison. Page 191

...this author's favorite, humility, to imitate Jesus and Socrates.
Benjamin Franklin, *Franklin Autobiography, 1771-1775* (Garden City, New York: Garden City Publishing Co., Inc., Reprinted in 1916), pp. 147-149. Page 193

...natural-law jurisprudence and Christianity is well-noted.
Mark David Hall, "Bibliographical Essay History of James Wilson's Law Lectures." In *Collected Works of James Wilson,* Kermit L. Hall and Mark David Hall, eds., Vol. 1 (Indianapolis, IN: Liberty Fund, Inc., 2007), Vol 1, pp. 401-413; Mark David Hall, *The Political and Legal Philosophy of James Wilson, 1742-1798* (Columbia, MO: University of Missouri Press, 1997); Robert Green McCloskey, *Introduction to the Works of James Wilson*, Robert Green McCloskey, ed. (Cambridge, MA: Harvard University Press, 1967), Vol. 1, pp. 1-48. Page 195

...human law is the human application of natural law.
See Saint Thomas Aquinas, *Summa Theologica. Vol. 1-Vol. 5;* Joan Neumann, *Natural Law and The Constitution: The Law of All Laws,* Chapter 4; Justin Buckley Dyer, *The Christian Natural Law Tradition and James Wilson's Lectures on Law*. Prepared for 2019 Berkeley Natural Law Workshop, Draft Date: January 23, 2019, accessed on March 19, 2020, www.law.berkeley.edu, 20. Page 197

...then the natural law would come back into force.
William Blackstone, *Commentaries on the Laws of England* (Oxford: Clarendon Press, 1766), Bk 1, p. 91. Page 198

...natural moral laws and are subject to these laws.
Charles Page Smith, *James Wilson: Founding Father (1742-1798)* (Chapel Hill: The University of North Carolina Press, 1956), pp. 324-341. Page 198

...island of Nevis in the British West Indies.
Ron Chernow, *Alexander Hamilton* (New York: Penguin Press, 2005). See Chernow for a fascinating account of Hamilton's birth and early childhood in Nevis, and his subsequent immigration to the United States in 1773 at the age of sixteen. Page 198

...in the whole of human nature by the hand of Divinity."
Alexander Hamilton, "Farmer Refuted," 1775; quoted in Nathan Schachner, *Alexander Hamilton* (New York: Barnes & Co., 1946, 1961), p. 38. Page 198

...versatility of man conversant in vast areas of knowledge."
Ron Chernow, *Alexander Hamilton* (New York: Penguin Books, 2005), p. 110. Page 198 & 199

...received from a duel with Vice-President Aaron Burr.
Ibid. Page 199

...opposition to the Constitution after the Convention.
David G. Smith *The Convention and the Constitution: The Political Ideas of the Founding Fathers* (New York: University Press of America, 1987). For a complete list of the Convention delegates listed according to their states, and a brief biographical sketch of each delegate see the Appendix pp. 93-97. See also a reprint of the Constitution of the United States, pp. 99-113. Page 200

...the universe and are antecedent to governments."
John Adams, *"A dissertation on the Canon and Feudal Law,"* August 12, 1775. http://founders.archives.gov/documents/Adams/06-01-02-0052-0004. Accessed on July 11, 2019. Page 201

...the revival of the British Constitution in this country."
James Madison to Thomas Jefferson, June 6, 1787, in *The Papers of James Madison,* William T. Hutchinson, William M.E. Rachal, Robert Rutland, et al., eds., (Chicago and Charlottesville. 1962-1991) 17 vols. (covering 1751-1801). 10:29-30. Page 201

...used by the delegates rather than "natural law".
Records of the Federal Convention, Max Farrand, ed., in Four Volumes, (New Haven and London: Yale University Press, 1911, 1937, 1966) Vol. I p. 48, 124, 135; Vol. II, p. 56. Page 203

...must also be protected in the national constitution.
Ibid., Vol. I, p. 437, 440, 493. Page 203

...power in order that a union of states may be formed.
Ibid., Vol. II, p. 666. Page 203

...also maintained their freedom, power, and integrity.
The Constitution of the United States of America, Amendment X, and Amendment XIV. See Donald S. Lutz, *The Origins of American Constitutionalism* (Louisiana: Louisiana State University Press, 1988), p. 153. Page 204

...immutable and universal principle of our existence.
Robert J. Morgan, "Madison's Analysis of the Sources of Political Authority," in *The American Political Science Review* 75 (September 1981): pp. 613-625. Page 205

...enter into the very definition of good government."
James Madison, *The Federalist Papers* (New York: Signet Classics, 1961), No. 37, p. 223. Page 206

...i.e., the President of the United States.
Alexander Hamilton, *The Federalist Papers* (New York: Signet Classics, 1961), No. 70, p. 422. Page 206

...powers which are requisite to supply that energy."
Ibid., No. 15, p. 103. Page 206

...adequate provision for its support; and competent powers."
Ibid., No. 70, p. 422. Page 206

...delegates wanted the states to retain their sovereignty.
David G. Smith, *The Convention and the Constitution: The Political Ideas of the Founding Fathers* (New York and London: University Press of America, 1987), pp. 35-36. The terms 'national' and 'federalists' later became the terms 'federalist' and 'anti-federalist' during the state debates over the ratification of the Constitution. Page 208

Chapter 11 Endnotes

...otherwise published, or communicated without leave."
The Records of the Federal Convention of 1787, Max Farrand, ed., (New Haven and London: Yale University Press, 1966). Vol. I, p. 15. Page 209

...were bound by an oath to support the articles of Union.
Ibid., Vol. I, pp. 18-22. See also: David G. Smith, *The Convention and the Constitution: The Political Ideas of the Founding Fathers* (New York and London: University Press of America, 1987), pp. 38. Page 210

...and liberty in the U. S. to pass away unimproved."
Ibid., Vol. I., p. 23. Page 210

...central government with power and authority.
Ibid., Vol. I, p. 16. See also: David G. Smith, p. 36; and Andrew C. McLaughlin, *A Constitutional History of the United States*, Vol. I (Safety Harbor, Fl.: Simon Publications, 2001), Vol. I, pp. 157-158. Page 210

...and outlined how to proceed for ratification.
David G. Smith, *The Convention and the Constitution: The Political Ideas of the Founding Fathers* (New York and London: University Press of America, 1987) pp. 36-38. Page 210

...proposed for the government system under consideration.
The Records of the Federal Convention of 1787. Vol. I, Max Farrand, eds. (New Haven and London: Yale University Press, 1966), Vol. I, p. 240. Page 211

...powers of the central government rested with the states.
David G. Smith, *The Convention and the Constitution: The Political Ideas of the Founding Fathers* (New York and London: University Press of America, 1987), p. 37. Page 211

...equality of votes without giving up their liberty."
Records, I, p. 437-438. (Luther Martin, June 27, 1787). Page 211

...natural rights of individuals, and in perfect equality."
Ibid., p. 440 (Robert Yates, June 27, 1787). Page 212

...for the Rights of States in the National Constitution."
Ibid., p. 493 (Rufus King, June 30, 1787). Page 212

...delegates must compromise as a body "to make a joint."
Ibid., p. 488 (Benjamin Franklin, June 30, 1787). Page 212

... over the military establishment, taxation and commerce.
Ibid, Vol. II, pp. 176-187. Page 213

...other clauses protected the rights to private property."
John P. Kaminsky, "The Constitution Without a Bill of Rights,'"in *The Bill of Rights and The States: The Colonial and Revolutionary Origins of American Liberties,* Patrick T. Conley and John P. Kaminsky, eds., (Madison, Wisconsin: Madison House, 1992), pp. 22-23. Page 213

Chapter 12 Endnotes

...because the Constitution itself is a bill of rights.
Alexander Hamilton, *The Federalist Papers* (New York, Signet Classics, 2003), No. 84, pp. 509-520. Page 217

...defended through experimental or empirical reasoning.
Morton White, *Philosophy, The Federalist, and the Constitution* (New York, Oxford: Oxford University Press, 1987), pp. 195-197. Page 218

...which all such institutions must be sacrificed."
James Madison, *The Federalist Papers,* No. 43, p. 276. Page 220

...are both the ends of government.
Ibid., No. 51. Page 220

...be done and pursued, and evil is to be avoided.
St. Thomas, *Summa Theologica*, I-II, q. 94, art. 2. Page 224

...according to reason, and to know the truth about God.
Ibid., q. 94, art. 3. Page 224

...we are not angels, nor are we depraved.
James Madison, *The Federalist Papers,* No. 51, p. 319. Page 225

...permanent and aggregate interests of the community.
James Madison, *The Federalist Papers,* No. 10, p. 72. Page 226

...faction is an unequal distribution of property.
James Madison, *The Federalist Papers,* No. 10, pp. 73-74. Page 226

...relief can be sought by controlling its effects.
Ibid., p. 75. Page 226

...great object to which our inquiries are directed."
Ibid., p. 75. Page 226

...and then betray the interest of the people."
Ibid., p. 77. Page 226

...and to which all such institutions must be sacrificed."
Ibid., No. 43, p. 276. Page 226

...keeping each other in their proper places."
Ibid., No. 51, p. 288. Page 226

...connected with the constitutional rights of the place.",
Ibid., pp. 289-290. Page 227

Chapter 13 Endnotes

...Constitution, rights can be considered to trump power.
Calvin R. Massey, *The Ninth Amendment and the Constitution's Unenumerated Rights* (Philadelphia: Temple University Press, 1995), p. 90; 218. Page 230

...social structures, and cities that are broken and unsafe.
Reverend Bill Owens, *A Dream DeRailed: How the Left Highjacked Civil Rights to Create a Permanent Underclass* (A New Dream Publishers, 2019). Page 233

...because they are threatened, intimated, and bullied by the left.
I urge my readers to research the individuals who are conspiring to remove our duly elected President, and take powers for themselves, and those who take a leadership role at Black Lives Matter, and ANTIFA. See, for example, https://www.revolver.news/2020/09/meet-norm-eisen-legal-hatchet-man...-central-operative-in-the-color-revolution-against-president-trump/ Page 234

...In hell, there will be nothing but law."
Grant Gilmore, *The Age of American Law* (New Haven: Yale University Press, 1977), pp. 110-111. Page 234

Chapter 14 Endnotes

...of a statute emanating from the sovereign people."
Edward S. Corwin, *The "Higher Law" Background of American Constitutional Law* (Indiana: Liberty Fund, Inc., 1955), p. 84. Page 238

...form has been backed up by judicial review.
Ibid., p. 85. Page 238

...the principle of things, the real order of the universe."
Orestes A. Brownson, *The American Republic: Its Constitution, Tendencies and Destiny,* Americo D. Lapati, ed., (New Haven Conn.: College & University Press, 1972), p. 35. Page 242

...for example, ancient Greece, and ancient Rome.
Freya Stark, *Rome on the Euphrates* (London: John Murray, 1966). Page 243

...and other clauses protected the rights to private property."
John P. Kaminsky, *"The Constitution Without a Bill of Rights," in The Bill of Rights and The States: The Colonial and Revolutionary Origins of American Liberties,* Patrick T. Conley and John P. Kaminsky, eds., (Madison, Wisconsin: Madison House, 1992), pp. 22-23. Page 243 & 244

...construed to deny or disparage others retained by the people."
See, The Constitution of the United States of America, Amendment IX. Page 244

...to bear in the framing of the United States Constitution.
See, for example: Charles A. Beard, *An Economic Interpretation of the Constitution* (New York: Macmillan, 1913) Page 247

Note: For a full bibliography please visit Joan's website at Socratesplace.com

Meet the Author

Joan Neumann holds a Doctor of Religious Education degree from Destiny University, a Master's Degree in Constitutional History from Wayne State University, and an undergraduate degree in Philosophy. The author can be reached at her blog at Socratesplace.com.

Made in the USA
Monee, IL
04 November 2026

67380521R00164